DRAGON MULTINATIONAL

DRAGON MULTINATIONAL
A New Model for Global Growth

John A. Mathews

UNIVERSITY PRESS

2002

OXFORD
UNIVERSITY PRESS

Oxford   New York
Athens   Auckland   Bangkok   Bogotá   Buenos Aires   Cape Town
Chennai   Dar es Salaam   Delhi   Florence   Hong Kong   Istanbul   Karachi
Kolkata   Kuala Lumpur   Madrid   Melbourne   Mexico City   Mumbai   Nairobi
Paris   São Paulo   Shanghai   Singapore   Taipei   Tokyo   Toronto   Warsaw

and associated companies in
Berlin   Ibadan

Published by Oxford University Press, Inc.
198 Madison Avenue, New York, New York 10016

Oxford is a registered trademark of Oxford University Press

Library of Congress Cataloging-in-Publication Data
Mathews, John A. (John Alwyn), 1946–
Dragon multinational : a new model for global growth / by John A. Mathews.
    p.   cm.
Includes bibliographical references.
ISBN 0-19-512146-5
1. International business enterprises.   2. Corporations, Asian.
3. International trade.   I. Title.
HD2755.5 .M376   2002
338.8'8—dc21   00-068467

9 8 7 6 5 4 3 2 1

Printed in the United States of America
on acid-free paper

PREFACE

This book is a contribution to the present debates over globalization, widely seen to be the dominant economic issue of our time. One influential view of globalization sees it as a process driven by giant multinational firms from the Triad—North America, Europe, and Japan—shaping the world in their own image. This is an outcome to be feared by all: it spells convergence, uniformity, centralization, and in particular loss of autonomy in the parts of the world outside the Triad, designated as "the Periphery." This book contests such a pessimistic view. *Dragon Multinational* describes the extraordinary success of a handful of multinationals from the Periphery in globalizing their operations extremely rapidly and becoming major players in industries as diverse as steel, cement, information technology, and general manufacturing, as well as in services such as finance and hotels. The firms involved have had to devise skillful strategies and organizational forms to achieve global coverage and compete with established giants. My argument is that in conditions of enhanced worldwide interfirm connections, these companies from the Periphery have been able to utilize strategies of international linkage and leverage to accelerate their global coverage—and that these strategies complement the multiply interconnected character of the global economy itself. In this sense they are organizational pioneers of a new kind of global firm from the Periphery, equipped with a global perspective and with a new model of global growth. Their success indicates that the business civilization being created in the twenty-first century is likely to be pluralistic and diverse, as well as global, and that this offers unprecedented opportunities for firms that are smart enough to work their way into proliferating global networks.

"Dragon multinationals" are companies that start with disadvantages as latecomers, but they devise clever strategies of linkage and leverage to take advantage of the worldwide web of interfirm connections that characterizes the global economy. They thereby accelerate their global coverage to become formidable competitors. This is a "good news" story that offers hope not just to multinational firms from the Periphery (which according to the conventional wisdom can expect nothing but crushing defeat and marginalization) but to all firms that can find ways to enmesh themselves in the growing tissue of interfirm connections and networks that characterize the emergent global economy.

My own interests in this topic go back several years, to a series of case studies I have conducted on strategies of globalization and technology enhancement developed by firms in the Periphery. Why choose such companies, given the common view that they are less interesting than the industry leaders in the Triad? My motivation is that these are firms (and countries) that start from behind and overcome their deficiencies to emerge as industry leaders, in sometimes astonishingly short periods of time, without any of the advantages of the incumbent industry leaders. They do so without initial resources, without skills and knowledge, without proximity to major markets, and without the social capital that is to be found in regions like Silicon Valley. But they succeed in spite of these initial disadvantages, indeed by turning initial disabilities into sources of advantage—by leapfrogging to advanced technological levels, for example, or by leveraging their way into new markets through partnerships and joint ventures.

To me, it is much more interesting to account for how Samsung became a world leader in the memory chip industry within 10 years of entering the industry than it is to account for how IBM remains a major player in the industry. IBM has a wealth of resources to explain its success, but Samsung started with very little. It was able to use what little it had to insert itself in world production networks to acquire and adapt the technological and market know-how needed. Likewise, I find it much more interesting to account for how Acer became a worldwide player in the PC and IT industry, using strategies of market leverage and partnership to expand in peripheral markets, rather than to account for the continued international success of a Compaq or HP. I find working with firms from the Periphery to be a much more rewarding research challenge than studying the well-endowed firms from the Triad. It is not just a descriptive exercise, but an engagement with the very fundamentals of management and organizational scholarship.

Dragon Multinational, then, is a work that locates itself in the literature of international business and in particular in the literature on international strategy, organization, and management. But here a paradox presents itself. These literatures are concerned with the creation and sustaining of competitive advantages at an international level. Indeed they are concerned almost overwhelmingly with how *existing advantages* are maintained, rather than with how outsiders may break into already occupied markets. Is it controversial to claim that these literatures place far too much emphasis on the strategies and perspectives of the incumbent firms, and not nearly enough on the perspectives of the newcomers and latecomers? It is precisely the latecomers that face the challenge of breaking into international markets already heavily populated by incumbent multinational enterprises (MNEs). To succeed they need to devise ingenious strategic and organizational innovations that are quite different from those developed and practised by the incumbents. This is why to me they have much greater intrinsic interest than firms that have already arrived and are merely exploiting their existing advantages.

Acer, Inc. offers a glimpse of the kind of possibilities and strategic innovations I am alluding to. It is a company founded only 25 years ago in Taiwan by a young entrepreneur named Stan Shih. Acer is now a global giant in the Information Technology industries, expanding rapidly into various kinds of internet and worldwide web-based businesses, in the Triad regions of North America, Europe, and Japan, as well as in major emerging markets like China, India, and Central and Southeast Asia. Stan Shih has emerged as a tireless champion of nonorthodox approaches to managing global corporations from the Periphery. He has received honors too numerous to mention in his native Taiwan and was named "Foreign Businessman of the Year" by the Academy of International Business at its meeting in South Carolina in 1999.

Mr. Shih utilizes the Chinese board game GO to explain some of the strategic innovations he has utilized in devising Acer's global growth—such as the principle of building strength through interconnections and the strategy of building strength in the Periphery before tackling the competition in the Center. Mr. Shih has a four-character expression to describe Acer's global business organizational architecture: a circle of dragons with no head. (His own depiction of this phrase, in his personal calligraphy is shown on the cover.) This can be interpreted to mean a group of independent and autonomous businesses (the dragon symbolizing strength and nobility) working together but with no head dragon giving orders. In other words, the member firms are expected to make their own business decisions and initiatives and to coordinate their behavior through close interaction and common rules. This is an uncommonly effective—and pithy—formula for building and managing a global organization at a time of great networking opportunities.

Acer and the other companies I deal with, such as Ispat, Cemex, Hong Leong, and Li & Fung, are all becoming global giants at a time when the conventional wisdom would suggest that it is becoming harder and harder for latecomer firms from the Periphery to make their mark. The fact of the success of these firms is in itself a kind of miracle, and one that cries out for an explanation. I was driven to write this book, and its related volume

Tiger Technology: The Creation of a Semiconductor Industry in East Asia, co-authored with Dong-Sung Cho, to try to make sense of these improbable successes, with a view to generalizing the lessons learned.

The subject matter of the two books concerns novel phenomena generated by the rise of East Asia—in the first case, the accelerated uptake of advanced technologies by firms in countries like Taiwan, Korea, or Singapore (and now by China), and in the present case, the accelerated internationalization by firms to acquire global coverage so quickly. The approach taken in the two books is complementary—in the first case, looking at the novel strategies adopted by firms in the East Asian countries to leverage knowledge and technologies from their more advanced competitors and in this present case, at the novel strategies adopted by firms to accelerate their internationalization as a competitive goal.

Fundamentally, both books base their argument on the notion that latecomers can overcome their initial disadvantages and indeed can draw advantages from their latecomer status—provided they can formulate the strategies and organizational forms which allow them to do so. In the case of technologies and technological enhancement, latecomer firms have been able to formulate strategies of resource leverage that enable them to acquire technological insights through providing services such as contract manufacturing to established players. This approach has been put to good use in East Asia in enabling firms to enter one area of advanced technology after another, such as the semiconductor industry described in *Tiger Technology.*

In the case of internationalization, a comparable argument is deployed—namely, that latecomer firms can utilize the existing and latent interfirm connections of the global economy to accelerate their global growth. By drawing themselves into such linkages, they can leverage entry into new markets far more rapidly than by following the stolid entry strategies of their multinational predecessors. The argument of the present book, then, may be summarized as follows. The globally interlinked structure of the latecomer MNE is the outcome of its strategic commitment to accelerated internationalization through linkage and leverage, and both strategy and structure in this case complement the multiply interlinked character of the global economy. The chapters to follow explore how this was accomplished and then seek to confront the existing international business literature with the challenges posed by these latecomers' unexpected success. But the general context should always be held in focus: the firms involved can achieve accelerated global coverage through identifying and exploiting latecomer advantages, which then become, in principle, strategies available to firms everywhere. By examining latecomers from the Periphery, we are in fact examining the future of all firms seeking to become players in the global economy of the twenty-first century.

Acknowledgments

My first acknowledgement must be to Stan Shih, founder and inspiration behind Acer, Inc. Stan Shih has been unstinting in the time he has offered to me, on my own and in collaboration with Professor Charles Snow, in explaining the strategic and organizational origins of Acer's success. He has also opened doors to Acer's managers, enabling me to conduct interviews and discussions with them in Taiwan as well as in the United States, Japan, Hong Kong, Singapore, Malaysia, and Australia.

I am also grateful to my collaborator at Penn State University, Professor Charles Snow. Chuck and I have shared much of the thought that goes into this book, as well as a critical two-day interview with Stan Shih in Taipei published in a joint article carried in the scholarly journal *Organizational Dynamics*. Although Chuck dropped out of the writing of the book, his insights and friendly criticism have always been challenging and sustaining.

At Oxford University Press in New York, I am particularly grateful to a wonderful editor, Herb Addison, for his faith in this project. We shared many long lunches as the themes of this book were elaborated. The writing of it seemed to stretch beyond all acceptable time horizons, yet Herb was always encouraging. In the final stretch he moved to a well-earned retirement, and I have been pleased to see the project ably taken up by Paul Donnelly, together with Martha Cooley and Robin Miura. It is a pleasure to work with such sophisticated and professional editors.

Within the companies studied, I wish to thank K. C. Tan from the Hong Leong group in Singapore, Litva Lazaneo Molina from the Cemex company in Mexico City, and William Fung from Li & Fung in Hong Kong. Within Acer I have many debts apart from those mentioned to Stan Shih. George Hsu provided initial contacts and was a most congenial host; Simon Lin, now CEO of AIPG, and K. Y. Lee, CEO of API, freely shared their insights; York Chen, originally as a vice president of ACI in Singapore and more recently as head of Acer's venture capital group, was an unstinting source of insights and ideas; and I had most constructive discussions with many other executives including Mike Culver, Ronald Chwang, H. B. Chen in Malaysia, Johnson Hsiung, George Huang, Tony Huang, Frachard Lung, T. Y. Lay, Teddy Lu, Jeff Tsao, Jerry Wang, Lance Wu, and Arthur Yeung. The head of Stan Shih's private office, Eugene Hwang, was a cheerful guide around the Acer networks and indefatigable in tracking down Acer documents.

This kind of global research project is dependent on sound financial backing, and in this I have been fortunate in the support secured from the Australian Research Council and from the Macquarie University Research Grant scheme. Young scholars such as Elizabeth Thurbon, Jane Ford, and Craig Reucassel have provided me with timely research assistance.

I have had the good fortune to test the ideas and arguments of this book in numerous seminars and academy meetings. Professor Orjan Sölvell at the

Institute of International Business at the Stockholm School of Economics and Professor Magnus Blomström at the School's European Institute of Japan Studies were wonderful co-hosts during a visiting professorship in late 2000, when many of the ideas were tested against the earlier Scandinavian experiences of internationalization. Participants provided useful feedback when I presented papers at the Academy of International Business meeting in Charleston (South Carolina) in 1999, at the meeting of the European Academy of International Business held in Maastricht, The Netherlands, in 2000, and at seminars held in Stockholm and Uppsala in October 2000. Further insights and feedback have been generously provided by my scholarly colleagues at various stages of the project. Mention should be made in particular of Chris Bartlett, Magnus Blomström, Shin-Horng Chen, Wan-wen Chu, Mark Dodgson, Yves Doz, Dexter Dunphy, Mats Forsgren, Henrik Glimstedt, Peter Hagström, Bob Hayes, Jan Johanson, Peter Katzenstein, Sanjaya Lall, Stefanie Lenway, Lars-Gunnar Mattsson, Ulf Olsson, Frederic Richard, Alan Rugman, Hubert Schmitz, Jon Sigurdson, Örjan Sölvell, John Stopford, Poh-Kam Wong, Ivo Zander, Udo Zander, and Jonathan Zeitlin. Linda Weiss remains as ever my most trusted and constructive critic; I thank her from the bottom of my heart for her wisdom and insights freely offered at every stage of this long project. I now launch the book to seek its fortune in the worlds of international business and the international academy of scholars.

Sydney   J. A. M.
April 2001

CONTENTS

ACRONYMS

ABO	Acer Brand Operations (2001)
ACI	Acer Computer International (Singapore)
ACLA	Acer Computec Latino America (Mexico)
ACMG	Acer Communications & Multimedia (global) Group
ADSG	Acer Digital Services (global) Group
ADT	Acer Display Technology
AI	Acer Inc.
AIG	Acer Infosystems (global) Group
AIPG	Acer Information Products (global) Group
ALAP	Africa Latin America Asia-Pacific marketing division (Acer 1989–1992)
ALI	Acer Laboratories Inc. (semiconductors)
AMN	Acer Mobile Networks Inc.
AMTI	Acer Media Technologies Inc.
APG	Acer Peripherals Group
API	Acer Peripherals Inc.
ASCG	Acer SoftCapital (global) Group
ASMI	Acer Semiconductor Manufacturing Inc.
ASSG	Acer Sertek Services Group (China)
CDL	City Developments Ltd. (Hong Leong Group)
CD-ROM	Compact Disc-Read Only Memory (PC peripheral)
CRT	Cathode Ray Tube (computer monitor)
C-S	Client-Server
DFI	Direct Foreign Investment (also FDI)
DMS	Design, Manufacturing, and Services (Acer OEM spinoff, 2001)

DRAM   Dynamic Random Access Memory (integrated circuit)
DRI   Direct Reduced Iron (used by Ispat)
DVD   Digital Video Disc
ETBF   Entrepreneurial technology-based firm
FDI   Foreign Direct Investment (also DFI)
FPD   Flat Panel Display (portable PC peripheral)
GBU   Global Business Unit
GI-LR   Global Integration–Local Responsiveness (dilemma)
GSU   Global Start-Up
IB   International Business
IDP   Investment Development Path
IJV   International Joint Venture
INV   International New Venture
IPO   Initial Public Offering
IT   Information Technology
ITRI   Industrial Technology Research Institute (Taiwan)
MEDC   Multinational Enterprise from a Developing Country
MNC/E   Multinational Corporation/Enterprise
NIC   Newly Industrialized Country
OEM   Original Equipment Manufacturer (industrial contractor)
OLI   Organizational, Locational, Internalization factors (conventional framework for discussing sources of MNE advantage)
OLI*   Outward-oriented, Linkage and leverage, Integration*
PAM   Pacific Asian Multinational
PC   Personal Computer
RBU   Regional Business Unit
RBV   Resource-Based View (of the firm)
SBU   Strategic Business Unit
SME   Small- or Medium-sized Enterprise
TFT-LCD   Thin Film Transistor–Liquid Crystal Display (FPD technology)
TNC/TNE   Transnational Corporation/Enterprise
TWM   Third World Multinational
UNCTAD   United Nations Conference on Trade and Development
UNIDO   United Nations Industrial Development Organization
VAP   Value-adding Partnership

*Nonstandard terminology introduced in this text.

DRAGON MULTINATIONAL

1

INTRODUCTION
Globalization from the Periphery

As we enter the next century, it is fair to say
that nearly all countries are navigating a single
economic sea.
>   Bruce Kogut,
>   "What Makes a Company Global?"

Globalization is . . . not just some passing trend.
Today it is the overarching international system
shaping the domestic politics and foreign
relations of virtually every country.
>   Thomas Friedman,
>   *The Lexus and the Olive Tree*

Stan Shih was obsessed with his "Dragon dream"—the dream of building his tiny Taiwan-based computer firm into a global giant. Never mind that he lacked all the ingredients considered essential—a strong brand name, a network of global suppliers, and markets around the world. His company, Multitech, had only been started in 1976, and it took until 1983 to develop its first major product: an IBM-compatible PC. But by the mid-1980s, Shih was fired up to go international and was already fantasizing about global conquests.

Renamed "Acer," Shih's company in fact blossomed and over the 10 years from its first steps across national borders, it grew at an annual rate between 25 and 35 percent, achieving the unlikely target of worldwide sales of $5 billion by 1995. It was by then the largest and most successful Chinese technology company in the world and well on the way to becoming the "Asian IBM." Sales revenues doubled again in the next five years, reaching just short of $10 billion by the turn of the century. Acer had diversified into a PC company, producing desktops, laptops, and components such as flat panel displays, CD-ROMs, and chips, as well as internet appliances and other electronic consumer goods such as cellular telephones. More than this, it was diversifying into internet services and becoming an incubator for high technology spin-off companies. It was indeed a global player in the fast-evolving Information Technology (IT) industry.

Acer achieved global coverage and a leading market position in dozens of countries in Asia, Latin America, and Central Asia in a fraction of the time taken by earlier multinationals emanating from the Triad countries—the United States, Europe, and Japan. Acer had built a global brand that helped to hold its dozens of independent businesses together in a coherent whole. Shih became a player in the worldwide computer industry through clever leverage of technology, international expansion via partnership, and through an organizational model of a global cluster that maximized the responsibility, initiative, and focus of his managers. All this meant that Acer was a completely different kind of multinational. By the turn of the century, Acer had most improbably arrived as one of the first of a new breed of "Dragon Multinationals" from the Periphery with a new model for global growth.

Acer is just one of hundreds of companies that are flourishing in the new conditions of the global economy. No one asked Acer or any of these other firms to join the party. Acer became a player by sheer determination and persistence and by devising strategies and organizational structures that were highly innovative. It did not achieve global coverage through simply emulating what incumbents like IBM or Compaq had done. This is what makes the achievements of an Acer so interesting—they rest on innovations, but they are strategic and organizational innovations rather than the product or process innovations that are viewed conventionally as driving economic change.

The latecomers and newcomers are developing global reach in some of the most unlikely or unpromising industries, where domestic competition has traditionally been paramount. Consider the steel industry, where it has long been considered that huge global corporations would drive out all competitors. Yet the world's first truly global steel firm, Ispat International, came from the periphery. It started in Indonesia and has risen in the space of a decade to become one of the world's Top 5 steelmakers, with a worldwide network of ultramodern minimills, supplying global customers like General Motors with steel tailored to their needs anywhere it is needed. This global operation was built by the corporation's founder, Lakshmi Mittal, through purchasing run-down state-owned steel plants in Latin America, Southeast Asia, and Central Asia and integrating them into a global network. On the basis of this platform, Ispat was in the late 1990s able to extend its network into the heartlands of the United States, Europe, and Japan.

Or consider the cement industry, hardly a global industry, where national companies continue to compete on their home turf. Yet a Mexican multinational, Cemex, has blazed a globalizing trail here, rising to become the world's number one cement trader, buying and selling cement in over 60 countries, and the world's third largest producer, owning or controlling over 50 cement plants in more than 10 countries spanning Latin America, Southeast Asia (The Philippines and Indonesia), the Middle East (Egypt), as well as Europe (Spain) and the United States. Cemex has achieved its distinction precisely because it pursued a global vision in a largely domestic-oriented industry. It backed this with innovative use of information technology (including the use of Global Positioning Satellite systems to locate all its cement deliveries worldwide) and integration of service planning and delivery to give previously unattainable levels of customer responsiveness. Indeed, the company boasts that you can order wet cement anywhere and it will arrive faster than a pizza!

These globalizing firms are coming from everywhere. The Hong Kong–based trading firm, Li & Fung, has turned itself into one of the world's largest and most successful industrial contractors, operating a global network of customer firms and supply chain contractees with razor-sharp efficiency. In the year 2000 it was leading the contract manufacturing sector into internet-based operations, expanding its global reach from a few hundred large customer firms to thousands of small customer firms. From Singapore, the Hong Leong Group has expanded into industry and manufacturing, property, finance, and, in the 1990s, into global hotel chains. Kwek Leng Beng, son of the group's founder, has put together the Millennium & Copthorne chain, now one of the world's Top 10 hotel chains. Listed in London, it is serving as the platform for Kwek's construction of a global hospitality chain, encompassing budget accommodation to six-star luxury.

It would be tedious to extend the list too far. It is clear that there exist a number of interesting new players in the global economy that are sufficiently different from conventional, large, resource-rich MNEs as to command analytical attention. Acer and these other firms, like Ispat, Cemex, Li & Fung, or the Hong Leong Group, all come from the Periphery. Yet they are profiting from the conditions created by globalization. In each case, these latecomers have utilized their late arrival as a source of advantage, overtaking the incumbents through their integration capabilities and their strategic and organizational innovations. They aspire to achieve and quickly acquire global scale of operations. They are not held back by comfortable assumptions that their domestic market is huge—an assumption that tends to hold back firms from the Triad markets of the United States, Europe, and Japan. They either have tiny domestic markets—like Acer in Taiwan—or they have no domestic market at all, like Ispat, and they are thus forced to view the world as their market.

The sudden appearance of these firms, and their capacity to create a competitive position in the teeth of opposition from giant incumbents, is the phenomenon that has provided the central puzzle and topic of interest for this study. It is indeed a puzzle that at a time of unparalleled interest in giant firms and globalization, these latecomers should make their dramatic entry. Their appearance and their model for global growth cannot be explained by conventional multinational strategies; these served the present incumbents but could not work in the face of incumbent opposition. Nor can their appearance be attributed to a new form of small-firm–large-firm dependence, since many of the newcomers and latecomers, like Ispat, are shaping the emergent form of a global market and acting as the vanguard for globalization. They are not simply occupying space vacated by incumbents, because in many cases they are creating new economic space by their own organizational and strategic innovations.

This book is concerned about how to unravel this puzzle and in so doing to develop a plausible account of the accelerated internationalization of firms from the Periphery. This account will involve elaborating and extending the existing frameworks utilized in the international business literature to discuss the process of internationalization, including the definition of internationalization itself, the impulse to internationalization, the processes through which internationalization is accomplished, and the sources of advantage of international firms over their domestic rivals. Much of this literature and these existing frameworks were developed for the situation obtaining two and three decades ago, when the multinational corporation was a species under siege. In many ways the international business literature still reflects concerns over internationalization developed at the height of the scare about "multinationals" in the 1970s, when the issue was posed in terms of a threat to national sovereignty. The fear was that giant corporations, striding across national borders, would reduce the nation state to subservience.[1] But this fear has not been realized.

The situation today is quite different. The latecomers and newcomers do not start out in a cautious way, feeling their way through foreign markets, but tend to regard a highly integrated world as their market from the outset. The international economy at the start of the twenty-first century is a very different kind of beast. It is inhabited by a few giants, true, but mostly by a large number of small- and medium-sized multinationals active across national borders through direct firm-to-firm interactions.[2] Their modes of internationalizing, their reasons for doing so, and their organizational and strategic innovations are scarcely captured by existing theories and conceptual frameworks, which were couched for different conditions in a different era.

The argument to be developed is that it is changes in the character of the world economy and in particular its globally interlinked character (what could be called the *worldwide web of interfirm connections*) that can be seen as responsible for driving the new approaches to and patterns of internationalization and global growth. Moreover, the strategies of interorganizational linkage and leverage that are most likely to succeed in this interlinked global economy are precisely those that would be favored by firms which lack substantial prior resource bases. In other words, they are ideal strategies for latecomers and newcomers and for small- and medium-sized firms rather than for established, large incumbents. My aim is to demonstrate that this argument provides a satisfying way of resolving the puzzle that initiates this investigation.

The Contradictions and Possibilities of Globalization

Every significant, complex social and economic system that we know of generates two complementary and contending forces. There are the forces of continuity and incremental change espoused and championed by the incumbents; and there are the forces of radical change and disruption fostered by the outsiders, the latecomers, and the newcomers. Every real system is in a state of dynamic evolution under the pressure of these contending forces. The world economy is one such system.

As we enter the twenty-first century, the world economy is one of the most important systems shaping our lives and aspirations. Some see it as headed inevitably and overwhelmingly toward a uniformity and convergence, where the great multinational corporations rule and everything else accommodates to their designs: this is the process popularized with endless gusto as *globalization*. But there are other futures, other pressures, other designs, that are generated not at the center but from the periphery. While it is no doubt true that all countries are "navigating a single economic sea" at the beginning of the twenty-first century, some are turning out to have much better navigation tools and insights than others.[3]

The successes of firms like Acer, Li & Fung, Ispat, Cemex, or Hong Leong, of many more like them, and of countless more to come, expose some of the contradictions and complexities of globalization. Far from creating a world of giant corporations devouring all before them, as is popularly believed, the process of globalization is actually creating a world of opportunities of vast potential—for those smart enough, and agile enough, to take advantage of them. These are the new multinationals from the Periphery. They can aptly be called, like Acer, the "Dragon Multinationals."

This book focuses on two of the tensions in globalization exploited by these firms—one a tension in space, the other a tension in time. The first is the tension between Center and Periphery—where the "Center" is taken to be the Triad countries (United States, Europe, and Japan) and the "Periphery" is taken to mean the former developing countries of East Asia and the present NICs. Despite some dissenting voices, most observers see the process of globalization as being driven by multinational firms from the Center—after all, they are the incumbents, they have the resources, they have the global reach.[4] The traditional focus on the Periphery is to see it as developing through a process of dependence on the Center—after all, this was the source of so much hostility by "the South" to the countries of the "North" in the failed "decade of development" of the 1970s. To focus on Acer and other "Dragon MNEs," as instigators of their own passage to global status, is to take a quite different stance—namely, one that sees the Periphery as exercising a countervailing power and promoting tendencies that complement those from the Triad but are not dependent on them. "Internationalization from the Periphery" is a concept that thus promises rewarding insights into the dynamics of globalization.

The second tension emerges in time between incumbents and latecomers. Latecomer firms like Acer had to find a way to compete globally in the computer business, without all the prior resources and experience of an IBM, a Compaq, or a Hewlett-Packard. Being a latecomer was not a strategic choice on Acer's part, but a constraint it had to live with and if possible exploit. Compaq too was a new firm in the computer industry, as was Dell. But these are best described as "newcomers" that are able to draw on a considerable body of resources and experience (e.g., customers, staff) within the industry as soon as they make their entry. These are advantages denied a latecomer. But there are ways that latecomers can draw advantages from their position, and Acer, Ispat, Li & Fung, and the Hong Leong Group, as well as many others, have very ably exploited these advantages to the full. As latecomers, they were able to leverage advantages from the incumbents they dealt with. Acer, for example, was able to act as a contract manufacturer of PCs for IBM and other leading brands and drew assiduously on this experience to ensure that its own production systems were as advanced as anywhere in the world. Furthermore, as latecomers, they are not tied to past technologies and practices; they are able to adopt the most advanced process and product technologies. Ispat illustrates this aptly with its capacity to leapfrog the world steel industry through adoption of an advanced process technology well before other large steel companies, and its attention paid to integration of its operations worldwide.[5]

The idea that latecomers from the Periphery might be able to exploit their position to advantage is an adaptation and elaboration for the late twentieth century of the process adumbrated by the Russian historian, Alexander Gerschenkron, in relation to the rise of latecomer industrial nations in Europe in the nineteenth century. Gerschenkron argued that latecomer nations like Germany and Russia were able to draw advantages from their latecomer status, such as the possibility of being able to draw on the latest technological advances in establishing new industries, thereby "leapfrogging" established rivals, or accelerating capital investment in new industries through such novel institutions as large-scale investment banks and state finance.[6] The same kind of idea can be applied not only to latecomer countries in the twentieth century, such as East Asian countries that utilized novel institutions for accelerating their uptake of advanced technologies, but to their firms as well, which can be characterized as "latecomer firms."[7]

The Dragon Multinational

By "Dragon Multinational" I mean a successful latecomer firm that internationalizes from the Periphery. It is a latecomer, rather than a newcomer or incumbent, and suffers the initial lack of resource endowment associated with this state. It internationalizes from the Periphery, rather than from the Center, and again suffers from the resource shortages and the distance from customers and suppliers that this entails. But the Dragon Multinationals are *successful*, in terms of their rate of growth and expansion into new markets, precisely because they overcome these obstacles. This is what makes them such an interesting case to investigate. To examine Acer or Ispat or Li & Fung or Hong Leong is not to look at yet another case of a firm mobilizing the appropriate resources, forging good links with other firms in its value chain, and serving its customers well, that is, building sustainable competitive advantages. All these features, which are taken for granted in the conventional discussions of competition and strategy and internationalization, are missing in the case of the latecomers from the Periphery.

Latecomers, by contrast, have to create advantages that did not exist; they have to turn their disadvantages into potential sources of advantage. To do so, they need to craft clever and innovative strategies and organizational forms. They cannot succeed merely by replicating what an IBM or HP or other incumbents did. First, they do not have the same resources, so it is beyond them. But even more important, they can hardly hope to succeed by pursuing strategies that incumbents like IBM or Compaq know full well, for then counterattack is predictable and easy. They need to develop novel and surprising strategies and organizational forms—which in many cases they are able to do. This is why Dragon Multinationals make such interesting cases to study. They develop the innovations—and thereby become players on the world stage—that then become available for other firms to replicate in their turn. But by then the Acers and Ispats are part of the elite and have access to the resources and sources of advantage that are conventionally described.

The hypothesis that launches this study, and which is to be investigated in detail, is that the arrival of the Dragon Multinationals is to be traced not to conventional sources of success, such as product or process innovation, but instead to innovations in strategy and organization. These are likely to be the sources of explanation for these firms' capacity to sustain breakneck speeds of internationalization, achieving global coverage in a fraction of the time taken by the earlier MNEs that are today's incumbents. Such an approach implies that some kinds of explanation are not available. For example, it implies that Dragon MNEs did not succeed simply because of low costs. Certainly, as peripheral latecomers from NICs, they enjoy cost advantages in their domestic base—but these are rapidly dissipated and in any case are of no consequence as soon as these firms expand into the Triad regions and pay the same as any other firm for labor and supplies. So the common assumption that costs are their only advantage is of little help in explaining their sustained success. Another explanation concerns continued dependence of Peripheral latecomers on the networks within which they insert themselves. For example, it might be argued that the subcontracting networks through which Acer was able to learn act as a fetter, constraining the firm's further development, if not in Acer's case, then perhaps in the case of other firms. Again the evidence, to be presented, indicates that latecomer firms from the Periphery are able to exploit network connections to accelerate their global coverage—but that they know how to disentangle themselves in order to pursue autonomous rather than dependent development.

These kinds of explanations and others like them, such as that governments were able to create special advantages for these latecomer firms, derive from the debates of two and three decades ago, when there was a fear that giant MNEs would stride across the planet and obliterate all competitors or else colonize some firms and maintain them in a state of permanent dependence. But these fears have simply not come to pass. It is time to move on and to examine the *successes* and achievements of the latecomers expanding internationally from the Periphery, rather than their predicted sources of failure.

Aims of This Book

This book engages with three sets of issues and seeks to contribute fresh ideas to each, based on the experiences of latecomer multinationals from the Periphery. The first set of issues concern the multinational enterprise (MNE) itself, as an institution that has come to public prominence in recent decades. The experience of Acer and other latecomer firms internationalizing from the Periphery—the Dragon Multinationals—is quite distinctive when compared with the experiences and characteristics of earlier MNEs, now the incumbents in the global economy, and indeed with earlier "Third World Multinationals." The primary aim of this book is to flesh out what these features are and to demonstrate their distinctiveness.

Second, the book aims to cast in a fresh light the ideas, concepts, and theoretical frameworks that have been built over the course of the past four decades in the field of international business studies. These are informed largely by the experiences of the incumbent MNEs that emanated from the United States—although the experiences of European and Japanese MNEs have also contributed to these frameworks. Theoretical accounts of the impulse to internationalization, of the advantages of international firms over their domestic rivals, and of the process of internationalization—all these tend to reflect the earlier experiences of the MNEs as they expanded abroad from a home base in the Triad. In this book I demonstrate that these frameworks fail in certain important ways to accommodate the quite distinctive experiences of latecomer MNEs from the Periphery. More to the point, the existing frameworks fail in significant ways to illuminate the experiences of the latecomers. They overlook significant features of the experiences of these firms and make it difficult to explain why some latecomer MNEs succeed admirably, and why others fail miserably. A second aim then is to contribute to the development of new conceptual and theoretical frameworks that can accommodate the wider range of internationalization experiences now to be found within the global economy.

A third area of intellectual concern is that of the global economy itself and the set of issues surrounding the notion of globalization. This is one of the most contested areas in current scholarship in international business and international political economy. Much of the debate, however, seems to be informed by an exaggerated notion of the power and reach of MNEs and their ability to influence events, to face down sovereign states, and to fashion a world that converges on a single model of doing business. In its ideal form, what is seen by many as emerging is a single global business civilization and global culture (for which read: Mickey Mouse, McDonald's Golden Arches, and the NASDAQ Stock Exchange). Now the set of experiences of the latecomers from the Periphery again generates a quite distinctive perspective on this issue and on the nature of the global economy itself. The latecomers have globalized very rapidly, taking full advantage of the exploding patterns of interfirm linkages that now characterize the international economy. The latecomers are not the only ones to do so: other newcomers, such as "global start-ups" and most recently, dot.com start-ups, have also been expanding operations across borders through alliances, partnerships, and various kinds of interfirm linkage and leverage. But they do so with the resources available in their home base, such as the richly endowed Silicon Valley. But the latecomers have had to do it without this resource base, and so their achievements are all the more remarkable. Thus, the experience of the latecomer MNEs from the Periphery forces a recognition that globalization creates wholly new kinds of possibilities for small- and medium-sized enterprises to become global players exceedingly rapidly, provided they have the wit and ability to take advantage of the opportunities offered. In this sense, it would be more correct to say that globalization is creating and sustaining multiple worlds rather than a single convergent world order. This is an attractive theme to explore.

Three objectives are therefore pursued in this work. First, I seek to establish the distinctiveness of the latecomer MNEs internationalizing from the Periphery, both with respect to the incumbent MNEs and to the other newcomers that have stormed onto the stage of the international economy in the past decade. This is both a descriptive and analytic task. Second, I develop a conceptual and theoretical framework that builds on the established frameworks in the international business (IB) literature for dealing with these distinctive characteristics. The existing frameworks shed little light on which latecomer strategies seem to work, and which don't, and why. Alternative frameworks that seem better adapted to accommodating the experiences of the latecomers, as well as sundry newcomers to the world stage, will be discussed. Third, I develop the proposition that globalization is an open-ended process, creating multiple outcomes rather than the single, convergent global system that is assumed by so many of the participants in the debates. I make the case that the latecomers from the Periphery are actually among the first firms to act on this insight and to take advantage of the opportunities inherent in globalization. They are, in fact, prime innovators in fashioning their strategies and organizational architectures in ways which complement and build on the networks and multiple interfirm connections that are the key features of the emergent global economy.

This book then is an attempt to engage with these puzzles and paradoxes of globalization. It is concerned with how outsiders—latecomers—may overthrow incumbent advantage and help to reshape the world economy.[8] This concern appears to be a very large project—as indeed it is—the overturning of incumbent advantage, through which the entire international economic system renews itself. This is the grand issue that should properly be the subject of sustained reflection by mainstream economic and management scholarship. It is a plea that goes back to Schumpeter and his claim that competitiveness analysis should be concerned with how firms survive the incursions of new technologies and new markets rather than with static considerations of price effects.[9] It is a plea that has become increasingly insistent, with the rise of new approaches such as evolutionary economics, industrial dynamics, and dynamic capabilities theories of the firm. In these approaches, the focus is not just on the exploitation of existing internal and external firm-specific capabilities (as is done in other strategic paradigms), but on how the firm can develop new ones. Such approaches are concerned with the specifics of "how some organizations first develop firm-specific capabilities and how they renew competencies to respond to shifts in the business environment. These issues are intimately tied to the firm's business processes, market positions, and expansion paths."[10]

Fundamentally, incumbents are concerned to extend and sustain their existing advantages. The business literature reflects this concern in its quest for the determinants of "sustainable competitive advantage" whether at the domestic or international level. The advantages of incumbents rest on their superior resources, that is, their existing assets and capabilities that are stretched across numerous national markets. Existing theories of internationalization and the sources of international competitive advantage reflect for the most part the experiences of dominant incumbent firms. Given such a state of affairs, this book not only seeks to document the experiences of a representative sample of newcomers and latecomers, but also seeks to engage with the existing theoretical frameworks, bringing the perspectives of these outsiders to the task. In this enterprise, the present work builds on an emerging and promising literature that emphasizes the novel strategies and organizational forms devised by multinationals from Peripheral countries to break into world markets.[11] Important parallels can be established between this literature and the emerging scholarship that describes and analyzes the internationalization of small- and medium-sized firms and the internationalization of entrepreneurship.[12] The same kinds of unorthodox strategies can be found common to all three groups of firms.

Using the language of resources (i.e., the resource-based view (RVB) of the firm), there is a clear distinction to be made between the strategies of incumbents and those of newcomer and latecomer multinationals. The strategies of incumbents reflect their desire to exploit their existing resources—their assets and capabilities, such as their technologies, their market presence, their overseas affiliates. The strategies of newcomers and latecomers, by contrast, are driven more by the quest to enhance their competitiveness by securing access to resources which they do not possess—such as through links with other international firms or through joint ventures with partners in new markets. The proposition that newcomers and latecomers expand abroad to secure resources and thereby enhance their competitiveness is central to the argument of this book.

A subsidiary aim of this book then is to put the resource-based view to new and potentially far-reaching applications. The emphasis is shifted from the conventional concern with firms' sustaining existing advantages to firms' creating new advantages—through the search for and acquisition of the appropriate resources. These resources are generally to be found in the wider world economy and under the control of incumbents. Gaining access to them has required newcomers and latecomers to move boldly into the international domain and devise ingenious strategies and organizational forms to sustain their quest. International outsiders—latecomer and newcomer MNEs—prove to be ideal vehicles for exploring the phenomena of competitive, accelerated internationalization. As outlined in the preface, this book forms a pair with my earlier book, *Tiger Technology*, coauthored with Dong-Sung Cho.[13]

Outline of the Chapters to Come

The argument as sketched here is fleshed out through subsequent chapters, according to the following schematic. Part I opens up the prospect of new kinds of players in the international economy and the implications of their arrival. Chapter 2 is concerned with the facts of the matter and with the range and variety of the new players. It seeks to order them in terms of their novel strategies in a new "zoology" of species and subspecies. Initial hypotheses are advanced through which the proliferation of newcomers and latecomers might be accounted for, referring both to the character of the international economy itself (and in particular the explosion of interfirm connections that has been characteristic of the last decade of the twentieth century) and to the strategies and organizational innovations of the newcomers and latecomers. This complementarity between the nature of the international economy and its worldwide web of interfirm connections, and the dramatic appearance of so many newcomers and latecomers as international players, is the motif that runs through the entire book.

Chapter 3 delves in detail into the case of one of the latecomer MNEs, namely, the Acer Group, which originated in Taiwan and has now become a global and very successful firm competing in a variety of IT product markets. Acer's case is of particular interest because it has moved through not just one model of internationalization in its brief international career, but through three very different organizational and strategic trajectories. In doing so, it illustrates all the options and choices open to latecomers and newcomers and thus engages with the point at issue: What are the most effective means through which newcomers and latecomers can fashion strategies and organization to take advantage of the new opportunities presented by the global economy?

In part II, the argument is fleshed out through the analysis of the characteristics of the latecomers and newcomers set against the theoretical frameworks of the international business literature. The argument proceeds through the firms' capacity to accelerate their internationalization, then considers their strategic innovations, followed by their organizational innovations, and finally discusses how these can be held together in a coherent whole. Chapter 4 starts by looking at the process of internationalization itself, to find clues as to how it can be accelerated so successfully and to what extent this departs from current conceptions of the process of internationalization. Here the experience of recent latecomers and newcomers finds an interesting counterpart in the experiences of firms internationalizing from the Scandinavian and Nordic countries in the early years of the twentieth century. They were the latecomers of their time, and they devised internationalization patterns that bear striking resemblance to those observed today among latecomers and newcomers but at a slower pace of expansion. Scandinavian researchers have captured this internationalization experience in a model of incremental expansion dubbed the "Uppsala model." This chapter addresses the question: How relevant is the Uppsala model to the more recent experiences of latecomers and newcomers? Again a resource-based view allows us to generalize the question and provide fresh insights based on latecomer experiences.

Chapter 5 tackles the question of the strategic innovations devised by Dragon Multinationals to break into international markets. The novel features of these strategies are captured in the notions of linkage and leverage—so that firms are able to accelerate their internationalization and cover the globe in latticelike formations. Stan Shih, chairman and CEO of Acer, characterizes the strategic innovations of Acer in terms of parallels with the ancient Chinese game of GO. These all provide a handle on the fundamental strategic departures exhibited internationally by the newcomers and latecomers. Again these approaches are contrasted with the existing literature on global strategy.

Chapter 6 addresses the organizational innovations and, in particular, the capacity of firms like Acer and Li & Fung to "bundle" their activities into discrete business units that are called (in this text) "cells" and then expand internationally through the creation of clusters of these business cells. This global cellular cluster organizational template is a dramatic departure from the conventional MNE organizational structure, where national subsidiaries were created under close supervision of headquarters and the whole was held together through structures of hierarchy and control. This chapter explores the management challenges of developing a global cellular organizational architecture, together with some of the pitfalls encountered by pioneers like Acer. The point is that while firms expanding internationally from the Periphery have many potential advantages, they must, in order to capture these advantages, display management and organizational capabilities of a high order.

In part III, we move to the impact that the experience of latecomer multinationals from the Periphery is having on the conceptual and theoretical frameworks of the international business literature. Chapter 7 engages with the general issue of the theories of international organization and internationalization, to see to what extent they shed light on the experiences of the new multinationals in the new global economy. Issues such as the definition of internationalization, the impulse to internationalize, the process of internationalization, and the sources of international advantage are all considered. The chapter critically appraises the existing theory from the perspective of its applicability to the experiences of latecomers and newcomers. It develops a framework that can more effectively accommodate these latter firms' choices and strategies.

Chapter 8, by contrast, engages with the literature on the process of internationalization itself. It provides a historical account of the theoretical frameworks that have been developed for this purpose and provides an overview of the basic dimensions of the internationalization process. Such a framework provides the setting within which quite different internationalization pathways may be identified, and their strategic goals compared. These different strategic approaches are then linked to their economic setting, namely, the global economy itself, and their effectiveness compared.

Finally, in chapter 9, the various strands of the argument of the book are woven together within a discussion of the key features and opposing tendencies of globalization. It queries whether the process termed "globalization" is creating a single, convergent, uniform world business system—as claimed by many of the evangelists of a new global order. It suggests that it is actually much more plausible to see globalization as being driven by multiple players and agents, among whom the global start-ups, the newcomers, and latecomers must be counted as significant participants. From this perspective, the latecomers from the Periphery are actually prime innovators, in that they have grasped the dialectic of globalization and fashioned strategies that build on, complement, and extend the strategies of incumbents. In this way, they have overturned their latecomer and Peripheral disadvantages and turned them into sources of strength. The book closes by discussing the relevance of these conclusions for firms more generally seeking to make their mark in the emerging global economy of the twenty-first century.

Notes

1. In their very different ways, Vernon (1971) and Barnet and Mueller (1974) reflected these tendencies in their accounts of the "storm over the multinationals." Both authors reviewed their conclusions from the perspective of the 1990s and found surprisingly little change: Vernon (1998); Barnet and Cavanagh (1994).

2. The United Nations Conference on Trade and Development (UNCTAD) in its *World Investment Report* for 1999 counted 60,000 firms with activities crossing national borders and controlling 500,000 national subsidiaries. Only a small minority of these firms are the global giants of popular imagination—as discussed for example by Stopford (1998) and in chapter 2.

3. The phrase is from Kogut (1999: 165).

4. One such dissenter is Rugman (2000). He argues that firms that emanate from the Triad have sufficiently large domestic markets that they do not have to aspire to global reach. This is a neat complement to the argument I develop in this text, namely, that it is firms from the Periphery which seek competitive advantage precisely through their global vision and global aspirations.

5. Ispat was an early adopter of Direct Reduced Iron (DRI) process technology, at a time when it was largely untested by the incumbent steel firms. As a latecomer, Ispat could afford to take a technological risk—which turned out to be a prescient move.

6. See Gerschenkron (1962) for the original formulation of this thesis. It has been much discussed since then in the historical literature.

7. See Hobday (1995) for an account of "latecomer firms" and Mathews and Cho (1999; 2000) for an elaboration in the context of the management and organizational literature.

8. There are several antecedents for such a venture, in the form of the books and articles published in the 1980s and early 1990s on the emergence of multinationals from developing countries, variously called "Third World Multinationals" (TWMs) or "Multinational Enterprises from Developing Countries" (MEDCs) or "Pacific Asian Multinationals" (PAMs). Notable are the studies by Ghymn (1980); O'Brien (1980); Lecraw (1977; 1981); Kumar and McLeod (eds) (1981); Chen (1981) on Hong Kong MNEs in Asia; Kumar (1982); Encarnation (1982); Lall (1982); Wells (1983); Lall et al. (1983); Agarwal (1985); Lall (1986); Monkiewicz (1986); Khan (1987); Vernon-Wortzel and Wortzel (1988); Buckley and Mirza (1988); Aggarwal and Agmon (1990); and Tolentino (1993). The works by Wells (1983) and Lecraw (1977; 1981) on the one hand, and Lall et al. (1983) and Lall (1986) on the other, set the tone for these studies, with their careful case studies and systematic comparisons between the "Third World" multinationals and those from the advanced countries. These studies generally saw multinationals from developing countries as drawing on their cost advantages to engage in competition with incumbents or else seeking some advantage in exploiting redundant technology or ethnic links. Wells and Lecraw saw TWMs as destined to die out unless they upgraded their strategies, while S. Lall and R. Lall tended to see TWMs as already developing distinctive strategies of their own, which prefigure what I am calling "latecomer strategies" in this book. At the time these debates reflected the prevailing realities; it remains the case for

the newer generations of NICs emerging onto the world stage, particularly from China. Indian MNEs occupy a special case, as their international expansion appeared to be driven more by domestic considerations (e.g., escape from Indian national regulations) than by aspirations of global reach; moreover, Indian MNEs tended to gravitate toward other NICs rather than toward advanced markets (Encarnation 1982; 1989; Kaplinsky 1997). This study moves beyond formerly prevalent cost concerns to consider how MNEs from the Periphery can confront incumbents on their own terms through organizational and strategic innovation rather than through endless reliance on cost advantages (which are in any case rapidly eroded). See Yeung (1994a); Dunning, van Hoesels and Narula (1997); and Vegado, Yu, and Negandhi (1996) for a review of these issues, and the collections of articles edited by Schmitz and Cassiolato (1992), Lall (1993), and by Yeung (1999c).

9. The claim was formulated by Schumpeter in his 1942 work, *Capitalism, Socialism and Democracy*. This provides one of the principal currents that has led to evolutionary economics.

10. Teece, Pisano, and Shuen (1997: 515). Their paper provides an overview of the dynamic capabilities approach, which in turn draws on the evolutionary economics perspective, which was given its definitive form by Nelson and Winter (1982), and the resource-based view, to be discussed below. The collection of papers edited by Montgomery (1995) provides an introduction to the overlaps between evolutionary economics approaches to the firm and the resource-based view.

11. Notable contributions include those by Buckley and Mirza (1988) on "Pacific Asian Multinationals" which anticipate many of the features described here as belonging to "Dragon Multinationals"; Tallman and Shenkar (1990) on SMEs from Korea expanding abroad through cooperative joint ventures; Chen (1992) and Chen and Chen (1998a;-b) on Taiwan firms' foreign direct investment and their utilization of overseas network linkages; Yeung (1994b; 1998; 1999b) on Hong Kong and Singaporean firms' innovative expansion strategies; and Young, Huang, and McDermott (1996) on emerging Chinese multinationals. Craig and Douglas (1997), Mytelka (2000), and Bartlett and Ghoshal (2000a;-b) review many of the relevant cases and strategies employed by these new global late movers.

12. On the internationalization of SMEs, see for example the contributions by Fujita (1995a;-b; 1998) at UNCTAD and by OECD (1997a), as well as by Acs and Preston (1997); Acs, Morck, Shaver, and Yeung (1997); Kohn (1997); Gomes-Casseres (1997); Gomes-Casseres and Kohn (1998); Coviello and Munro (1997); Coviello and McAuley (1999); Hamid and Wright (1999), and Prasad (1999). This vibrant literature is concerned to bring out the distinctive features of SMEs' internationalization, or globalization, as compared with the dominant IB literature of the past four decades that has equated international reach with large size. On the internationalization of entrepreneurship, which deals with "born global" technology-rich and knowledge-rich start-up firms or new players, see for example the several contributions by McDougall and Oviatt (1991; 1997; 2000) and Oviatt and McDougall (1994; 1995; 1997; 1999); Zacharakis (1997); Preece, Miles, and Baetz (1999); Hamid and Wright (1999); Jones (1999); Anderson (2000) and Burgel and Murray (2000). This literature highlights the net-

work connections made by entrepreneurial firms in the global economy. My approach in this text is to make the case that many of the strategic and organizational innovations that can be identified among the latecomers can also be found among these kinds of newcomers, and for the same kinds of reasons—namely, that they are drawn into the global economy by networks of interconnections rather than by their possession of overwhelming prior resources.

13. See Mathews and Cho (2000) as well as Mathews (2001a). For an insightful review of the book, see Geoffrey Owen, "Leapfrogged by leverage" in the Inside Track column, *Financial Times*, 24 July 2000.

Part I

THE ARRIVAL OF MULTINATIONAL
NEWCOMERS AND LATECOMERS

2

THE NEW ZOOLOGY OF THE
INTERNATIONAL ECONOMY

The global landscape is . . . no longer the sole
domain of multinational behemoths originating
from the Industrial Triad. It is now populated
by an array of companies, including a growing
number of small- and medium-sized companies.
Domestic market leaders from emerging
economies are venturing into international
markets as once-protected home markets open
up to foreign competition.

> C. Samuel Craig and
> Susan P. Douglas,
> "Developing Strategies for
> Global Markets"

Market entry in (the international network)
view is not so much a matter of choosing
modes of entry but a laborious process of
acquiring a rudimentary understanding of the
character of the network, of timing of activities
regarding different relationships, and of
responding to actions by other actors in the
network.

> Mats Forsgren and
> Jan Johanson,
> *Managing Networks in
> International Business*

The multinational corporation is the most familiar character in the globalization drama. It is the most admired, most feared, yet most elusive of the
actors shaping the world of the twenty-first century. The global corporation
is the central driving force, so it is held, of the dominant process of our
time, which is globalization.[1] As conventionally viewed, this process is
driving the world economy to a state where a few hundred dominant multinational enterprises (MNEs) interact with each other and define a new
global organizational and management model that sets new standards which
others must reach or perish. Global reach, global capabilities, global synergies achieved through global strategies—these are seen as becoming the
preeminent sources of advantage. In the popular literature as much as in

the management and organizational literature, this is a globalization process that is widely seen to be unstoppable. It is grounded in technological changes that provide global firms with unprecedented opportunities for integrating their far-flung operations while maintaining responsiveness to national markets. They are shaping the world, we are told, in their image.[2]

Yet even a cursory look at the management literature and the popular business press shows that these same large, dominant firms are finding it difficult to keep up with the changes that they are supposed to have unleashed. Peter Drucker claims correctly that new "transnational" corporations are emerging for whom the global economy is simply the place where they do business. Some scholars point to the inability of most global firms to develop "transnational" organizational structures and processes that take them beyond their domestic models and relations.[3] Others point to the pace of change that leaves most of the world's large firms floundering in the wake of smaller, more nimble but equally global firms that drive technological innovation and diffusion.[4] Many question whether so-called global firms are in reality as geocentric as they might think. Scratch the typical giant U.S., European, or Japanese MNE, and you find a national firm engaged in international operations.[5]

What is of greatest interest is that today's transnationals are emerging from the unlikeliest places. In the past decade, a host of new firms have arisen which are active in the global economy while bearing little resemblance to the lumbering giants of popular imagination. According to the United Nations Conference on Trade and Development (UNCTAD), by the end of the 1990s, there were over 60,000 firms operating internationally, controlling at least 500,000 foreign affiliates.[6] They produced goods worth around $11 trillion in 1998 (compared with world trade in that year of almost $7 trillion—meaning that international production by MNEs has overtaken world trade as the dominant international dynamic). The trade between these firms has been increasing faster than world trade overall, while investments by these firms (foreign direct investment) is also increasing faster than world trade growth. It is the activities of these firms that define the emergent global economy. This economy in reality shows few points of resemblance with the uniform, convergent, giant MNE-dominated economy of popular imagination.

How much do we know about these 60,000-odd firms—in terms of their origins, their mode of operation, their strategies and organization?[7] Certainly, they include typical MNEs that have vast resources, operations in more than 100 countries, and multiple sites covering R&D, production, logistics, marketing, and customer support—the General Electrics, the GMs, IBMs, Motorolas, NECs, Siemens, Unilevers. But they also include firms which are quite different from these conventional and resource-rich MNEs. They include, for example, much smaller MNEs, both in terms of resources, staff, and capital—what we might christen as "micro-MNEs."[8]

They include the "latecomer MNEs" from formerly developing countries, for example, which have pursued accelerated internationalization over the course of the past decade and acquired global reach in a fraction of the time taken by their predecessors. Acer is a good example—as are others from late-developing countries such as Li & Fung from Hong Kong or the Hong Leong Group from Singapore and Southeast Asia. Ispat International, started by an entrepreneur from India, is now the world's most globalized steel company, while Cemex from Mexico has emerged as the world's third largest producer of cement and the world's most global supplier and producer. These are global corporations; they are definitely not marginal players.[9]

That these latecomers are not anomalies—exceptions that prove the rule of incumbent superiority—is proven by the fact that the last two decades have also seen a proliferation of newcomer firms following equally innovative strategies. These include small- or medium-sized firms which originate from the advanced industrial countries but attack the world market with such vigor and with such clever strategies of integration that they must be classified as a new species of "newcomers." Firms like the Dutch foodstuffs firm Nutreco, or the German renal dialysis machines firm-turned global health services provider, Fresenius, or the U.S.-based CMS Energy, which became a global energy giant within a decade, are all examples of this new phenomenon. Other firms are included that almost bypass internationalization as a "process," since they are started and operate from day one in global markets as global players, servicing their customers wherever they are to be found; these are the "born globals" or "international new ventures."[10] An emerging literature points to the fact that many of these, quite small players, are internationalizing faster than their earlier competitors and much earlier in their corporate careers.[11]

Take the case of CMS Energy, which was at the beginning of the 1990s a relatively small Midwest utilities company generating electric power for Michigan state and operating a small non-U.S. oil and gas business. But under new management it went into globalization overdrive. By the end of the decade, it was an energy giant, operating worldwide businesses in electric and natural gas; independent power production; natural gas pipelines and storage; oil and gas exploration and production; and energy marketing, services, and trading. CMS Energy had acquired assets totaling around $14 billion throughout the United States and in 22 countries around the world and was generating revenues worth more than $6 billion—all this in less than a decade. This is a newcomer with a vengeance. It shows what can be done by established companies in advanced countries like the United States when they want to get serious about globalization.

Europe too has generated a good proportion of such global newcomers. Fresenius was a modest health care products firm which developed a business in renal dialysis machines, starting out as an agent and importer, and moving through the 1980s to build up its own domestic manufacturing resources. Like CMS Energy, it went into globalization overdrive in the 1990s. Under its new CEO, Gerd Frick, Fresenius expanded rapidly through growth and acquisition; it acquired a major U.S. dialysis equipment and services company and then consolidated its worldwide operations as Fresenius Medical Care, with public listings in New York and Frankfurt. It thus turned itself into a global health services operation.[12]

The Dutch-based Nutreco is another case of a rapidly globalizing group of companies focused on the worldwide animal feedstuffs and fish farming businesses. Nutreco has emerged as the world's largest salmon fish farming entity, for example, with major operations in Norway and Chile, now the world's leading suppliers of farmed Atlantic salmon. In 1999, Nutreco expanded its reach further through the acquisition of the Chilean and Scottish salmon-farming operations of Marine Harvest Salmon, which itself had achieved global scale rapidly through the purchase of these operations from the MNE Unilever. This is international leverage strategy at work.

Yet more firms have always been "global" but kept quiet about it, focusing their efforts on maintaining a commanding position in a very narrowly defined niche market. Firms like Hauni, which after several decades continues to supply 90 percent of the world market for cigarette-making machines, show that suitably focused geocentric firms can sustain their world position against the efforts of even huge multinational competitors like a General Electric. These are the species "global niche players" and "hidden champions."[13]

There are yet other forms in this new "zoology" of the global economy. One type is what we might call the "contractor MNEs," which are the many firms that serve as industrial contractors to existing MNEs, providing the components or the final assemblies that big name firms then brand and market.[14] Moreover, they supply them anywhere in the world, from numerous production and logistics points which the firms create as part of their attraction for global customers. Supply firms are established in Singapore or Mexico to provide parts and equipment or maintenance services to multinationals and are drawn abroad with their customer firms. This pattern of internationalization increasingly involves the firm being "pulled" into international connections rather than internationalizing through its own "push" efforts. Thus is the global economy being created and enriched through such kinds of global interfirm linkages and connections.

These then are some of the inhabitants of the global economy that is emerging at the start of the twenty-first century—the newcomers and latecomers, whose modes of operation appear to be very different from those of the conventional incumbents.[15] The newcomers and latecomers have carved out a space for themselves in the global arena, not by replicating the strategies of the incumbents, nor seeking to compete with them head to head, but by fashioning novel strategies of containment and encirclement, combined with collaboration—by making themselves indispensable to the incumbents, for example, as contractors and suppliers. They effortlessly regard the world as their market and have no trouble in devising global organizational and management structures of great power and novelty. These newcomers and latecomers are successful precisely because they have adapted faster than others to the new features of the global economy—to its interconnectedness, its multiple linkages—which create the networking opportunities that latecomers and newcomers have seized. *The newcomers and latecomers are the vanguard of the new transnational corporation.*

The Global Economy and Its Inhabitants

The emergence of a relatively uniform world business system, within which MNEs (and increasingly, transnational corporations) are able to make confident investment and planning decisions, actually provides the ground within which the newcomer and latecomer MNEs of interest to us can flourish. It is the openness of the world trading system that provides the fundamental platform for this development. It should not be a source of surprise that it is internationalizing firms from the Periphery that are able to take advantage of this new open global system—for this has been the driving force behind East Asian industrialization for most of the past four decades.[16]

The more the global economy opens up possibilities for rapid economic integration, the more we find firms inventing new ways to organize their international expansion and their integration within the worldwide web of interfirm connections. It is their very diversity that provides them with competitive and collaborative advantages. While there may have been some uniformity in the patterns of expansion, organization, and management of the giant MNEs which pioneered the exploitation of the international economy (e.g., in terms of headquarters-subsidiary relations or approaches to entering new markets), any such uniformity has clearly been dispensed with as newcomer and latecomer firms engage with the challenge of transnationality. It is the variety of approaches that has generated successful models of expansion as well as failures. This is the evolutionary process at work.[17]

The networked global economy is itself a new phenomenon of the 1990s—or at least, a return to the integrated world system whose progress was interrupted by the First World War. Kobrin (1997) captures the essential twin features of this global economy. By *global* is meant a fusion of markets that have gone beyond a collection of national markets linked by trade. By *networked* is meant an economic space that has gone beyond the distinction between market and hierarchy but is concerned largely with the direct links between firms.[18] Thus, a networked global economy is focused on the direct interactions between firms that engage with each other in a continuous economic space.

Let us define the global economy in terms of the activities of the 60,000-odd firms that UNCTAD counted in 1999 as being engaged in cross-border trade or production.[19] These firms are the drivers of foreign direct investment—for purposes of conducting production across borders, or R&D, or marketing, or customer service, or regional coordination. All are now frequent forms of cross-border business activity. These are the firms that form the heart of the global economy—in fact, *they are the global economy*. These firms form multiple linkages and interconnections with each other. They interact with a host of suppliers and customer firms, drawing them too into the ambit of the global economy. They add value to components; they provide services; they produce final assemblies; and they market them. All this activity can in principle be computed and the resultant value-added constitutes the "global economy," which overlaps with each of the world's national economies and forms a growing proportion of total world economic activity.[20]

Picture this global economy as a teeming mass of multiple interactions and linkages between firms—a "network of networks." The focus of interest is not just the firms themselves, but the shifting linkages between them. Firms expand internationally, according to such a picture, by forming new linkages with firms that are already active in the global economy. They are "drawn" into the global economy; they are "pulled"; they are "integrated." These are all much more powerful metaphors for describing what actually goes on with these newcomers and latecomers than traditional notions of firms overcoming "barriers to entry" and "pushing" themselves past numerous obstacles to become internationally active. Such pictures belong to the period when the international economy was dominated by trade, whereas today it is dominated by criss-crossing value chains encompassing R&D, production, logistics, marketing, as well as exchange, where all the links are between firms rather than between countries.

In fact, one can argue that the global economy forms today an economic "system" in the same way that nation states form an international system. By this is meant that the main protagonists preferentially recognize each other as players and downgrade their recognition of, or involvement with, other kinds of players. This happened in the international state system, as nation-states asserted their authority in the fifteenth and sixteenth centuries over competing forms such as city-states and trading leagues; the system was formalized as a system of nation-states with the Treaty of Westphalia in 1648, bringing to an end the terrible Thirty Years War in Europe.[21] The same kind of argument can be leveled at the global economy at the end of the twentieth century, where global firms treat preferentially with each other. A global bank, for example, looks to global IT firms to supply and service its computing requirements, rather than having a variety of local suppliers in its different spheres of operations. A global automobile manufacturer like General Motors looks to global suppliers of steel and other raw materials as its preferred suppliers, who can cope with global production and logistics requirements, rather than an assortment of local suppliers—as was underlined by General Motors' call for global steel supply tenders in 1998. These pressures from existing global firms on other firms to likewise become global is in fact one of the critical—and underrecognized—drivers of globalization today. My point is that latecomers (and new-comers) are some of the earliest firms to recognize these pressures and trends and are thus powering a new dynamic in the globalizing world economy.

The Network Economy

The standard economic view, where firms are treated as atomistic entities engaged in highly individual production operations, is misleading at the best of times, but in the case of the global economy, it is dangerously aberrant. For firms engaged in international production, exchange relationships are all-important. This is true in practical terms, for the firms themselves, and in theory, for the purposes of analysis. Firms then are best understood as engaged in exchange relationships with each other. One industrial firm supplies another with needed components; in turn, it is supplied with components or subassemblies by another firm. All this happens in the industrial economy before final goods get to consumers through retail outlets. In fact, this is the bulk of economic activity: retail trade accounts for only a small proportion of the value-added in an economy.[22]

Sequences of such supply links, with each one adding-value to what has gone before (or working backward) each one supplying a value-added component or subassembly, form value-adding chains. Such chains may be based on minimal interfirm interaction, and the individual units may be varied frequently. But such variations in linkage constitute a source of transactions costs, insofar as firms have to search for new suppliers or customers and then search out their capabilities, pricing structures, and availability. Such costs can be minimized by the firms entering into longer-term relations with each other, based on knowledge of their operations and capabilities developed in cumulative fashion over time. Insofar as the firms engaged in such long-term contracting become partners, one can speak of a "value-adding partnership" (VAP).[23]

A picture then of the industrial economy as populated by thousands of firms cross-linked with each other, with chains of linkages constituting a first-order form of aggregation in VAPs, is one that will help us to make sense of the extraordinary growth and evolution of the international economy. The links might run vertically or diagonally and might criss-cross each other where firms belong to more than one VAP simultaneously (which will frequently be the case). The global economy, with these multiple linkages and criss-crossing VAPs, then looks as shown in Fig. 2.1.

This is the kind of multiply connected economy that has emerged internationally, and in which a host of new kinds of multinational enterprises are thriving. Newcomers like CMS Energy or Nutreco and latecomers like Acer, Ispat International, Li & Fung, or the Hong Leong Group have flourished in these conditions. They are part of what might be called the new "zoology" of the networked global economy. Let us look at them a little

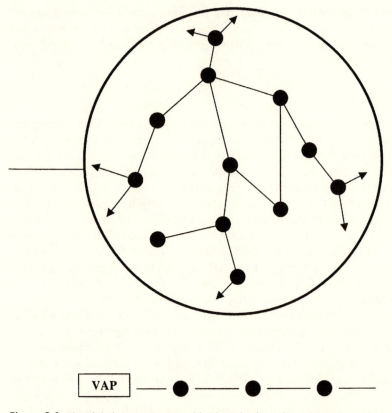

Figure 2.1 The global economy: A worldwide web of interfirm connections.

more closely to see what it is that enables them to internationalize so quickly and so thoroughly, taking maximum advantage of the network characteristics of the global economy.

Micro-MNEs

Despite the image of MNEs as being huge conglomerates, the majority of the world's 60,000 transnationals are quite small; indeed, most of them employ fewer than 250 people. Let us call these firms "micro-MNEs" since they are smaller even than "mini-MNEs." Their patterns of expansion, and their strategies, are being recognized as quite distinctive.[24] It is the thickening interconnections within the global economy that enable such small firms to operate globally. They do so largely by offering highly specialized services to existing global firms—services for which there would not in fact be an adequate market in the firm's domestic sphere. Thus, it is *only in a global context* that such micro-MNEs can survive. Their degree of specialization reflects the emergence of a global market and the outsourcing habits of established MNEs.[25]

Micro-MNEs are feasible as global players because of the astonishing developments in information technology—fax, cheaper telephone calls, the internet and the worldwide web—which enable companies to operate with minimal overheads and customers scattered around the globe. But technology is the facilitator of the development, not its cause. Such firms have also benefited from the changes in the world's trading systems, the breaking down of tariff barriers, and the opening up of markets to competition.[26] These provide the opportunities, but it is up to the agile microfirms to take advantage of them.

Born Globals/Global Start-Ups

An increasing number of internationally active firms can be described as "born global" high tech start-ups and international joint ventures in high tech sectors—variously called "international new ventures" or "global start-ups."[27] The formation of such ventures that are international from inception is an increasingly important phenomenon that clearly does not fit either an incremental theory of expansion nor a large firm expansion model. A typical example would be the firm Logitech, founded in 1982 by three entrepreneurs, two Italians and a Swiss, which was involved immediately in supplying mouse pointers for PC-producing MNEs in Taiwan and Europe, from production plants which were located close to its customers. Companies like Logitech rarely sell to final retail markets, but are industrial suppliers with only a very few industrial customers. Thus, they operate within well-defined industrial networks, in close partnership with these customer firms (and also with their own industrial suppliers). In this sense, their "instant" overseas expansion can be said to be implemented through partnerships— where the partners are their industrial customers and suppliers.

Contractor MNEs

A closely linked phenomenon is that of firms which contract to established MNEs, producing either components or subassemblies (as in the case of Logitech) or supplying full products on an Original Equipment Manufacturer (OEM) basis to companies which place their brand on the finished product.[28] The highly successful Taiwan PC industry, for example, is largely made up of such contractor MNEs, which supply fully produced PCs to specification for majors like IBM, Compaq, Apple, or Hewlett-Packard. They are MNEs because they are required to supply and deliver at any point in the world where the established firm specifies. Examples are First International Computer from Taiwan or Natsteel from Singapore. Such firms are becoming an increasingly important and expanding part of the growing global economy with its dense contracting interconnections.

Other Novel MNEs

Some firms are drawn into the global economy because they supply global MNEs and thereby become MNEs themselves. Consider the cases of firms that supply equipment and services to MNEs in the semiconductor industry, originating in emerging markets like Singapore and Penang in Malaysia. Firms such as Advanced Systems Automation (ASA) or LKT begin as local suppliers but expand abroad as they receive more and substantial orders from MNE semiconductor producers like Siemens or Intel.[29] From another perspective, firms become active internationally not just through engaging globally with customers, but also through contracting globally with suppliers. The interconnections that proliferate through such global networks expand as much toward suppliers as toward customers; they are all-encompassing, and a principal driver of internationalization by firms.

Latecomer Multinationals

One set of these "new" MNEs is going to engage our detailed attention, namely, the "latecomer" MNEs. Latecomers originate from the late-developing countries, typically in East Asia (as in our sample cases of Li & Fung, the Hong Leong Group, and of course Acer) but also from Latin America (as in the case of Cemex from Mexico) or South Asia (as in the case of Ispat International). Latecomers have to overcome their original lack of resources through strategies of linkage and leverage that maximize the impact of their few initial advantages, such as low costs and openness to new technological trends.[30] The common element in the appearance of these new forms of MNE is their engagement with the networks of firms constituting the "international economy." In each case, connections are established (such as industrial supplier, or industrial customer, or partner, or agent) that take a firm into a new set of relationships, and thus a role in a new and expanded network that at the same time spans borders and thus carries the firm into engagement with the international economy. For the latecomer MNE, the international economy is viewed not so much as a mass of competitors but as a plentiful source of collaborators and partners that can supply the resources and networks that the latecomer lacks.[31]

The Acer Group

Acer is a prime example of a latecomer multinational enterprise originating from Taiwan. By the late 1990s, it was commanding a position in the Top 5 of the world's PC firms.[32] As against the conventional view of the MNE, driven by a global headquarters conceiving and implementing a global strategy for the enterprise, Acer has evolved as a worldwide cluster of independent corporate entities. They are united by a common brand, but each strives to grow and expand its own business, collaborating with each other where convenient and sometimes competing with each other as well. Some of these business units specialize in chips and computer components, some in systems, some in internet business applications, while others are marketing companies focused on maximizing Acer's penetration of markets around the world. These business units are separately incorporated, and many of them are publicly listed on local stock exchanges. Their managers and workers own a considerable stake in these businesses and work hard to make them prosper. The founder and chairman of Acer, Stan Shih, likes to say that the less he owns of Acer's growing cluster of worldwide businesses, the richer he becomes—because the business overall grows and prospers through the efforts of these owner-managers and workers. Acer has 40 or 50 growth engines in place of one that powers the conventional MNE.

Acer's two principal business units, known in the 1990s as Acer Information Products Group (AIPG) and Acer Peripherals Inc. (API), were themselves global corporations that grew and diversified, spinning off new business units as they sought out and entered new businesses and markets. Adaptation through changes in the business processes or strategies of these units, combined with regular new business formation through spinning off (or "budding" new enterprises), means that Acer as a global group is constantly changing its configuration and organizational structure. It has no problems with "subsidiary initiative"—the absence of which plagues conventional MNEs (or its complement, wayward subsidiary initiatives, that are out of line with overall strategies).[33]

Acer keeps its operating parts together not through hierarchical relations of authority but through interdependence and agreed rules of behavior—what Stan Shih called in the 1990s a "client-server" organizational architecture and by 2000 was referring to as an Internet Organizational Protocol—that is, interconnected, heterarchical, and coordinated autonomy, fused by partnership.

Acer's partnership model extends beyond its own companies and employees to its suppliers and industrial customers and distributors. Whereas the conventional MNE views market entry in terms of a decision between establishing a greenfield site or acquiring an existing business, many of Acer's successful market incursions have involved partnerships with existing PC distributors. Acer grew rapidly to market leadership in Mexico, for example, through its partnership with Computec, and it has reached second position in India likewise through partnership with Wipro. Partnership is used by Acer as a means of accelerating global coverage.

We will have much more to say about Acer as a latecomer multinational; about its accelerated internationalization through partnerships; its strategic innovations in tackling Peripheral markets and consolidating there before driving into the Triad; and its organizational innovations as a successful

global cluster of highly focused but interdependent firms that are themselves becoming global in scale and scope. The salience of Acer is underscored by the fact that it is just one of these new kinds of latecomer MNEs
from the Periphery. Others have tackled the global challenge in equally ar-
resting and innovative fashion.

Ispat International

Ispat International in the 1980s was a small, Indian-based company looking
to become involved in the steel industry.[34] When Ispat's founder, Lakshmi
Mittal, surveyed his options for becoming (improbably) one of the Big 10
steel producers in the world, the first option discarded was to pursue a
conventional strategy based on large, integrated steel works maximizing
economies of scale. The capital resources required were far too large, and
in any case this would take him into head-to-head competition with giants
that had much better connections and resources than he could muster. Instead, Lakshmi Mittal spun a worldwide web of small-scale plants close to
their final customers, thus replacing a business model based on trade (with
the strategic goal of minimizing trade-related costs) to one based on local
supply and customization. Within a decade of its internationalization, Ispat
duly entered the lists of the world's Top 10 steel producers. As a "latecomer" it realized that it had to employ novel strategies and business models and maximize its "latecomer advantage"—in this case, its freedom from
the burden of large, integrated plants as assets. It would be much harder for
the giant incumbents to pursue such a strategy of interlinked small-scale
plants, precisely because of their existing assets acting as a curb or brake
on such organizational innovation.

Ispat International pursued a strategy of growth in the Periphery at first,
where it built up its formidable management and technical skills. It expanded initially into Indonesia, then into Central America, and then into
the periphery of Europe via Ireland. From modest beginnings, its revenues
had grown to $440 million by 1992. Then began its explosive accelerated
growth, through major acquisitions in North America and Europe, principally France and Germany. Revenues climbed rapidly to $2.2 billion in 1997
and $3.5 billion in 1998, with steel shipments capacity approaching 20 mil-
lion tons by the end of the decade. Access to capital has also been of prime
concern. Ispat International was listed publicly on the New York and Amsterdam Stock Exchanges in 1997, thus consolidating its global status.

The key strategy employed by Mittal to grow internationally was purchasing struggling (often state-owned) steel operations at a fraction of their
value and turning them around by injecting new investment and advanced
technology, as well as modern management and the global connections offered by his expanding group. Mittal bought troubled Irish Steel for a token
1 punt (but had to pay off millions in accumulated debt). He secured Mexico's loss-making Sicarsta mills in 1992 for $220 million (the country's third

largest and built by the Mexican government for $2 billion, less than a decade before). After the Mexican purchase, Mittal himself moved there and worked in the plant for six months to bed it down.

Ispat's purchases began in the Periphery but by the late 1990s had moved directly into the industrial heartlands. In October 1997, Ispat acquired the long products division from German Thyssen for $16.4 million, and in 1999, it closed a deal to acquire the Unimetal, Trefileurope, and Societe Metallurgique de Revigny (SMR) steelmaking subsidiaries from France's Usinor Group. This gave it substantial capacity in Europe, indeed, becoming the first truly pan-European steel firm. In the United States in 1998, it closed a lightning deal to acquire the Inland Steel operation from Inland Steel Industries for a consideration of $1.4 billion. The entire North and Central American operations were then restructured as Ispat America, headed by the former CEO of Inland Steel. With this purchase, Ispat also inherited two joint ventures that Inland had entered with the Japanese steel giant NKK which gave Ispat also a foothold in Japan. Thus, Ispat has consolidated its global reach, starting in the Periphery, where it builds its capabilities and reach, and then moving in determined fashion into the industrial heartlands. This is a characteristic global expansion and coverage strategy of the latecomers.[35]

Ispat's growth has indeed been phenomenal through internal expansion and judicious acquisition. Over five years from 1992 to 1997, its compound growth was 55 percent per year. Ispat has become the steel industry's first truly global firm. Lowest cost and highest quality have always been Mittal's twin business standards. Ispat International has integrated vertically up its supply chain, buying iron mines in Mexico to supply its iron ore, which is reduced on-site through technology that Ispat has spent 20 years perfecting. Indeed, Ispat is the world's leading producer and user of Direct Reduced Iron (DRI), a cheaper raw material for steel production than scrap metal used in most minimills or the various grades of ore used in integrated steel plants. The company is widely perceived in the industry to be the "Nucor of the 21st century"—just as innovative as Nucor was seen to be in the 1980s but adding the crucial international dimension that Nucor has lacked so far.

Cemex

No less impressive in an equally unpromising industry is the performance of Cemex, Mexico's largest MNE and the third largest cement company in the world. It is also the most global of the world's cement firms, in an industry that has opened up to internationalization only slowly. Cemex repeatedly wins awards as one of the world's best-managed firms.[36] Founded in 1906, Cemex began exporting from Mexico in 1976 and grew by domestic acquisitions to become Mexico's largest supplier. It subsequently became a major cement trader, buying cement where it was produced cheaply such as in China and selling it where it could fetch a higher price. Thus, it was positioned by the mid-1980s with substantial experience in cement production, trading, and market expansion. But Mexico's national policies at the time kept the company to a domestic production focus.

Cemex's globalization began in earnest in the late-1980s when Mexico removed protective trade barriers and opened up to the world economy. Cemex started out by making important acquisitions of cement-producing firms in Spanish-speaking countries. Cemex acquired the two most important cement producers in Spain (Valenciana and Sanson) in 1992, and then made further acquisitions in Venezuela, Panama, the United States (Texas), the Dominican Republic, and Colombia. Up to this point, all its acquisitions had occurred in Spanish-speaking countries or in states like Texas with a strong link to its Spanish origins. In 1997, it expanded its acquisition drive in the Asia-Pacific region, taking advantage of depressed asset prices due to the Asian financial crisis, and acquired a 30 percent stake in the Philippine cement company Rizal Cement; then in 1998, it purchased a 14 percent stake in PT Semen Gresik, Indonesia's largest cement producer; it subsequently raised its stakes in these firms to 70 percent and 20 percent, respectively. In 1999, it purchased a majority stake in another Philippine company, APO Cement, in conjunction with Philippine partners, making it overall the Philippines' second largest cement producer.

At the same time, Cemex was expanding its cement-trading activities to become the premier cement-trading company in the world. Its operations by the end of the 1990s spanned more than 60 countries. These acquisitions and expansion strategies mean that Cemex has become not only the world's no. 1 cement trader, purchasing cement from other producers (particularly in China) and selling it in over 60 countries, but it has also become the world's third largest producer in its own right and the most globalized cement company. By the end of the 1990s, Cemex operated 50 cement plants around the world in 10 countries, covering Latin America, Europe (Spain), the United States, and Southeast Asia (Indonesia and the Philippines). It held a leading position in virtually all the markets in which it produces.

Cemex backs its expanding global reach with a capacity for management integration and a uniform level of high customer service. It guarantees ready-mix concrete to be delivered to a site within 20 minutes—just like a pizza—or the customer can claim their money back. This relentless concentration on efficiency has translated into lower costs and greater customer loyalty. By the end of the 1990s, Cemex was pioneering e-commerce in the cement industry, providing a pilot internet-based system that links clients, suppliers, customers, agents, and Cemex executives around the world. Thus, Cemex has used the most advanced process cement technology, modernizing plants as they are acquired, and the most advanced IT technology to leapfrog its way to its leading world position as an integrated worldwide cement producer and trader.

Cemex further consolidated its global position by listing on the New York Stock Exchange, which gave it access to cheaper capital and also allowed the firm to spread its financial risk away from Mexican pesetas. Globalizing financial dealings in order to spread risk and maximize opportunities is certainly one of the goals of the accelerated internationalizing strategies of the latecomer MNEs from late industrializing countries.

Li & Fung

Li & Fung is another example of a latecomer MNE from Hong Kong which has used strategic and organizational innovation to secure a place for itself as a worldwide trading company or "industrial supply" company.[37] Its business is managing a global logistics chain that links its 350 customers with around 7,500 suppliers found throughout Asia and particularly in mainland China. The customers are largely retail chains or other retail outlets, but in fact Li & Fung will satisfy any customer's order for a specified article. Li & Fung took a giant leap forward in globalization in 1995, when it acquired the operations of Inchcape Buying Services (IBS), one of the former blue-blood "hongs" that grew wealthy in the rich colonial waters of Hong Kong. IBS brought to Li & Fung an established network of offices in India, Pakistan, Bangladesh, and Sri Lanka (i.e., all countries of the former British Empire). The strategic issue was that there were three major industrial supplies companies in Hong Kong—Inchcape, Jardines, and Li & Fung. When Inchcape announced their intended withdrawal from the business to concentrate on their European operations, Li & Fung pounced before Jardines swallowed their longtime British rival. It was a strategic masterstroke that nearly doubled the global reach of Li & Fung.

Li & Fung shares many features with Acer, in that it is organized along largely cellular lines and in its capacity to organize extensive logistics supply chains around the world. But its strategies have been quite different, in its focusing on extracting value from its supply chain management rather than through brand promotion. Its expansion through acquisition also differs sharply from Acer's more organic growth through partnership with PC dealers in different countries. It is such variations on the theme of accelerated international expansion that make these latecomers so interesting.

Hong Leong Group

Consider finally the Hong Leong Group, which by the end of the 1990s had grown from a small base in Singapore to be a large conglomerate with assets of U.S. $16 billion and annual revenues of $2.5 billion. It encompassed a worldwide hotel chain (under the Millennium & Copthorne brand among others), a worldwide property development company, and numerous other financial services and industrial interests in the Asia-Pacific region, Europe, and North America.[38]

From humble beginnings in 1941 as a general trading company, founded by Kwek Hong Png, the core of the group took off in Singapore's miracle industrialization decade of the 1960s as a building supplies operation through the formation of joint ventures with Japanese giants Mitsui and Onoda Cement. This resulted in the formation of Singapore's first cement-grinding plant, which was part of the Singapore government's strategy of building self-sufficiency in the fragile young city-state. In the 1980s, the company expanded further through acquisition, taking over the Asian operations of the Australian Hume Far East group of companies (a producer of cement products like pipe and slab) and then of the Rheem Far East group of companies. These operations were consolidated under Hong Leong Corporation Ltd. (HLCL) in 1982, which expanded to encompass companies and operations in building and construction materials, packaging and container products, trading, distribution and manufacturing, and consumer products. Toward the end of the 1990s, revenues from HLCL exceeded $1 billion, and the group was actively diversifying and expanding internationally.

Hong Leong Group diversified into property development, hotels and tourism, and finance in the 1970s, when Kwek Leng Beng, the founder's son, entered the business. He built up first a property development company, City Developments Ltd. (CDL), which grew to become the largest commercial property developer in Singapore and a major force in the region. By the end of the 1990s its operations spanned Malaysia, Indonesia, China, Australia, and New Zealand. Hong Leong acquired in 1979 a financial services firm, Singapore Finance, and built this and the related Hong Leong Finance into one of Singapore's strongest financial houses. The group embarked on a major diversification into the leisure industry in the late 1990s through a joint venture with the U.S. global bowling center operator AMF Bowling Worldwide. This pattern of diversification into related service-oriented activities, utilizing joint ventures as a means of getting started, is a characteristic approach of innovative latecomers. I discuss these patterns of international expansion in detail in the chapters to follow.

It would be tedious to list too many of these fast internationalizing companies by name.[39] By now the pattern is clear. Whether the multinational companies are latecomers from late industrializing countries, or newcomers which have just been formed in advanced countries or been revitalized from previously dormant firms, or global niche players which steadily build a global market and maintain their hold on it, they share important features. They all clearly maintain a relentless global focus and a capacity for operating globally. They have a penchant for doing things differently—for engaging fearlessly in strategic and organizational innovation. They sometimes ride on the back of technological innovation, where this is one of their core assets, but in general they innovate more in terms of marketing, strategy, or organization. They can accelerate their international expansion through acquisition, or they can choose to grow through other mechanisms such as partnerships. One thing they always have in common is that they see their future in terms of being a world player in a carefully defined world market.

These then are the empirical facts with which our investigation must start. We have assembled a representative sample of "new" MNEs, consisting of latecomers, buttressed by other cases of newcomers and niche players, which share a set of characteristics that present a *prima facie* case for explaining their rapid arrival and success in the world economy. The stories of these representative firms seem to replicate the major features observed in other newcomer and latecomer cases.[40] Our task now is to tease out these common features and identify the strategic and organizational innovations in greater detail. We seek to develop a plausible account of these firms' global success and accelerated internationalization that is consistent with a view of the evolution of the global economy itself. The argument will be strengthened if we can establish a link between these distinctive features of the firms and the characteristics of the emergent global economy.

Common Features in the Emergence of the Newcomers and Latecomers

Three features in the internationalization of latecomers and newcomers are immediately worth noting. First, all the firms discussed utilized various forms of accelerated market entry and international expansion. Acer was able to expand rapidly into many emerging markets as a leading IT supplier through partnerships with distributors—such as Computec in Mexico to form Acer Computec Latino America or Wipro in India. Ispat International, by contrast, utilized a strategy of buying up unwanted and underperforming steel mills at a fraction of their book value and turning them around through judicious investment in updated technology and globalization of customer and supplier logistics. Li & Fung took a great leap forward in internationalization with its acquisition of the trading business of Inchcape.

Accelerated Internationalization

Accelerated internationalization is not a luxury for the latecomer but a necessity. Its goal is catch-up—through various ingenious stratagems—but while it is seeking to catch the incumbents, they too are moving ahead. Global coverage that lends competitive advantage, through generating long production runs for example, cannot be achieved through the solid build-up of one subsidiary after another. It can however be achieved through the kinds of innovative acquisitions and partnerships demonstrated by Acer, Ispat, Li & Fung, and Cemex.

Accelerated internationalization is a feature common to newcomers and latecomers. In some newcomers it is so striking that it may accurately be described as "born global" firms—even very small ones. This is becoming one of the most intensively studied features of the emerging global economy.[41] The strongest internationalizing tendencies can be found in early-stage technology-intensive firms. Recent work argues that such firms seek to compete in technological niche markets that are global in character.[42] Keeble et al. surveyed 100 such firms in the Oxford and Cambridge areas of the United Kingdom, and found that their level of internationalization was far higher than for equivalent-sized firms not specializing in technology-intensive products. Such firms also tend to grow faster and to seek involvement in multinational interfirm networks and consortia than their domestic-focused equivalents. The survey of early-stage technology-based firms in the United States by Preece et al. (1999) concurred that such firms seek international involvement very early as their way of establishing themselves in global technology-based niche markets.

Strategic Innovation

Second, the firms have relied not so much on technological or market innovation to drive their expansion (like an established MNE might do) but on strategic innovation.[43] For Ispat, strategic innovation lay in its pattern of purchasing existing plant sites rather than building greenfield sites, plus building a worldwide network of steel minimills rather than huge integrated steel complexes, and finally, utilizing Direct Reduced Iron (DRI) as high quality but cheaper raw material than scrap steel. None of these represented an innovation in itself, but their synthesis into a global strategy represented a profound innovation in business practice and one which has proven to be extremely effective. For Acer, strategic innovation lay in its developing a global logistics system modeled on the "fast food" approach of assembling 'fresh' " components at the last minute. For Li & Fung, strategic innovation lay in the Fung brothers' capacity to respond to manufacturing orders faster than anyone else through their network of industrial suppliers located around Asia and particularly in China.

In this sense, the latecomers and newcomers represent a challenge to the conventional thinking on competitiveness, which starts with the assumption that the creation of competitive advantage is founded on innovation of the technical or marketing kind.[44] No such advantages are available to the latecomers and newcomers, in general.[45] They clearly rely on something different, namely, their ability to fashion linkage and leverage strategies that complement the strategies of the incumbents and "fit" well with the interconnectedness of the emerging global economy.

Organizational Innovation

The third common factor is organizational innovation. The latecomer MNEs have not achieved rapid global coverage by building solid structures with bureaucratic hierarchies for the control of slowly changing procedures. On the contrary, they have demonstrated enormous ingenuity in devising non-hierarchical, latticelike structures that optimize the possibilities of achieving rapid global spread. Many of them have developed some version or other of a global "cellular" architecture. This is most evident in the case of Acer, which maintains its competitive edge through creating a tightly integrated network of business units, modeled on what Stan Shih called a "client-server" organizational architecture in the 1990s and an "Internet Protocol" architecture in 2000. We shall examine Acer's evolving cellular structures in the next chapter.

But Acer is not alone in this form of organizational innovation. Li & Fung is also organized along cellular lines. It consists of around 60 business cells (called divisions) which are customer-focused—usually on one customer or related group of customers. For example, there is a "theme-store division" (or cell) which deals exclusively with theme-store customers like Rainforest Café or Warner Brothers stores. Each division does business worth between $20 million and $50 million and is run by a lead entrepreneur that the company calls a "little John Wayne" because they have to defend their wagon train! Take the Gymboree division as an example, which serves the needs of a single customer Gymboree. It consists of around 40 staff, led by Ada Liu in her Hong Kong office in the late 1990s. Each staff member has a computer linked directly to Gymboree and Li & Fung's supply chain management system. The staff within the division are organized into teams along functional lines, covering aspects such as technical support, merchandising, raw materials purchasing, quality assurance, and shipping. Ada also has dedicated sourcing teams within the Li & Fung branch offices in China, The Philippines, and Indonesia, because Gymboree has large volume business in those three countries. So there is a dedicated team for Gymboree in perhaps five of Li & Fung's 26 branch offices. She hires these people herself; they are a part of the Gymboree division, although located in their different branch offices.

This is a remarkable organizational structure for a trading company, which traditionally has been organized exclusively along geographic lines, with branch offices in each country as the profit centers (and competing against each other). It is very difficult to optimize along the supply chain in such circumstances. With Li & Fung, by contrast, the customer-centric cells (divisions) shape the supply chain according to the customer's specific needs, seeking maximum performance in terms of logistics and delivery as well as quality. The leader-entrepreneur operates the cell (division) just like their own small business. They have the financial resources and administrative support of a large organization, but apart from that they have a great deal of autonomy in meeting the needs of their customer.

As Victor Fung puts it, for the creative side of the business (meeting customer needs, attracting new customers), they want as much entrepreneurial behavior as possible. They rely on very substantial performance bonuses, which have no upper cap—so the harder people work to make a customer satisfied, and the higher the profit, the greater their individual reward. But there is also tight operational integration.[46] There are tight operating controls over inventory, and all cash flow is managed centrally through Hong Kong. All letters of credit, for example, are sent to Hong Kong for approval and are then reissued by the central office. In this way, Li & Fung is guaranteed payment before they execute an order. It is a totally customized operation.

Likewise, Ispat International is successful not only because of the brilliant strategy pursued, but also because new mills, once integrated in the Ispat worldwide network, have new managements installed which enjoy maximum autonomy in running the plants to their capacity performance. Ispat's emerging international structure is one of a weblike integration, where the entire network grows through organic accretion. Each new mill acquired is rapidly modernized, subjected to new management, and integrated within the existing Ispat networks, such as through a restructuring of its supply linkages and its customers. Thus, the new mill is "accommodated" within the existing networks. This is an excellent illustration of global "integration."

Thus, we can point to factors in the emergence of these latecomers that go beyond the kind of technological or marketing innovations usually identified as sources of competitive advantage for firms which are globalizing their operations. While such factors are certainly important in the cases of the Compaqs or the Dells, which are truly formidable competitors for latecomers like Acer, they cannot be seen as driving the expansion of latecomers, which by definition lack such initial advantages.

The common features in these three cases revolve around the capacity of the latecomer to overcome its initial disadvantages by exploiting its potential advantages such as lack of institutional inertia. The outstanding competitive advantage available to a latecomer firm in the international domain is the possibility of *expanding globally with an exclusively geocentric approach* (utilizing the terminology of Perlmutter 1969), thereby skipping or leapfrogging the ethnocentric and polycentric phases that earlier MNEs have had to go through. This focus has the potential to lend significant competitive advantages to the latecomer MNE, provided it can develop the organizational resources needed to accomplish such a development.

As they acquire global reach, how do these latecomers and newcomers resolve, for example, the "global integration–local responsiveness" (GILR) dilemma? Insofar as their strategic and organizational innovations create business units with enhanced autonomy, the firms we are studying find the task of global coordination to be a central issue—and one which needs to be resolved without sacrifice of local responsiveness. While some global incumbents appear to have found ways to resolve this GILR dilemma, through their "transnational" organizational processes, we find that newcomers and latecomers can deal with it quite distinctively. Authors like

Bartlett and Ghoshal call firms that are active in the international economy multinationals and internationals, but reserve the term "transnational" for those which successfully integrate their activities globally and resolve the GILR dilemma.[47] The latecomers however can resolve the dilemma as they expand (rather than seeking to resolve it once they have acquired global reach), and moreover, this appears to facilitate their accelerated internationalization.

This discussion would not be complete without a consideration of the issue of internationalization itself, seen as a general process (as opposed to the economic analysis of why internationalization occurs, a subject we turn to in chapter 7). We need to demonstrate the distinctiveness of the latecomer approach in terms of the definition of internationalization and the impulse behind it.

What Is Meant by "Internationalization"?

In keeping with the emphasis of the international business (IB) literature on the constraints operating on international firms, scholars have tended to use a "push-oriented" concept, with the outward movement of the firm propelled by some strategic objective. Thus, Welch and Luostarinen (1988: 36) define internationalization as "the process of increasing involvement in international operations." This definition implies that internationalization is a unilinear sequential process of "increasing" involvement—which excludes the cases where firms actually cut back on their international exposure or follow an "oscillatory" trajectory of increasing then diminishing international involvement—as in the case of the Swedish MNE, Alfa-Laval, for example.[48]

Calof and Beamish (1995) sought a way around this problem with their definition of internationalization as being "the process of adapting firms' operations (strategy, structure, resource, etc.) to international environments" (1995: 116). This would appear to be a superior formulation, in that it does not pose any specific direction on the process of engagement with the international economy. A similar tack is taken by Hitt, Hoskisson, and Kim (1997), who link internationalization to diversification and define it as "expansion across the borders of global regions and countries into different geographic locations, or markets."

To accommodate the case of newcomers and latecomers, internationalization needs to be reconceived as a "pull" rather than a push. It is the multiple connections of the global economy which draw firms into involvement across national borders, through contracting, licensing, or other transacting relationships. Bearing this in mind, internationalization may be defined as "the process of the firm's becoming integrated in international economic activities." The term "integration" covers both cases of push and pull and provides a more comprehensive formulation, seeing the global economy as preexisting and offering resources to the firm that seeks strategic involvement at this level. In addition to covering the well-known and studied cases of export activity and foreign direct investment, such a broadly based definition encompasses the experiences of the latecomers and newcomers which are the focus of this book. It emphasizes the point that internationalization is a process of engagement with the prior existing interfirm linkages of the global economy.

A Global Perspective: Making the "Gestalt Switch"

What all the newcomers and latecomers share in their experience of internationalization is a global perspective unencumbered by any attachment to a domestic market. The successful outsiders are free of such residual attachments and thus able to develop a truly "global" perspective that gives them considerable advantages over incumbent MNEs. Think of this global perspective as operating like a "gestalt switch," changing the perceptions of the firm that has experienced it. A firm without this gestalt switch sees the international economy in terms of adding one foreign country to its domestic market, then another, and another in incremental expansion. In such a process, a global perspective emerges only slowly, if at all. Trade-offs between country operations, and the rotation of product strategies through the most relevant countries, are barely discernible as potential strategies.

A firm that makes the gestalt switch, by contrast, makes its first foreign foray as an initial step, not into one foreign market, but *into the world*. It starts out with a view that it will pursue customers wherever they are to be found, and preferably global customers, since they give maximum internationalizing leverage. Each move is seen as adding another piece in an expanding pattern that was global in scope from the beginning. It should not be surprising that it is firms from the Periphery which are most advanced in developing such an outlook, for this can be one of their few sources of advantage over incumbents from the advanced Triad countries.[49]

Ispat International, for example, has been able to attract global customers such as General Motors, precisely because of its global reach. Indeed, the option of dealing with global giants like GM was certainly one of the driving influences on Ispat's strategy. When GM made the decision to concentrate the steel supplies to its worldwide automotive operations to 30 companies, in 1998, Ispat through its purchase of Inland Steel in the United States was already on GM's doorstep—and was able to guarantee supplies elsewhere in the American continent, in Europe, in Asia, wherever GM was building cars or trucks. Ispat was operating with a global perspective, while other steel companies were content to do business with a domestic or at best a regional perspective. It had made the gestalt switch early on and was able to profit from its relentless pursuit of the global goal.

It is notable that in none of these cases of newcomer or latecomer international expansion has the traditional organizational solution of the firm's international activities being lumped together in an "international division" been adopted.[50] In all cases the international activities are the firm's activities; there is no distinction made between "domestic" and "international." This is the clearest possible evidence of the firms' genuinely global, or geocentric, outlook.

While the "switch" to a global focus can be executed rapidly, the process of building a global presence nevertheless takes time. The gestalt switch does not mean that the firm has to "globalize" its activities virtually overnight. On the contrary, it may follow a reasonably cautious, even incremental, approach to international expansion.[51] Ispat was quite fast, while Cemex has been a little slower in the cement industry. Hong Leong ventures into hotels has had to concentrate on building a global chain as and when acquisition opportunities present themselves. The key is not so much the speed of internationalization, as the goal that drives it.

Latecomers and the Dynamics of the Global Economy

We have now established a starting point for our exploration of the newcomers and latecomers in the global economy and their highly distinctive patterns of emergence. There is at least a *prima facie* case that the rapid growth of so many new forms of MNEs is linked (strongly linked) to the new dynamics observable in the emergent global economy. There has been an explosion of multiple linkages within this global economy in the past decade, that has acted as a magnet and template for the integration of new players within these networks. Earlier phases of internationalization by latecomer European firms, such as Swedish MNEs, exhibited similar kinds of patterns but at a much slower pace of development.

Our strategy now is to probe the three features of latecomer internationalization strategies and frameworks more deeply, looking at the processes and mechanisms involved in accelerated market entry, the construction of global cellular clusters, and the hatching and implementation of novel strategic approaches that knit together these internationalization demands. In each case, we shall be concerned to bring out any plausible linkage between the appearance and form of the latecomer and the character of the global economy within which it is operating.

The Global Economy: A Worldwide Web of Interlinked Firms

The key to considering this new "zoology" of the global economy is to develop a complementary perspective on the emerging global economy itself. The link that holds the strands of argument together in this book is the characterization of the emerging global economy as multiply connected networks and its complementarity with the structures and strategies we see latecomer MNEs like Acer utilizing. In brief, the world economy that is emerging at the beginning of the twenty-first century *is a worldwide web of interfirm connections.* It is a network of networks, expressed through "value-adding partnerships" (VAPs) and multiple value-adding pathways as elaborated above. This worldwide web of interlinkages is what underpins and indeed drives the novel strategies and organizational architectures developed by latecomers and newcomers with such success. Indeed, one can say that these innovations are successful *precisely because they are such good adaptations to the emerging network character of the global economy.* It is our task in the subsequent chapters to justify this assertion.

Interfirm Relations and Dependencies

Each firm possesses a unique set of linkages or relations that contribute to its resources and capabilities. The firm is able to improve or enhance its capabilities through attracting and sharing resources with the other firms with which it shares links. The firms with which a focal firm has linkages at any one point may be called its business partners. This set of firms is a subset of the wider network of firms found in the economy; it may be called the firm's "market context."[52] The firm's knowledge and capabilities are shared with the other firms in its market context and provide the appropriate perspective for viewing firms' involvement in international business networks.

Taking the entire worldwide set of firms and their linkages as our object of interest, we may make some critical distinctions between firms based on their degree of internationalization. The set of firms that have no cross-border links, whatever country they originate in, we term *domestic firms.* The set of firms that have cross-border links, we term *international firms.* But within this set are the firms of greatest interest, namely, the international firms with a global perspective and with multiple cross-border linkages termed *transnationals,* after Bartlett and Ghoshal (1989).

A network view of the economy, which can accommodate the perspectives of firms developing complementary strategies and accessing more mobile resources, needs to be contrasted with the conventional view, which sees firms as atomistic entities engaged in arm's-length transactions with each other, mediated through the price system. Such firms are viewed only as production entities, equipped according to the stylized economic description, with transparent technology in the form of a production function that converts inputs into outputs. This view may well have caught aspects of retail markets in the eighteenth and nineteenth centuries, but it certainly never caught the spirit of the industrial economy, where firms deal directly with each other, frequently through long-term contracts—and yet it has remained as an intellectual model through the twentieth century, in the face of so much counterevidence as to its vacuity and misleading propositions. One example: interventions to promote firms' sustainability have to be justified on grounds of presumed "market failure" rather than on the positive requirements and needs of directly interacting firms.[53]

Oddly enough, exchange at the level of the firm is banished in this conventional view; the exchanges take place purely within markets for factors of production and for outputs. This basic lack of realism is then compounded by further abstractions, such as viewing the firm as a bundle of contracts mediated between principals and agents or, alternatively, as an optimizing entity concerned only with moving along objectively given production frontiers. It would indeed be miraculous if firms survived by acting on principles derived from this kind of framework. The reality of course is that firms ignore them–they are honored only in the classroom. Firms understand that in reality they are connected to each other through long chains of linkages, and that their success or otherwise depends on their ability to manage these linkages as much as through their ability to manage their strictly internal affairs.[54]

The network perspective brings the focus onto these linkages and the various forms they may take, from purely supply arrangements with no further collaboration, to fully collaborative global alliances.[55] In the global setting, we see the emergent international economy as a network of networks—literally, as *a worldwide web of interfirm connections.*

Empirical support for the network view of the economy is overwhelming. Study of the global economy from this perspective has been pioneered in Scandinavia (linked to parallel studies of the process of internationalization of the firm) and it has resulted in an understanding of the dynamics of the interfirm linkages, their stability over time, as well as their evolution. This network view of the international economy really is a profound departure from conventional views. It is not a matter, as Mattsson (1998) rightly insists, of seeing the international networks formed by global firms as being some sort of unstable "hybrid" governance structure located somewhere between markets and hierarchies. This transactions view of network structures is, we suggest, completely misleading when it comes to understanding the dynamics of global firms and the networks within which they operate.[56] Strong support for the network view comes from East Asia and especially from studies of the workings of the Japanese economy and the overseas expansion of Japanese MNEs to form regional production networks.

A Resource-Based Perspective on Internationalization

The language of resources provides a powerful framework for holding together an argument concerning the impact of new transnational firms from the Periphery and newcomer firms from the industrial heartlands within this interlinked global economy. A resource-based view of international activity and international reach enables crucial distinctions to be made between the strategies of incumbents and those of latecomers and newcomers. The resource-based view emerged over the course of the past decade as a powerful analytical tool for explaining the origins and sustaining of competitive advantage by firms.[57] The resource-based view (RBV) is concerned

with firms in general. It makes no distinction between firms playing in domestic or international marketplaces. (Indeed, the international dimension
has for some reason been largely neglected by most RBV theorists and scholars.) Thus, a subsidiary aim of this book is to develop a RBV of internationalization, taking the cases of newcomers and latecomers as exemplary.[58]

The RBV holds that a firm acquires competitive characteristics not simply as a function of its industrial location (i.e., its position in the value
chain within a certain industry and its relationship to rival firms to supplier
firms, and to customer firms) but even more significantly as a function of
its inner "resources" and capabilities. A classic instance would be a Japanese firm like Honda, which is able to enter one new industry after another,
from motorbikes to small cars to large cars to power boats and finally to
domestic appliances like lawnmowers, all on the basis of its internal resources and capabilities in power train technology. Another instance would
be NEC, with its resources and capabilities in semiconductors, telecom-
munications, and computing, enabling it to bring out hybrid products spanning these three fields and thereby constantly renewing its competitive advantages.[59] This RBV turns out to be a powerful approach to understanding
the dynamics of interfirm competition, generating more insight than was
provided by earlier accounts linked to the industrial organization and structure traditions.

What appears to be novel in the current situation of the world economy,
and which appears to account for the success of so many newcomer and
latecomer MNEs, is this: firms can seek involvement—or "integration"—in
the global economy for purposes of enhancing their resource base. Latecomers seek industrial contracts, for example, which not only replenish their
cash flow but also expose them to superior organizational and technological
skills that they seek to acquire and adapt to their own purposes. Newcomers
seek global customers because they stretch their involvement around the
world, thus opening up more possibilities for attracting customers within
their chosen niche. This is an utterly different rationale for seeking global
involvement from the quest to exploit existing superior resources, which
motivated traditional MNEs.

The difference between these two perspectives is profound. For the incumbent, the world is seen in terms of threats to existing competitive positions. Incumbents therefore devise strategies to meet or circumvent these
threats. This is the stuff of endless analysis in the existing management and
organizational literature. For the latecomers and newcomers, by contrast,
the overwhelming need is to locate and access resources that will facilitate
the firm's growth, diversification, and international expansion. They
therefore devise strategies of access, of partnership, of complementarity,
which are designed not to extend existing advantages but to create competitive positions that do not yet exist. In place of seeing the world as full
of threats, they see it as full of opportunities. In place of seeking sustained
competitive advantage, they frequently seek no more than an initial com-

petitive foothold, some way of getting started that can lead to bigger and better things subsequently.[60]

The key then to the argument to be developed in this book is that latecomers from the Periphery have been able to develop successful and effective strategies for insertion in the global economy, through linkage, leverage, and learning, precisely because they have understood the fundamentals of the dynamics of this global economy.[61] They have developed strategies and organizational forms that actually complement and build on the kinds of changes being seen in the international economy. In this sense, they are genuine innovators. These issues will be elaborated in the following chapters, where hypotheses expressing these general approaches will be tested in the setting of our sample of latecomers (buttressed by many more cases of newcomers and niche players). Once they have arrived they have no hesitation in seeking to extend their reach and their advantages through conventional means. At this point, they become of less interest and relevance for the argument developed here. It is the *process of arrival* as an international firm, that is, the process of internationalization, that is of such interest and that calls for analysis. The practical side to this is that many firms attempt internationalization and fail badly—as did the firms we shall discuss in this book—on numerous occasions. Acer, for example, had three attempts at internationalization before finding a formula which worked well. Understanding how these firms have succeeded obviously provides valuable lessons for those firms looking to become engaged in the global economy.

Concluding Remarks

Innovative firms, whether from the Periphery or from the Triad, are drawn into a networked global economy through linkage and leverage possibilities that were unknown just a few years ago and add their own multiply linked contributions. This creates so many more possible patterns of internationalization and thus again opens up opportunities for newcomers and latecomers that may well be more nimble in seizing the opportunities created. So the global economy is certainly changing, but the sources of advantage for global firms may be very different from those conventionally depicted. It is plausible to suppose that it is the newcomers and latecomers, like Acer, Ispat International, Li & Fung, and the Hong Leong Group, which form part of the vanguard of the emergent global economy precisely because they are equipped with a global outlook and because they are prepared to experiment with strategic and organizational innovations, that place global considerations ahead of all others. In this they may perhaps be holding up a mirror for the incumbents, showing them what the future may hold.

Before exploring the characteristics of these newcomers and latecomers in more general terms, let us look in some detail at the processes that one of them, namely, the Acer, Group, has utilized in order to achieve the status of a global player. Acer has employed not one but three models of global reach and global architecture in its short trajectory of 15 years as a firm internationalizing from the Periphery. Its story is full of surprises, of strategic and organizational leaps, of brilliant victories and crushing setbacks. Acer is the case par excellence of the Dragon Multinational.

Notes

1. The globalization literature is becoming vast, and much of it travels into regions such as global financial integration and cultural integration which are not of direct interest to this study. Popular accounts of globalization, which depict it as an unstoppable force, include those by Friedman (1999) or Yergin and Stanislaw (1999). Much of what they say is factually well grounded and analytically sound, but in their enthusiasm for the trends described they downplay, or ignore, alternative scenarios emanating from the Periphery. It is these aspects, and in particular the role played by new kinds of multinational corporations, which form the focus of this study. More nuanced studies see globalization as a multifaceted process replete with its own contradictions: see for example Luttwak (1999).

2. The literature on multinational enterprises (MNEs) and their economic effects is also vast. Much of the popular concern about their potentially destabilizing and damaging effects stems from the literature of the 1970s, which ranged from the sober and thoughtful (e.g., Penrose 1968, 1971; or Vernon 1971, 1977) to the hysterical (e.g., Barnet and Mueller 1974). In the 1980s, much of the literature was collected together in the 18-volume *United Nations Library on Transnational Corporations*, under the general editorship of John Dunning; individual volumes are cited below where directly relevant. Recent collections of papers that bring the situation up to date, and place MNEs in the context of wider trends in the global economy, include Dunning (1997); Sölvell and Zander (1995); Chandler, Hagström, and Sölvell (1998) and Kozul-Wright and Rowthorn (1998).

3. See for example Bartlett and Ghoshal (1989) and Ghoshal and Bartlett (1997). Similar themes have been raised by Hedlund (1986; 1993a;-b) and Hedlund and Kogut (1993).

4. See Prahalad and Hamel (1990); Hamel and Prahalad (1994); and Doz and Hamel (1998) for representative discussions.

5. See Hu (1992) who utilizes this phrase. Doremus, Keller, Pauly, and Reich (1998) provide a comprehensive exposition of this theme; see Kogut (1999) for an extended review of their book. Fleenor (1993) provides a comparable skeptical perspective, drawn from a roundtable involving scholars such as Sumantra Ghoshal, John Stopford, and George Yip.

6. UNCTAD *World Investment Report* (1999).

7. Stopford (1998) provides an overview of this question.

8. The phrase was used by Hedlund (1993b); numerous Swedish examples investing in the United States were given by Agren (1990). Lindqvist (1991) referred to similar young, technology-based internationalizing firms from Sweden as "infant multinationals."

9. The situation contrasts dramatically with that described only a decade earlier, when Vernon-Wortzel and Wortzel could write: "The efforts of multinationals from the South or Developing countries (MEDECs) have been prodigious and their progress in international markets has been quite impressive. But most, if not all, are still fringe players in the world business arena; by global standards, none is a major player in its industry and there are only a small number of industries in which MEDECs are even significant participants" (1988: 28).

10. The phrases "born global" and "international new ventures" (INVs) are used by Oviatt and McDougall (1994; 1995; 1997); McDougall, Shane, and Oviatt (1994); Knight and Cavusgil (1996); Bloodgood, Sapienza, and Almeida (1996); Kohn (1997) and Madsen and Servais (1997). They are all referring to the accelerated internationalization observed in new, high technology ventures from the U.S. and elsewhere.

11. Much of this is summarized in the OECD report on globalization and SMEs (OECD 1997).

12. On Fresenius and CMS Energy, see Korine (1999a; 1999b).

13. See Simon (1996) for an interesting survey of 500 of these global "hidden champions."

14. See Andersen, Blenker, and Christensen (1997) for a discussion of international contracting linkages.

15. See Craig and Douglas (1996a; 1996b) and Stopford (1998) for comparable assertions that the world economy is peopled by many more forms than can be accounted for by traditional, large MNEs.

16. The point is underscored by Sachs and Warner (1995), and Rodrik (1999), who argue that continued industrialization from NICs depends on their ability to adapt to the institutional features of an increasingly integrated world economic system.

17. See Dunning and Narula (1996; 1997) and Narula (1996) for a similar argument concerning divergence of a "second wave" of multinational investment from formerly developing countries, along what these scholars call the "investment development path."

18. Powell (1990) described a network in these terms, without any necessary reference to global scale.

19. UNCTAD (1999).

20. On the production side, international firms and their affiliates accounted for around 25 percent of world output in 1998, a proportion that is steadily growing: UNCTAD (1999).

21. This evolutionary and systemic perspective on the international system of states is the subject of a flourishing scholarship. See for example Spruyt (1994) for a treatment which relates the rise of the nation state over its principal organizational competitors, city states (e.g., in Italy) and trading leagues (e.g., the Hanseatic League in Germany).

22. See the series of papers by Johanson and Mattsson (1988; 1991; 1992; 1994), as well as Mattsson (1995; 1998), which pioneer application of the network view of firms in industrial markets to the issue of internationalization. On the more general features of the "Uppsala" industrial network perspective, see Forsgren and Johanson (eds) (1992) and Håkansson (1982; 1989) for a comprehensive account.

23. "Value-adding partnership" is the phrase used by Johnston and Lawrence (1990) in their analysis of the multiple linkages making up an industrial economy. Porter (1985) popularized the notion of the value-adding chain as an analytic category.

24. See for example, Calof (1993); Baird, Lyles, and Orris (1994); Fujita (1995a;-b; 1998); Acs, Morck, Shaver, and Yeung (1997); Coviello and Munro (1997); and Liesch and Knight (1999) for specific treatments of small- and medium-sized firms internationalizing in the 1990s.

25. See Gomes-Casseres and Kohn (1998).

26. See Oviatt and McDougall (1999) for a discussion of such issues, where the emphasis is placed much more on technological factors in favoring the emergence of SMEs as global players.

27. See for example, Oviatt and McDougall (1994; 1995; 1997); McDougall, Shane, and Oviatt (1994); and Kohn (1997) for discussions of the "born global" phenomenon, and Knight and Cavusgil (1996) for a review. Bloodgood, Sapienza, and Almeida (1996) provide systematic empirical investigation in their study of 61 new high technology ventures in the U.S., all of which internationalized very rapidly.

28. Andersen, Blenker, and Christensen (1997) discuss international contracting linkages as a new form of internationalizing factor. The same theme is picked up in the internationalization of service firms, as discussed for example in Aharoni (1996).

29. These examples are drawn from Mathews & Cho (2000) and Mathews (2001a).

30. The term "latecomer" was first used by the historian Alexander Gerschenkron (1962), to describe patterns of industrialization in the nineteenth century in countries like Germany, Russia, and the United States, which differed from the patterns observed in early industrializers like Britain. Gerschenkron's point was that the latecomers had to overcome disadvantages in lacking fundamental productive capabilities and being excluded from markets, but that they had certain advantages which would help them to close the gap if used intelligently. These advantages included the absence of institutional impediments that arose from earlier phases of industrialization, and the possibility of using state agencies to act as collective entrepreneur and accelerate processes that would otherwise take too long to accomplish. While the concept remains debated by European historians, it has proven to be fruitful in explaining patterns of East Asian industrialization and is now being taken over by the management literature in the form of the concept of the "latecomer firm"—see Hobday (1995) and Mathews (1998; 1999) and Mathews and Cho (1999; 2000) for an elaboration. In the context of internationalization, a principal advantage available to the latecomer firm is absence of earlier "ethnocentric" or "polycentric" attitudes and instead a truly global or "geocentric" attitude from the outset—to use the terminology introduced by Perlmutter (1969).

31. In this way the latecomers that have come to prominence in the 1990s differ from an earlier generation of "Third World Multinationals" which were discussed in the 1980s in a flourishing literature. As representative examples, see Wells (1977); Lecraw (1981); Kumar and McLeod (1981); Wells (1983); Lall (1986); Khan (1987); Vernon-Wortzel and Wortzel (1988); Aggarwal and Agmon

(1990); and Tolentino (1993). For representative overviews and collections of articles, see Lall (1993) and Yeung (1999c).

32. Documentary sources on Acer are given in chapter 3.

33. Subsidiary initiative is an issue discussed in the current IB literature by scholars concerned to show that the rich interplay between subsidiaries and headquarters in conventional MNEs is not captured by notions of hierarchical authority. See Birkinshaw and Hood (1998a; 1998b), Forsgren Holm, and Johanson (1995), or Forsgren, Pedersen, and Foss (1999) as representative. The issue is discussed in chapter 6.

34. On Ispat, see various magazine articles such as Manik Mehta, "Steel's still-growing giant," *Industry Week*, January 18, 1999, pp. 120–123. An extensive case analysis is available: see Sull (1999).

35. Contrast this with the failed international expansion strategy of BHP Steel, emanating from Australia, where the focus was almost entirely on becoming a player in the U.S. steel industry through expensive acquisitions and joint ventures. BHP Steel announced that all its overseas steel plants were for sale in October 1999.

36. For the fourth year in a row, Cemex was selected by *Industry Week* magazine in 1999 as one of the 100 best-managed companies in the world. A case analysis of Cemex is available in De La Torre, Doz, and Devinney (2000).

37. On Li & Fung, see sources such as the HBR interview with Victor Fung in Magretta (1998) and the Harvard Business School cases: *Li & Fung (A)*, HBS 396-107 (1996) written by Diane Long and Richard Seet, under the direction of Professor Michael Y. Yoshino; and *Li & Fung: Beyond 'filling in the mosaic' 1995–1998*, HBS 9-398-092 (1998) written by Anthony St. George under the supervision of Carin-Isabel Knoop and Professor Michael Y. Yoshino. Li & Fung is not strictly speaking a "latecomer" in that it traces its origins to a business founded in Canton in 1906 by the Fung brothers' grandfather, but its international expansion from Hong Kong only started in earnest when the Fung brothers returned to Hong Kong in the 1970s armed with their Harvard degrees.

38. On the Hong Leong Group, see for example Yeung (1999b).

39. Many other potential candidates are described in the international business literature. Bartlett and Ghoshal (2000b), for example, in their "lessons from late movers" in going global, mention cases like the Indian pharmaceutical firm Ranbaxy or the Indian small boilers firm Thermax, both of which broke into very competitive world markets, and the Philippines-originating fast food chain, Jollibee, which emulated McDonald's, but tailored the product to different Asian tastes. Yeung (1999a) mentions successful internationalizing Chinese conglomerates in Asia, such as the CP Group in Thailand, and the Salim Group in Indonesia, which expanded abroad through the First Pacific Group in Hong Kong. Then there are numerous Korean cases, including Samsung, Hyundai, and LG, as well as the counterexample of Daewoo, which overreached itself and collapsed after the Asian financial crisis, described in Ungson, Steers, and Park (1997). The point is that the sample of firms to draw on in illustrating the characteristics of latecomer multinationals from the Periphery, is potentially very large.

40. Representative studies concerned with patterns of internationalization of firms from the Periphery, that parallel the present investigation, include the

study of Thailand's CP Group (Pananond and Zeithaml 1998); the study of Taiwanese firms' expansion into SEAsia (Chen and Chen 1998a;-b); and the study of international expansion by Hong Kong firms in SEAsia (Yeung 1997; 1998) and by Singaporean firms (Tsang 1999; Yeung 1999a;-b). See Williamson (1997) for an interesting overview of the strategies of what he calls a "new breed of local competitors" in Asia's expanding markets, many of which are seen to be rapidly expanding internationally, and Ulgado, Yu, and Negandhi (1994) for a discussion of the management and organizational characteristics of MNEs from Asian NICs. Note how all these stories of international expansion differ from those attributed to "Third World" multinationals in the 1980s, a decade earlier.

41. See Coviello and McAuley (1999) for an overview, and Oviatt and McDougall (1999) and McDougall and Oviatt (2000) as well as Zahra, Ireland, and Hitt (2000) for the links between accelerated internationalization and entrepreneurship.

42. See, for example, Preece, Miles, and Baetz (1999); Keeble, Lawson, Lawton-Smith, Moore, and Wilkinson (1998).

43. See Markides (1997) for a discussion of strategic innovation as a general category.

44. See Porter (1985; 1990) for the most elaborated statement of this assumption. While it was clearly the case that firms which became multinationals in the nienteenth and twentieth centuries generally had technological or marketing innovations as their core resource, this has become less and less a precondition for international success, and it seems to be of only marginal relevance for the latecomers and newcomers discussed in this study.

45. Some newcomers do have new technologies to exploit—such as Gemplus with its smart card technology. But these cases are exceptional. Firms like Fresenius or Nutreco have no technological advantages in renal dialysis machines or animal feeds, respectively—other than their ability to construct global niche strategies.

46. See Magretta (1998) for further details.

47. See Bartlett and Ghoshal (1989) and Ghoshal and Bartlett (1997) for their major books, based on scholarly articles such as Bartlett and Ghoshal (1987). The *World Investment Report 1998* issued by UNCTAD makes a similar point when it argues that the successful MNEs are ones that develop their strategies from "simple integration" to "complex integration."

48. On Alfa-Laval, see Zander and Zander (1997).

49. Rugman (1999; 2000) makes a similar point in arguing that Triad MNEs are more likely to be regional in their outlook than global. The incumbent MNEs with a genuinely "global" or geocentric perspective are still relatively rare.

50. See Stopford and Wells (1972) for the classic description of this organizational pattern of internationalization. Chapter 4 discusses the matter in detail.

51. Gomez and Korine (1999) present a contrary viewpoint, where it is claimed that firms must internationalize through a "leap to globalization."

52. See Andersson, Johanson, and Vahlne (1997) for elaboration of the notion of "market context," and Welch and Welch (1996) for a strategic perspective on internationalization, and networks.

53. Kogut and Zander (1993) developed a view of multinational firms that made an explicit break with "market failure" considerations and instead based

the firm's multinational development on the capacity to manage international knowledge flows. See Mathews (2000; 2001b) for an elaboration on this point.

54. To see the firm as an exchange unit means bringing the firm and its relations to the center of analysis–something conventional economics has never done. As Teece (1998) puts it pithily:

> . . . Coase (1937) has referred to firms as "islands of conscious power." Coase's metaphor needs to be transformed from islands to archipela- goes to capture important elements of business organization. This is because firms commonly need to form strategic alliances, vertically (both upstream and downstream), laterally, and sometimes horizontally in order to develop and commercialize new technologies. (1998: 148)

55. See Doz and Hamel (1998) for a comprehensive treatment of global alli- ances and their management.

56. Mattsson suggests that "the basic coordinating mechanism in a market is interaction within and between connected exchange relationships between ac- tors" (1998: 243).

57. See Wernerfelt (1984) for the original argument concerning the resource- based view, and Barney (1986; 1991; 1995; 1997) for an influential exposition. Foss (1997) provides a useful overview of the RBV of the firm, while Collis (1991) and Collis and Montgomery (1998) show how the RBV can be applied to strategic industry analysis and the formulation of corporate strategy.

58. For a discussion of firms' internationalization as a search for external resources, utilizing the RBV of the firm, see Mutinelli and Piscitello (1998) for the case of firms internationalizing from Italy, and Chen and Chen (1998a;-b) for the case of firms internationalizing from Taiwan.

59. See Prahalad and Hamel (1990) for these and other examples.

60. As Chen & Chen (1998b: 446) put it, this is a perspective which sees firms investing abroad "as an attempt to access external resources in order to offset the weaknesses of the investor." The *World Investment Report 1998* rec- ognized this same effect in what it called "competitiveness-enhancing FDI," where multinational corporations seek not only cost reduction and bigger market shares, but also seek access to technology and innovative capacity. These latter are "man-made resources" rather than natural resources; they are what UNCTAD calls "created assets" (i.e., resources and capabilities), and they are seen to be critical to internationalizing firms' success.

61. These terms have been taken up and elaborated by the United Nations Industrial Development Organization (UNIDO) in the context of its forthcoming *World Industrial Development Report* (UNIDO 2002).

3

THE ACER GROUP
A Dragon Multinational

I think it is normal that crisis happens in
enterprises. It is abnormal if there is no crisis at
all. Therefore, a company has to continuously
accumulate strength and cultivate talent even
though it is not needed immediately.

Stan Shih,
Me-Too Is Not My Style

Acer is the world's largest and most successful Chinese high technology
company—and it is barely 25 years old. Established in Taiwan in 1976 by
entrepreneur Stan Shih, Acer has grown to become a diversified IT group
and a world leader in the Personal Computer industry. It is the world's third
largest PC producer (of both branded and original equipment production)
and is one of the Top 10 branded PC producers. It offers a range of IT
products, including high-end servers, multimedia PCs, notebooks, computer
peripherals, components, and semiconductors, as well as cellular telephones, internet service providers, and a range of web-based services. By
the end of 1999, the Acer Group encompassed over 120 offices spanning 41
countries and employing more than 35,000 people. The group operated 21
manufacturing sites and 20 assembly plants in 21 countries. Acer group
revenues were U.S. $6.7 billion in 1998, growing to $8.4 billion in 1999
and $9.9 billion (provisionally) in 2000. By the turn of the century, it was
thus a $10-billion-plus global enterprise moving rapidly to a position of
leadership in new IT areas such as third generation mobile telephony base
stations.

These are the bare statistics of success, for which Acer has become Taiwan's most famous company and its founder, Stan Shih, the country's most
honored entrepreneur. But behind these data lie a fascinating story. Acer is
a completely new kind of multinational enterprise. It has devised novel
organizational and management solutions to the problems of achieving
global scale, and in organizing a global scale of operation once it is
achieved. While firms can potentially gain enormous competitive advan-

tages from achieving global scale and scope, these gains can prove elusive if the firm cannot generate a style of management that Perlmutter described and anticipated back in 1969 as "geocentric."[1] The case can be made that Acer, as a "latecomer" MNE, has leapfrogged its more traditional rivals. It has utilized strategic innovation, such as peripheral expansion before tackling the Triad markets, and organizational innovation, in devising its network organizational structures, which have generated a genuinely geocentric approach to management.[2] It has arguably devised an approach to international expansion that resolves organizational dilemmas such as the goal of achieving global integration and local responsiveness simultaneously.[3] As we shall see, Acer placed more emphasis on local responsiveness in the mid-1990s and then more emphasis on global integration in the later 1990s. This was all driven by founder Stan Shih's "Dragon dream"—a dream of Acer taking its place as one of the world's great global enterprises.[4] Acer is thus a case of exceptional interest. It is a "Dragon Multinational" par excellence.

Acer is a case of great interest also in that its founder and chairman, Stan Shih, is one of the most brilliant of the new business figures to have emerged from East Asia. He is tireless in explaining and defending his organizational philosophies and entrepreneurial style. Shih is remarkable in that when he says he has not done it all on his own, he really means what he says. Shih has been able to motivate employees, customers, and suppliers in sharing responsibility for Acer's fortunes, because they are all allowed and encouraged to share in its wealth. By the end of the 1990s, managers and employees owned around 30 percent of Acer's businesses. Shih boasts that the more he shares ownership of Acer with others, the wealthier he gets—because the company grows through the efforts of others.

Shih's greatest legacy is likely to be a worldwide Acer Group that can function very effectively without him, enriching its managers, shareholders, and employees (who all share in the wealth, through widespread stock ownership plans) and generating new businesses as fast as opportunities present themselves. It is this entrepreneurial and strategic dynamic that keeps a worldwide entity like Acer alive and self-sustaining, and which constitutes such a rich source for the study of the processes that are needed to keep *all firms* alive and self-sustaining.

Finally, Acer is of great interest because it has experimented not with just one model of internationalization, but with at least four quite different models—or "four and a half"—depending on how they are counted. All this in no more than 15 years of international expansion. It is the capacity to evolve *at a global scale* and to learn quickly from mistakes that makes Acer of such compelling interest.

Acer's evolution through several stages of internationalization is depicted in Fig. 3.1. The corporation started as a purely domestic operation, while it acquired the necessary capabilities to make its launch on the world.

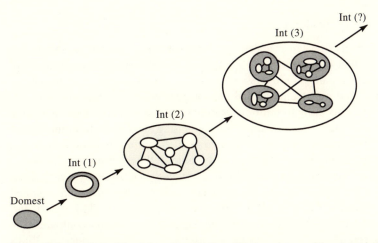

Figure 3.1 Acer's evolving internationalization. This is a picture of Acer's evolution through several stages in its internationalization experience.

It evolved from this to a first phase of international expansion, with a centralized organizational structure. This was a perfectly traditional organizational architecture, involving no more than a functional division of labor. When this reached its limits, Acer evolved to a second phase, in which cellular business units (BUs) become the primary site of the corporation's activities, interacting directly with each other (e.g., supplying components and subassemblies) and with external customers. This organizational architecture too reached its limits, in the late 1990s, when the corporation evolved to a third phase, involving four overarching global BUs, each again containing constituent BUs or cells. This phase can be expected to evolve to yet another form, or realization of the cellular architecture, when the time is ripe. Indeed, by the end of 2000 a fourth phase had already been initiated, with the Acer branded business being separated from Acer's design, manufacturing, and services business, spun off as a new entity, Wistron.

Note how the degrees of interaction between Acer and the world have multiplied as one phase succeeds another. In its first internationalization phase, there was a single degree of interaction (Acer to the outside world). In the second internationalization phase, involving regional business units (RBUs) and strategic business units (SBUs), there were two degrees of interaction—inter-BU interactions, and interactions between Acer and the outside world. In the third internationalization phase, there are three degrees of interaction—intra-GBU; inter-GBU; and between Acer and the outside world. It is these multiple degrees of interaction that enable Acer to keep the lid on exploding complexity as it expands to become a global corporation—complexity that degrades the performance of conventionally structured firms as they expand internationally.[5]

Acer's First Phase: Domestic Operations

Acer spent its first ten years of existence establishing itself as one of Taiwan's leading high technology companies.[6] In this first phase of development, the company's founders and senior managers learned how to acquire organizational and technological capabilities; how to implement these in new businesses; how to build marketing channels and a branded business; how to implement cost controls and operating standards. In other words, in this first phase, Acer (not yet known as such, but trading under the name Multitech) acquired the character of a viable, self-sustaining enterprise.

In typical entrepreneurial fashion, Acer was established as a very small operation by Stan Shih and five associates, after he had acquired practical and technical knowledge of the Information Technology (IT) industry and had been frustrated by poor management decisions in the companies he had worked for. Acer was founded as *Hong Chi* (a name that refers to Shih's favorite game of GO, whose stratagems have been an inspiration for some of Acer's own moves) with $25,000 capital and just 11 employees. The early years saw Shih and his engineers eking out an existence as a contract R&D company, utilizing their knowledge of microprocessors, and providing services to electronics firms which could benefit from the introduction of microprocessors but lacked the expertise to design them into their products. This inauspicious beginning evokes similar experiences in now-great enterprises like Hewlett-Packard, which also took several years to find its eventual business niche.

Acer's early success was based on acting as Taiwan agent for U.S. microprocessor firms such as Zilog, whose products were used in the early 1980s by Taiwanese producers of electronic games. This burgeoning business was driven largely by intellectual property piracy (by the games producers, not by Acer), and it was stamped out by the Taiwan government in 1982. The effect was to drive many Taiwan firms toward personal computers, then getting started as a new industry. Shih was able to leverage technological assistance to design a proto-PC, the "Microprofessor," which was the company's first successful product, achieving substantial sales in Taiwan and abroad. It was in 1982 that the PC industry worldwide took a momentous turn, when Compaq demonstrated the world's first "IBM-compatible" machine at the Comdex trade fair to great acclaim. This presented the fledgling Acer with a new kind of opportunity. Rather than pursuing its own proprietary architecture, as Apple and some other U.S. firms were doing, and as the entire Japanese PC industry was doing, Acer could elect to become a low-cost producer of IBM-compatible machines on its own account, as well as under contract to other branded producers. Shih executed this strategic shift with great alacrity. Technological expertise was leveraged from outside the company, this time from Taiwan professors and from the country's public R&D laboratories, the Industrial Technology Research Institute (ITRI).[7] Shih's company, now trading in English as Multitech, produced Taiwan's first commercial IBM-compatible PC.[8] It has been the leading company in this industry in Taiwan ever since.

Entry into the PC business took the firm into mass production manufacturing for the first time. Over the course of several years, Shih and his managers learned the benefits of scale and speed, as well as the significance of brand and retail marketing channels. As the company's sales abroad expanded, it was confronted with a potentially ruinous dispute with a U.S. firm that was also trading as "Multitech." After much soul-searching, Shih eventually decided to abandon this brand name and start internationally afresh with a new one.

How Shih and his senior managers went about this task reveals their understanding of the significance of brand as a corporate asset—even before the company had acquired any significant international exposure. There were two options: fight the case and try to hang on to the name Multitech, or start again with something new. A quick search of the trademark literature and records revealed that the U.S. firm had indeed registered the name Multitech not only in the United States but in several European countries as well. A trademark legal dispute could drag on for years and could ultimately prove to be extremely expensive. It put all Shih's grand plans for internationalizing—for realizing his "Dragon dream"—in jeopardy. So he bit the bullet and went for the alternative option. His company's new internationalization push would be accompanied by a new name.

The international marketing and advertising agency, Ogilvy & Mather, was commissioned to come up with options. They generated hundreds of four-letter possibilities, evaluating them for readability, memorability, and English-language connotations. After prolonged discussion, within O&M and among the Taiwan company's managers, the name "Acer" was chosen. It is a Latin word, meaning "sharp or pointed," giving the brand a vanguard feel to it, an edge. It contains the word "ace" which means the strongest card in the deck. It also began with the letter "a," meaning it would be placed first in most directories, a nice advantage for trade fairs and technical exhibits and telephone listings. (Acer precedes all its major competitors, such as AST, Compaq, Dell, Fujitsu, HP, IBM, Sun, Toshiba.) "Apex" was another strong candidate, but it suffered from the disadvantage that it was already used as a brand name in some countries, creating multiple connotations and further potential legal disputes. The clear advantage of "Acer" was that it was completely new.

These factors were all taken into account in settling on the name. This in itself was an exercise in "geocentric" management, since the Chinese approach to creating English-language brands is utterly pragmatic, without regard to any home-country preferences. Then there was a logo to go with the name. For this, O&M contracted with an Australian design house well known for its company icons. Again, numerous options were tried, before Shih and his managers settled on the now-familiar four-letter Acer—with the large initial "A", followed by "ce" in lower case and a final "R" in upper

Figure 3.2 Acer logo, adopted in 1988.

case. This logo is highly distinctive (and adopted with an eye to catching counterfeiters who might put the final "r" in lower case) and when combined with the sharp-pointed chevron in blue and red, created a very satisfying and heavily coded image—as shown in Fig. 3.2. This was Shih's new coat of arms, announced with much bravado at a press conference in Taipei in September 1987.[9]

This brand and logo have been built with single-minded determination ever since (until the changes in 2001). A wholly owned retail chain of PC stores, named *AcerLand*, was built in Taiwan to accelerate sales as well as promote the brand. By Acer's tenth anniversary, it was Taiwan's leading IT firm; Acer was a household brand in Taiwan, and Shih was a local hero, the recipient of numerous national prizes. But internationally, Acer was seen, if it was noticed at all, as just another Taiwanese PC "cloner." This reputation is what Shih was determined to change.

Acer's "Dragon Dream" of Internationalization

By 1986, Acer was already an internationalized company, in the sense of earning more than half its revenue outside Taiwan. But this was from export earnings. Stan Shih's vision was of a totally internationalized company, operating through production, logistics, sales, and customer support in markets around the world. This he called the "Dragon dream," which carries connotations in Chinese of ambition, vision, and nobility. He startled his company, then earning a substantial $400 million in revenues, with an audacious 10-year internationalization plan, in which annual revenues for the group would expand more than tenfold to reach $5 billion. This plan was actually in two parts. In the first five years, the company would grow at an anticipated 35 percent per year, to reach revenues worldwide of $1.6 billion by 1991. It would then consolidate and continue at a moderated 25 percent annual growth, to reach $5 billion in revenues by 1996. These targets were greeted with derision in Taiwan at the time, both inside the company and outside. They were regarded as wildly optimistic. Yet as it turned out, Shih was over optimistic in his first-phase predictions (Acer reached just under $1 billion in 1991, a year of losses) but conservative in his second-phase prediction, which saw Acer's revenues soar to $5.8 billion by 1995. This was indeed a remarkable realization of the "Dragon dream."

Acer's Internationalization Phase 1: Centralized Model

Shih believed that to succeed internationally it was necessary to abandon many of the features that had proved successful in Acer's domestic expansion, such as a relaxed approach to managerial initiative, rapid diversification, and multiple systems of partnership, in favor of a tighter and more centralized approach. Acer's model of internationalization was patterned on what Shih took to be the superior examples available at the time—such as IBM, Hewlett-Packard, or Compaq. The more relaxed style of allocation of responsibilities that had propelled Acer to national dominance in Taiwan in its first 10 years were abandoned in the quest for global scale. A new chief executive was appointed, recruited from IBM, who brought with him the ideology, as well as many of the practitioners of what we might call "serious management."

This phase had its successes. Acer did indeed become a global PC company to be reckoned with. It did become established in the U.S. market, in both PCs and minicomputers (through two expensive acquisitions of minicomputer firms, Counterpoint and Altos). It spread its marketing presence throughout the emerging markets of Southeast Asia and Latin America, as well as securing a foothold in Europe. Its production facilities in Taiwan showed great manufacturing capabilities and flexibility in churning out PCs for a variegated world market. It widened its spread of activities to encompass more components, including motherboards and the key component of memory chips, through the creation of a dynamic random access memory (DRAM) fabricating joint venture with Texas Instruments.

But this global scale was bought at great cost. Acer's financing was stretched to the limit, and the revenues did not expand as needed to cover the interest charges and repayments. The U.S. acquisitions proved to be mistakes, which drained cash flow for years. The expansion into new lines of business, such as DRAMs, further stretched the company's fragile financial resources. By 1990, Acer was facing severe difficulties and by 1991 it was in financial crisis.

At this point, the Acer story could have come to a premature close. Acer's efforts to become a player in established markets and in many technologically advanced industries simultaneously were overambitious. Some other way was needed. The centralized, breakneck speed model had been tried and had failed. It represented an approach to international management that Shih and his colleagues had seen as being the necessary "medicine" to make Acer into a global competitor. It was "serious management," but it had brought the company to its knees. Shih had to find another way, or face extinction—or at the very least, retreat from his global aspirations and resume a career as owner of a domestic Taiwan company that had a substantial export portfolio. But this was unacceptable for Shih.

Acer's Internationalization Phase 2: A New "Client-Server" Model

It was at this point that Shih stepped forward and resumed executive responsibility for the group. He initially offered his resignation as company chairman, to take responsibility for the mistakes, but the board rejected this. He then stepped back into the chief executive's role and initiated a fundamental rethink of Acer's internationalization strategy and organizational methods. This led to a series of innovations, such as the reconceptualization of Acer's business units as "clients" and "servers" interacting in a nonhierarchical manner, combined with fundamental reengineering of the company's newly internationalized operations. Sweeping organizational changes that had been planned by the earlier regime but not brought to fruition were implemented, along with a series of daring and imaginative organizational innovations. Stan Shih "reinvented" Acer and through tireless argument and persuasion carried his senior management group with him. What emerged was a global group divided into several business units, with responsibilities allocated either for production of PCs or for specialized components or for sales in a specific region of the world.

The idea behind this organizational architecture was that it would encourage initiative and responsibility on the part of the business groups themselves. It was initiative and responsibility that had been found wanting in the first, highly centralized phase. The production-oriented business units would supply the marketing-oriented business units, with both being responsible for their own profit and loss statements and both responsible for growing their business as rapidly as possible. For the production units (SBUs), this meant taking on extra OEM business and selling through multiple channels, while for the marketing business units (RBUs), it meant driving hard to build market share and expand into new markets rapidly, frequently through the use of partnerships and joint ventures with existing and promising distributors.

This was Acer's new "cellular" organizational template, in which each business cell had substantial autonomy for its own profit and loss accounts, its own investment and marketing, and in which the cells interacted directly (rather than via a central hierarchy) through negotiated contracting relationships. It was this interaction between cells that inspired Shih to dub this a "client-server" organizational model, appealing to the computer argot of the managers of the Acer Group. The "client-server" analogy—one based on computer networks—drew attention to the fact that the SBUs would "serve" the RBUs as clients, while the relations could also be reversed (as in a computer network) when, for example, RBUs took new product initiatives and enrolled the SBUs as clients. This process was tested to its limits by the experience of producing the innovative new product, Acer Aspire PC by Acer America, a RBU, working with the SBUs Acer Inc. and Acer Peripherals Inc.

The cellular organizational architecture achieved by this phase of Acer's restructuring is shown in Fig. 3.3. This model depicts the major RBUs like

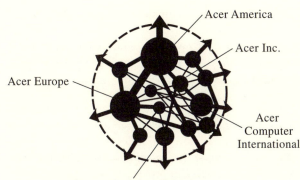

Acer America

Acer Inc.

Acer Europe

Acer
Computer
International

API (Acer Peripherals Inc.)

Figure 3.3 Cellular organizational architecture: Acer SBUs and RBUs, 1992.

Acer America, Acer Europe, or Acer Computer International interacting with external customers, as well as with the SBUs supplying them with product, mainly, Acer Inc. and Acer Peripherals Inc. These SBUs also have their external customers in the form of OEM orders from major PC vendors such as IBM.

The client-server model (or "cellular" architecture) was complemented by major initiatives in the reengineering of logistics, patterned on the "fast food" model of quick and "fresh" assembly of PCs as close to the customer as possible, rather than being shipped as fully built PCs from Taiwan. This second element, the "fast food model" was directly linked to the autonomy of the RBUs, who were responsible for forecasting demand in their own sales territories and for managing credit and inventory matters there.

A third element was the shift away from a conventional "battering ram" approach to new market entry via acquisition of an existing company or creation of a wholly owned national subsidiary. Instead, Shih and his senior managers fashioned a more graduated but still accelerated form of market entry via partnership with key distributors, in a self-propagating fashion, where partnerships in one country would expand to link with potential partners in neighboring countries. This strategy led Shih to characterize Acer as adopting a distinctive "national" or local identity in each market thus entered. This third element, involving local partnerships, was complemented by a powerful push to create Acer as an international brand and as the unifying factor for the whole group. These complementary strategies, based on Acer's highly decentralized structure, were captured by Stan Shih in his pithy phrase, "global brand, local touch." It is the counterpart to the theoretical problem enunciated by management scholars as the "global integration–local responsiveness" dilemma.[10]

The SBUs in this structure were given a global charter to pursue their own expansion–and they acted on it. The principal SBUs, Acer Inc. (AI) and Acer Peripherals Inc. (API), both internationalized their production and logistics operations. API opened major new production facilities in Malaysia and China, while AI opened a vast new production complex at Subic Bay in The Philippines. Acer's SBUs were fast acquiring the global reach that Stan Shih had envisaged for them.

New Business Formation   Two of Shih's key management lieutenants, the head of Acer Information Products, Simon Lin, and the head of Acer Peripherals, K.Y. Lee, were the principal drivers of the diversification and globalization of the Acer SBUs.[11] Simon Lin proved to be a dynamic instigator of new business formation through spinning off new ventures from the AI core. Examples included Acer Neweb, a consumer communications company focused on the TV set-top box business and wireless communication devices; Acer Netxus, a new business focused on computer networking products such as fast data switches; Acer Nexcell, a new business devoted to creation of long-life batteries for PCs; and Acer Softech, focused on the design and sales of software products. One of these spin-offs, Aopen, became involved in a celebrated product development battle with its sister SBU, Acer Peripherals, in the area of CD-ROMs. This potential competitiveness between business units for areas of new business is one of the critical issues that an organization with Acer's devolved structures and responsibilities needs to face. (The incident is discussed in chapter 6.) Under K.Y. Lee's guidance, Acer Peripherals was also an exemplary source of new spin-off businesses, such as Acer Display Technology (ADT) to design, manufacture, and sell various kinds of computer monitors and flat panel displays; Acer Media Technology (AMT) to design and create rewritable media for optical storage; and Darfon Electronics, for the design of flyback transformers and other critical components.

It is this process of new business formation, perfected by Shih himself and his senior managers Simon Lin and K.Y. Lee, that has proved to be the engine that drives the constant variation in business involvement and product development and enables Acer as a whole to respond so rapidly and successfully to shifts in market demand. This is truly a biological business model, employing notions of wide variety in order to cope with the selection pressures of markets, and "budding" processes to form new businesses out of existing businesses, rather than the conventional alternatives of new business acquisition as a means of diversification. As Simon Lin points out, diversification via the conventional route of corporate acquisition provokes inefficiencies in the form of incompatibilities between operating systems, between legal and accounting systems, and between corporate cultures and management styles.[12] The Acer budding method is more in tune with present understandings of the virtues of spinning off new enterprises as a way of maintaining business focus without losing corporate coherence.[13] Acer as a totality was "growing" in ways that responded to and in some ways anticipated market forces.

Growth Fueled by Global Devolution of Responsibilities   The new RBU-SBU organizational structure resolved many of the bottlenecks created by the first centralized structure and liberated new energies in the Acer Group, fueling rapid international expansion and revenue growth. Worldwide sales grew from U.S.$1.9 billion in 1993 to $5.8 billion in 1995, powering Acer into the Top 7 branded PC companies (and into the Top 5 overall) in the world. It looked as though everything was going right for Acer. Shih took his ideas of radical decentralization further through the formulation of the "21 in 21" concept, meaning that Acer Group companies would publicly list, separately and independently, on stock exchanges around the world—so that the group would come to consist of at least 21 separately owned entities by early in the twenty-first century. This is quite different from the normal MNE organizational model, where headquarters is constantly feuding with national subsidiaries for control.[14] The group would be tied together by common operating systems, interactions, common brand, and common goals. His ideas of devolved ownership as a means of resolving the motivation problem for the workforce were also taken further, with the share of employee ownership in Acer operations increasing to over 30 percent overall. Shih boasted that as his own shareholding in Acer declined, he became richer—because the value of the group as a whole was growing so fast.

But this rapid growth came to a halt in the mid-1990s. Sales worldwide in 1996 were $5.9 billion, barely more than the 1995 total, and edged up to $6.5 billion in 1997 and $6.7 billion in 1998, as shown in Fig. 3.4. The

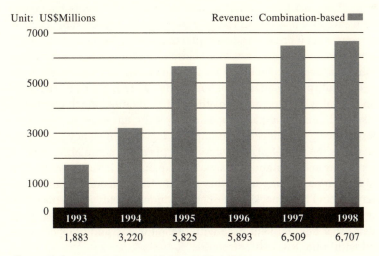

Figure 3.4 Acer revenues worldwide, 1993–1998.

Acer growth machine appeared to have ground to a halt. What was causing the problem?

Many factors could be blamed for this poor performance. There was a general difficulty faced by all leading PC firms in the conditions of hyper-competition that prevailed; few if any were making profits, particularly in the retail sales channels where Acer was focusing its efforts. (U.S. firms like Dell and Compaq were protected from the most vicious price wars in the retail sector by their strong sales to corporate customers.) There was the worldwide downturn in the semiconductor industry, and particularly the memory chip sector, which dragged down Acer's overall performance. The Asian financial crisis could also be implicated, in tightening credit conditions on Acer and depressing demand in its Asian markets. But even with all these excuses, Acer's organizational model must still carry some of the blame.

The particular "cut" of responsibilities associated with the RBUs and SBUs meant that initiatives taken anywhere in the Acer structure involved extensive negotiations if they were to be realized. RBUs, which tried to develop new products, as Acer America did with Acer Aspire, were frustrated by their having to coordinate with so many players, SBUs for design and production and RBUs for marketing around the world. The SBUs in turn were frustrated by the fact that they did not have direct access to customers in the principal markets but had to rely on the intermediary efforts of the RBUs—which they saw as sometimes being less than satisfactory. The main SBUs like Acer Information Products and Acer Peripherals developed their own "second" brands such as Aopen and Vuego precisely to get around this problem of the intermediation of RBUs.

Furthermore, the successful reengineering of Acer's worldwide logistics in the form of the fast food model, which had given Acer undoubted competitive advantages when first introduced, was rapidly emulated by its competitors. Pretty soon it became industry practice to emulate Acer in shipping components and modules for assembly close to final market. Acer's efforts to introduce further efficiencies in its logistics model were likewise frustrated by the multiple organizational boundaries that supply chain management had to deal with. Organizations that were structured much more centrally, like Dell and Compaq, appeared to gain an edge in terms of continuous process reengineering to improve logistics efficiency.

Thus, while the RBU-SBU structure had played a stimulating role in opening up new markets and accelerating expansion, it was now widely seen inside Acer as holding up further growth. It was generating unnecessary organizational bottlenecks. Acer had expanded worldwide to the point that it needed to consolidate and reinforce the coordination and integrating mechanisms that had not kept pace with the autonomy and independence generated within the RBU-SBU structure.

In 1997, Stan Shih initiated a fundamental reappraisal of Acer's organizational model. A top-level brainstorming session was held in Lungtan, at

Acer's futuristic Aspire Park, in November, attended by over 100 of Acer's senior managers around the world. (Note the contrast between this open way of dealing with a problem and the usual behind-the-scenes decision-making in the conventional divisionalized corporation.) After much discussion it was concluded that the SBU-RBU version of the client-server model, while giving Acer great flexibility and facilitating rapid expansion, was failing in generating and sustaining a strong identity for the global group. Integration, such as in driving efficient linkages between RBU and SBU development of brand focus, was failing. There was too much energy being consumed in RBU-SBU negotiations and not enough on promoting the business as a whole or in dealing directly with customers and their needs. In particular, the possibility of negotiating global deals with global customers, which was in the offing when Citicorp approached Acer for a comprehensive PC supply and servicing contract, was dashed due to the inability of RBUs to coordinate their pricing models and customer service standards. Thus, it was the multiplying incompatibilities between RBUs and SBUs that was identified as the key problem in need of an organizational solution.

Transitional Organizational Remedy: A Global Matrix   Early in 1998, Shih and his senior managers ushered in a transitional organizational remedy to deal with the perceived problems of the RBU-SBU structure. This solution involved a reorganization of some of the business "cells" and the introduction of new systems for global coordination. The gaps in coordination and the lack of product focus "end to end" across the entire value chain were remedied initially by the attempted introduction of a global matrix.

First, new global "lines of business" were created and overlaid across the existing RBU-SBU structure, in an attempt to provide focus for the key worldwide products of the group and reconnect with customer requirements. These "lines of business" were made the responsibility of senior managers, accountable directly to the chairman, and grouped into three "major business groups" that encompassed information products (i.e., PCs), peripherals, and semiconductors, plus a fourth "cross-business" category of all other businesses started at one time or another by Acer but which no longer fell within the three main business areas.

Second, the corporate headquarters were beefed up to provide a stronger global focus on such functions as internal information technology infrastructure, global brand management, and global logistics. In all these areas the RBU-SBU structure had led to loss of focus and proliferation of incompatibilities. It was time to rein in this profusion and get some global anchorage for Acer's now far-flung operations. Finally, a new Corporate Executive Committee was established to take charge of this process of consolidating Acer's corporate functions and effecting the coordination that had been lacking. The CEC was made up of seven of Acer's most senior corporate executives. It was to meet more frequently, and carried more authority, than the earlier twice yearly summits attended by heads of all business units.

Courageous as it was, this structural reform of early 1998 suffered from a lack of commitment on the part of Acer's senior managers, who saw—quite correctly—that this organizational template would create the familiar problems of cross-responsibilities associated with matrix organizations. Confusion continued to reign; revenues refused to improve; and the SBUs still chafed at their lack of access to their global customers. A more drastic and radical restructuring was clearly called for, driven this time by the CEC itself.

Acer's Internationalization Phase 3: Creation of a Set of Global Business Units

To the great credit of Stan Shih and his senior managers, the defects in the transitional matrix structure were quickly identified and action taken to correct them. The key issue, namely, a break with the RBU-SBU structure altogether, was seen by all as the necessary next step. With apparently little discussion, Acer's senior managers quickly decided on the next global structure. Thus was launched a much more radical organizational reengineering that broke with the RBU-SBU template altogether, replacing it by a cluster of global business units.

A new structure, implemented from the middle of 1998, created a new cut of Acer's expanded global activities. In place of a manufacturing and marketing oriented cut, there was now a consolidation into five global business units—four product-focused units, covering computer-related activities; peripherals; semiconductors; and services, with all the offline businesses grouped eclectically into a noncore cluster called XBUs. The cellular architecture of Acer's global operations remained unimpaired, indeed, strengthened. The various business cells, which by 1998 numbered over 40, were grouped into four global business units or "supercells"—as well as the cross-business unit (XBU) cluster—thus enhancing and consolidating their common objectives without jettisoning the autonomy and initiative that flowed from the basic cellular architecture.

The American and European RBUs disappeared in this reorganization to be absorbed by Acer Information Products in a new, global business unit (GBU) called Acer Information Products Group (AIPG). It incorporated the IP group within Acer Inc., as well as spin-off businesses such as Acer Netxus, Acer Neweb, and Acer Softech, as well as the former RBUs Acer America and Acer Europe. A second global business unit, Acer Peripherals Group, was formed by Acer Peripherals together with its spin-offs, Acer Display Technology (a very successful new business producing LCD displays for notebook PCs), Darfon Electronics, and Acer Media Technology. These two GBUs remained the core of Acer's current revenue-earning capability. A third global business unit was made up of the combined RBUs that had acquired separate legal quoted identities, particularly ACI (based in Singapore), ACLA (Latin America), Acer Sertek (Taiwan), and AMS (China), together with spin-off businesses such as AAsoft, AOpen, Servex, Weblink, VisionTech, and HiTrust. In typical pragmatic fashion, Acer turned these businesses into the core of its new thrust toward starting completely new service businesses, including internet service providers, on-line gaming services, on-line media content providers (such as games and audiovisual material), and future-oriented e-commerce businesses. A fourth global business unit was made up of Acer's semiconductor activities, which were consolidated as the Acer Semiconductor Group. This group badly needed to acquire some consistency and direction; its flagship, Acer Semiconductor Manufacturing, was drifting without a clear strategy after the sudden withdrawal of Texas Instruments from the venture (precipitated by TI's decision to withdraw globally from the DRAM business). As it turned out, this group was to have a short existence, being disbanded in 1999. Finally, a fifth unit was made up of assorted business units ("cells") that did not fit into the four GBUs. This structure is shown in Fig. 3.5.

The key difference introduced by this new organizational structure was that it provided the two core business groups, covering IT products and peripherals, with direct control over the entire value chain of their global businesses, from design, through production, logistics, sales and marketing, to customer support. It was the absence of this kind of "end-to-end" responsibility that had chafed in the previous structure. To reflect this new

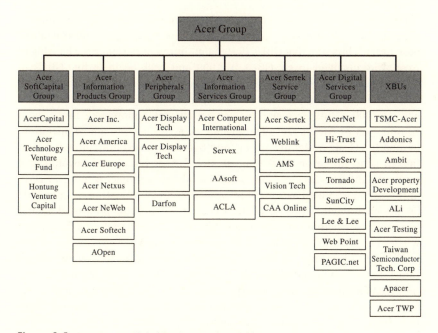

Figure 3.5 Acer Group Global Business Units, 1999.

customer-centric organizational design, the AIPG was vested with a new Branded Business Unit, whose responsibility was to steer the IP Group away from OEM and third-party business (which had been building up in the mid-1990s) toward supporting the basic Acer brand, with renewed emphasis on customer requirements and customer support. Likewise, Acer Peripherals was able to reengineer its operations toward gaining control over the entire value chain, and it created a series of internal product divisions which gave the same "end-to-end" customer focus.

The losers in this restructuring were the two principal RBUs, Acer America and Acer Europe, which now lost their separate identity. For some senior managers within these regions, this restructuring was perceived as a loss of status and as a restriction of career opportunities, so there was some attrition. But this is the inescapable price to be paid in any global restructuring: some will be seen to gain and some will be seen to lose. In fact, the AIPG has enhanced American and European marketing and customer support operations, around the core created by the former RBUs, while Acer Peripherals created two new marketing and customer support subsidiaries, Acer Peripherals America and Acer Peripherals Europe. In their first year these new entities were able to break even and were making profits in their second year. This proves that Acer can be profitable in these advanced markets, provided it gets its marketing channels and customer focus right.

New Phases of Acer's International Organization

No organizational structure remains relevant indefinitely. Acer continues to experiment with new ways of grouping and coordinating its multiple business units. Thus, the five GBUs designated in the mid-1998 restructuring of Acer were changed to six GBUs in 1999 and back again to five GBUs in 2000, reflecting changes in the emphasis of the business (and the decline of Acer's involvement in semiconductors, particularly DRAMs). Then at the end of 2000 a further major reorganization was announced, involving a spinning off of AIPG's OEM manufacturing activities into a new operation, termed the Design, Manufacturing, and Services (DMS) unit, allowing Acer Inc. to concentrate on marketing its global Acer brand and develop new products and services without worrying about manufacturing. The DMS unit was incorporated as a separate spinoff company, Wistron, in July 2001 (as the book went to press). Wistron is a term connoting both *wis*dom and elec*tron*ics—wisdom through electronics (e.g. the internet as a brain) and wisdom applied to electronics (through good design).

Thus, heading into the new century, Acer had again reconfigured itself into three fundamental global coordinating entities: Acer Branded Operations (ABO); the DMS unit, incorporated separately as Wistron; and all the other associated businesses grouped as the Holding and Investment Business (HIB). This latter group encompassed the former API, renamed Acer Communications and Multimedia (ACM), with its associated businesses such as Acer Media Technology, Darfon Electronics, and the very successful flat panel displays company, Acer Display Technology (renamed AU Optronics after its merger with Unipac in mid-2001)—as well as a series of Acer companies involved in components and modules, channel businesses (distribution and marketing), e-commerce, and venture capital. In all, there were over 40 separately incorporated businesses in the group, led by the new flagship, Acer Branded Operations, with its mission to turn Acer into the most respected IT solutions brand in emerging Asia and a strong competitor to the incumbents like HP, Compaq, NEC, or IBM in the Triad countries. The Acer Group business entities, grouped in this way as of July 2001, are shown in Fig. 3.6.

Benefits of the Global Restructuring

Customer Focus End to End across the Value Chain   The principal goal of the global restructuring at the end of the 1990s, and continuing into 2000 and 2001, was to generate a customer focus for the major business units, giving them "end-to-end" control over their value chain, from product development through production, logistics, sales, and marketing to customer support. This was further emphasized in 2001 with the spinoff of design, manufacturing, and services operations to Wistron, enabling the branded products operation within Acer to focus exclusively on customer service, marketing and new product development, and outsourcing its manufacturing—initially to its partner firm Wistron, but also to other external contract manufacturing firms. Likewise, Wistron was expecting to provide manufacturing services to Acer businesses, but also to major OEM customers, including IBM.

Acer has taken advantage of these restructurings to shift the focus of its marketing efforts away from retail channels in the United States, where it was losing money, to the emerging markets of Greater China and Asia, as well as to Europe and other parts of the world. Its individual business entities were encouraged to develop a global business vision, as done very successfully by Acer Peripherals (now Acer Communications and Multimedia). As described in the following sections, it has restructured into global product divisions with individual control over all their operations, "end to end" from design to marketing.

Corporate Coherence: Coordination through Standardization   The counterpart to the restructuring into a series of global business units (of varying names) and their efforts to coordinate operations was the role played by the global headquarters in developing coordination standards for the entire group. In 1999 Acer acquired a Corporate Executive Committee (CEC) that began to meet monthly and to stamp its authority on processes of standardization. The CEC systematically worked through the development of glob-

Figure 3.6 Acer Group entities in 2001.

Acer Inc.

Acer Brand Operations
With new focus on Greater China and regional offices throughout the world.

Wistron (formerly **Design, Manufacturing and Services** unit in AIPG)
Focus on provision of non-branded (OEM) manufacturing services, with additional expertise in design and R&D. World's #1 contract supplier of ICT products. Set to expand its manufacturing operations beyond PCs and laptops to servers, internet appliances, storage systems, communication, and network products. Incorporated as Wistron in July 2001, with 8,400 employees worldwide, five manufacturing sites around the world (in Taiwan, Philippines, China, Mexico, and Europe), and multiple service and technical support sites. Linked to Acer member companies including:
- Acer Netxus—design and manufacture of network products
- Acer NeWeb—design and manufacture of wireless communications equipment
- AOpen—motherboards, storage devices, and multimedia products (in distribution channels)
- Acer Pivotal—broadband multimedia solutions
- AnexTEK—sales of storage subsystems and
- Software businesses

Holding and Investment Business (HIB)

*HIB Acer Communications and Multimedia (ACM, formerly Acer Peripherals Inc.)
Design, manufacture, and sale of Acer mobile phones, scanners, LCD projectors, photo printers, CRT and LCD monitors, CD-ROMs, keyboards, and disk drives. Headquartered in Taoyuan, Taiwan, it has major manufacturing sites in Taiwan, Penang (Malaysia), China (Suzhou), and Mexico, with marketing and service sites in the United States, the Netherlands, and Japan. Employs more than 5,000 worldwide. ACM is Taiwan's top manufacturer of CD-ROM drives and #3 in the world in production of flat panel displays. It is associated with the spin-off businesses:
- Acer Display Technology (renamed AU Optronics after the merger with Unipac)—TFT-LCDs and plasma displays
- Darfon Electronics—flyback transformers, ceramic capacitors, etc.
- Acer Media—rewritable optical media such as CD-ROMs
- Acer Mobile Networking—third generation cellular telephone systems

*HIB Components and Modules
Encompassing the Acer businesses:
- Ambit—design, manufacture, and sales of compact power and communications modules
- Acer Laboratories Inc. (ALI)—logic, input-output integrated circuits (ICs)
- Taiwan Semiconductor Technology Corp (TSTC)—IC packaging services
- Acer Testing—value-added IC testing services
- Apacer—memory modules
- Animeta Systems—embedded Linux applications
- FormoSoft—multimedia and internet application software

Figure 3.6   Acer Group entities in 2001. (*continued*)

---

*HIB Channel Business

Encompassing the Acer businesses:

- Acer Sertek—assembly, marketing, and sales of Acer branded products in Taiwan
- Weblink—internet-based sales of personal digital assistants, computer peripherals, and software
- TWP (formerly Third Wave Publishing)—publishing of computer- and internet-related magazines
- Onking—digital information appliances
- PDA Hub—personal digital assistant application services

*HIB e-Solutions

Encompassing the Acer businesses:

- HiTrust—internet certification and authentication, payment gateway services
- Vision Tech—distribution of Unicenter software
- CAA Online—internet accounting software
- Acer Internet—internet technology and solutions
- Pagic—internet/telecom service provider
- Acer CyberCenter—internet data center
- EB Easy—B2B e-commerce services
- Acer eCard—Mondex e-cash
- Acer mSoft—mobile communications solution software

*HIB Venture Capital

Acer venture capital funds, encompassing:

- Fund 21—$60M fund, established in 1997 and managed by Acer Capital
- Acer Technology Ventures (ATV) Fund—$40M fund, established in 1998 and managed by ATV Management
- IP Fund One—$260M fund, established in 2000 and managed by
- ATVA (America) and ATVAP (Asia-Pacific)
- Acer Capital Corp—investment management services
- Acer Property development—developer and manager of Acer Aspire Park
- Acer Foundation—a nonprofit cultural and educational charity

Acer Inc. has varying levels of holdings in these associated businesses (as of July 2001), ranging from 41.4 percent in AOpen and 43.9 percent in TWP, to a medium 30.0 percent in Acer Communication, to as little as 5.7 percent in Acer Display.

---

ally consistent procedures and corporate operations, where it was perceived that lack of consistency was leading to loss of business or loss of focus. This was no consistency for its own sake, as a purely bureaucratic objective, but a consistency that ensured global focus and compatibility between operations within different business units. The price paid for autonomy and adaptivity within a widely dispersed group (with its rapid business responsiveness and entrepreneurship) is that efforts to ensure consistency have to be unremitting; otherwise, the different parts of the business rapidly move apart along different trajectories.

Global Organizational Architecture   The opening of the new century, then, saw Acer restructured according to a new organizational architecture, which Stan Shih christened as an "Internet Architecture for a Digital Economy." His depiction of this architecture, as of mid-2000, is shown in Fig. 3.7. The idea is that the business units are grouped together in weblike fashion, through multiple cross-linkages involving the units directly contracting with each other for services (such as the Acer branded operations contracting with the DMS unit for manufacturing and logistics services). The coordination is effected both through direct unit-to-unit transactions and negotiations, but also through a set of rules and procedures, binding on all units within the global group, which play the part of the interconnection standards within the internet. In both cases variety and flexibility is achieved through connectivity and autonomy, but the connectivity is underpinned by strict enforcement of standards for interoperability. The signs all point to this being a powerful organizational metaphor, for Acer and, more widely, in the twenty-first century.

Acer as a Global Cluster of Independently Owned Businesses

One of the most attractive features of Acer's organizational model has been Shih's emphasis on promoting separate and independent ownership of its constituent businesses. This is sought for three reasons. Partly, it emphasizes the autonomy of the cellular parts, allowing for considerable manage-

Acer Group Internet Organization

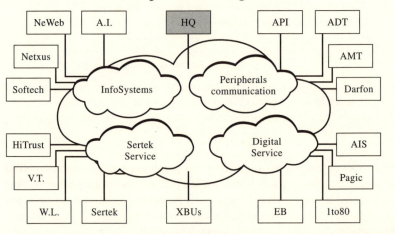

The Internet Organization for a Digital Economy

Figure 3.7 Acer Group entities in 2000. Source: Stan Shih, Acer.

ment and employee ownership within the business units. Partly, it allows for a sense of national ownership of Acer within each of its major spheres of operation, promoting its identification with each country—the "local touch" combined with a global brand. And partly, it is a pragmatic response to the need to raise capital. Shih argues, reasonably enough, that capital raised on a dozen different stock exchanges gives more room for investment options around the world than capital raised on a single stock exchange.

Shih announced his vision of Acer as a global group or cluster of independently owned businesses independently listed on stock exchanges in 1992. In characteristic fashion he coined a slogan for the model: "21 in 21." By this he meant that Acer would consist of at least 21 independently listed businesses by some time early in the twenty-first century. This was indeed a unique and daring organizational-cum-financial global model, and it attracted considerable attention.

The early steps toward realization of this dream were promising. The first public listing of an Acer business beyond Acer Inc. (listed in Taiwan in 1988) was that of Acer Computer International (ACI) in 1995 in Singapore. This RBU was responsible for sales, marketing, and customer support in countries in Asia-Pacific, Africa, the Middle East, and Central Europe and Russia. Even though ACI was 64 percent owned by Acer Inc., it met with an overwhelming response, with the issue being oversubscribed nineteen times. The Singapore Stock Exchange turned out to be extremely demanding in terms of information required and guarantees of noninterference in the affairs of ACI by other Acer businesses. This scrutiny provided some insight into potential pitfalls in Shih's ambitious model.

The ACI public listing was followed by further listings in Taiwan of Acer Peripherals Inc. (API) in 1996 and then of Acer Sertek in the same year. The next big public listing beyond Taiwan was of the Acer Computec joint venture in Mexico, another spectacularly successful Initial Public Offering (IPO). By the end of 1999, Acer had eight of its business units listed on local stock exchanges. These included AI in Taiwan, ACI in Singapore, API and Acer Sertek in Taiwan, and ACLA in Mexico City and New York. In 1998, Ambit Microelectronics went public, and in 1999, there were two further IPOs in Taiwan—the semiconductor firm ALI and Acer TWP (Third Wave Publishing)—the seventh and eighth IPOs. Both have the potential to become global corporations and contribute actively to the Acer Group worldwide. The process of public listing is proceeding, and future potential listings include AOpen, AcerNet, and many of the new internet and software services firms.

It has to be admitted that Stan Shih's target of 21 listings by early in the twenty-first century is going to be difficult to meet. Public listing has turned out to be far more arduous an exercise than even Stan Shih could have anticipated. The reason is not just the complexity and demanding nature of the information to be made available to stock exchange authorities prior to listing, which has certainly been a factor. The real issue is organizational. Acer's cellular structure, which gives it advantages and benefits in so many ways, works against it in the process of public listing. How is this so?

The essential assumption in a public listing is that the company seeking public quotation is in control of its own destiny. In order to protect potential shareholders, the applicant company has to show, in great detail, that it operates in an independent and autonomous fashion, without danger of some external party intervening to siphon off capital raised by the public listing. Thus, listing requirements are very strict on this point, pertaining to corporate control, and are very suspicious of any hint of external linkages. Thus, the Acer cellular structure, with its complex interlocking equity holdings and operational linkages, arouses a great deal of suspicion. Cellular structures and public listings on several exchanges just do not go well together.[18]

In making the "21 in 21" announcement, Stan Shih assumed that companies with local majority shareholdings would have no difficulty in listing on local exchanges. This has proven to be wide of the mark. The initial listing of ACI revealed how demanding and scrupulous the stock exchange authorities would be. In the end, ACI listed in Singapore with 64 percent of equity in the hands of Acer Inc.; 15 percent held by employees; and 22 percent in the hands of Singapore investors. It was the presence of Singapore-based investors that eventually swung the decision to list in Acer's favor. ACLA likewise had to include local investors in its IPO in Mexico City—but this experience was easier, because it was a joint venture with a genuine local partner taking 51 percent of the equity.

The project to list Acer America on the New York Stock Exchange proved to be most problematic of all. The NYSE is in a real sense the financial capital of the world, and so it is unthinkable for a subsidiary to be listed in the absence of its parent company. Thus, to list Acer America on its own was not an option. The lack of profitability of Acer America precluded listing in any case. This problem was overtaken by the absorption of Acer America into the new AIPG created in 1998. But Acer as a whole at the end of the 1990s still lacked a public listing on a major stock exchange such as London, New York, or Frankfurt—a blow for the global aspirations of the group.

The difficulties encountered by the cellular organizational form in seeking public listing are not confined to the requirements of stock exchange authorities. Institutional investors, likewise, face difficulties when confronted by cellular corporate entities. Take the case of a pension fund based in the United States that would like to invest in "Acer" as a growing PC force. Where does it place its investment? In Acer Inc., which is currently listed only on the Taiwan Stock Exchange? In ACI, which was listed in Singapore, or ACLA, with its joint listing in Mexico City and New York? Should it spread its investment across several of Acer's cellular entities—

and if so, in what proportions? These are genuine issues that the cellular organizational form raises and needs to resolve.

The "21 in 21" vision has had to adapt to Acer's global organizational restructuring in 1998 and 1999. The year 1999 saw the two separately listed RBUs—ACI headquartered in Singapore, and ACLA headquartered in Mexico City—reabsorbed into AIPG through privatization, with Acer Inc. buying out the existing public shareholders. This was undertaken in recognition that stand-alone RBUs were no longer compatible with the new global business units structure; their independence frustrated attempts by AIPG to achieve systematic "end-to-end" efficiencies and customer contact all around the world. The RBU-SBU structure had served its purpose in the early 1990s, but by the late 1990s, it was an organizational obstacle to further streamlining of Acer's worldwide operations. The "21 in 21" vision of separately listed companies had to bow to this overriding organizational requirement. But it was a bitter blow to the managers concerned, who had worked hard to build ACI and ACLA.

Stan Shih insists that the "21 in 21" vision is intact. What has changed is that purely regionally based companies, like ACLA or ACI, will no longer be formed. All Acer Group companies that list should have global expansion potential. This then clarifies the nature of the "global cluster" aspect of the Acer Group. It is a corporation with global reach, constituted by independent companies each of which, at least potentially, has global reach itself.[19] It remains an attractive vision of how to run a complex entity like a global business with maximum responsiveness and devolution of responsibility.

Management Preconditions for Success of the Acer Model

The management of Acer's new ventures, and of the internationalization process itself, calls for quite different management and organizational skills than those found in conventional MNEs. There needs to be a tolerance for ambiguity; a capacity to work with guidelines that leave a margin for initiative and for on-the-spot correction; and above all a capacity to understand what motivates the actions of other managers in the Acer Group companies, so that initiatives will not be cut off prematurely and new businesses, such as those budded off by AI and API, will be allowed to flourish. We consider many of these issues in the chapters that follow, particularly in chapter 6 on the workings of the cellularity principle. Here it is convenient to point to the kinds of issues that other scholars have raised as they start to interest themselves in Acer's organizational innovations.

Management scholars around the world are now interested in Acer's organizational innovations.[20] Questions are raised as to the efficacy of the innovations and the management capabilities and assumptions that must underpin them.[21] A first issue refers to the need for effective coordination mechanisms to be put in place when traditional hierarchical and division-alized means of control are dispensed with. It implies that Acer paid in-sufficient attention to this issue, and the criticism is answered in the way that Acer is applying much tighter global standards and procedures under its new GBU structure. Of course, it remains to be seen how effective these new standardization and coordination initiatives will turn out to be.

A second issue refers to the kinds of management norms that are needed to drive new organizational models like that employed by Acer. One way of answering this is to look to the norms dubbed "stretch, trust, discipline and support" by Bartlett and Ghoshal.[22] They are certainly called for in managing the global cellular organization of the kind developed by Acer. But there is something else, beyond this, which is perhaps captured in the notion of "fuzziness." Managers in Acer's structures need to be comfortable with a degree of ambiguity and fuzziness in the way in which their roles are specified and their performance measured. This certainly sets limits to its spread.

A third issue refers to the transfer abroad of new management practices and the influence on this of organizational processes. It implies that Acer's approach is likely to face difficulties in propagation. But a strong case can be made that conventional models face even greater difficulties. The clearest comparison is between Acer as a somewhat "messy" structure, growing or-ganically in partnership with different firms, and thus acquiring some of their characteristics in the process, and Dell Computer, which is a clear-cut American operation, highly controlled and divisionalized, now propagating itself around the world in the image of its American parent operation. Dell's success has been based on its efficiency in supplying PCs quickly to its U.S. customers through direct sales.[23] Insofar as this model can be replicated in other countries, Dell's strategy of cloning itself through wholly owned na-tional subsidiaries appears to be working. But there is little adaptive capa-bility within the Dell model. It does not seem well suited for China and even less so for India. The Acer approach, by contrast, is to adapt to the national conditions in these countries through partnership, while retaining a strong grip on its production and logistics operations worldwide. Acer's organizational approach emphasizes this balance between local adaptation and partnership with global coordination; it is potentially a more robust or resilient model of internationalization. But, of course, its success is bound up with a host of other business and strategic decisions.

Fuzziness of the Cellular Model: Conditions Governing Its Success

Compared with the clarity and unambiguous tracing of lines of authority and accountability in the divisionalized model, the Acer cellular organi-zational model appears "fuzzy." The responsibilities of business cells are not clearly defined, nor are territorial jurisdictions clearly demarcated.

Some BUs have overlapping product portfolios. This is all part and parcel of an organizational model that emphasizes autonomy and initiative and fast decision-making by managers who have a stake in reaching commercial accommodation with each other.

The fuzziness of the cellular model means that it can be operated only by people who are motivated to take the responsibilities and initiatives envisaged. If they are simply waiting for orders, then the clear lines of accountability of the divisionalized model are better suited to their disposition. But if they wish to expand markets or product lines, then a fuzzy structure which maximizes their autonomy—within broad operating guidelines and limits—is just what they need.

The fuzziness of Acer's cellular model is also ideally adapted to the demands of the fast-moving IT industry. The trends toward fragmentation of products, and the specialization of leading merchant suppliers such as Intel and Microsoft in components rather than systems, mean that an organizational model that can mirror or complement this fragmentation must have an advantage. This certainly seems to be the case with Acer—and it is the reason why leading IT firms such as Hewlett-Packard are devolving responsibilities into "cell-like" business units in place of conventional divisions.

The fuzziness of the Acer model means that managers who operate within it have to be "comfortable with ambiguity." This is not an easily learned trait, especially for managers reared in the divisional school of responsibility and accountability. Yet senior managers within Acer seem to thrive on the discretion and autonomy that fuzziness provides.

Concluding Remarks

Acer has arrived as a global corporation, or rather as a cluster of global businesses, focused on IT, PCs, PC components, IT services, and the internet. This achievement was not won easily. No one asked Acer to become a global player and join the world PC industry. It was not invited to the party. It had to muscle its way in, using an extraordinary variety of strategic and organizational innovations to do so. Nor was the achievement accomplished overnight. It took Acer several shots at the U.S. market (like many internationalizing firms before it), and it took several global organizational models before Acer could congratulate itself on its arrival. Nothing is determined in this most open-ended of processes as internationalization.

Chapters 2 and 3 have opened up to analysis the phenomenon of the sudden appearance in the world economy of a variety of new kinds of multinational enterprises. A representative sample of such firms has been chosen to illustrate the range of countries from which the firms are emerging, and the range of organizational and strategic innovations they have generated. In the case of Acer, we have demonstrated a rich set of experiences whose novelty strains the intellectual frameworks of international business.

In the next three chapters, these details are explored further, in relation to three sets of questions that present themselves as being prime features common to all the latecomer and newcomer firms' experiences: they have internationalized very rapidly; they have deployed innovative strategies; and they have devised innovative organizational architectures to underwrite their global expansion. The research question tackled is this: Can these features explain the sudden appearance and success of these firms or are there other factors at work? What then are the dynamics of accelerated internationalization, and how are they implemented within the different species of newcomers and latecomers?

Notes

1. See H.V. Perlmutter's classic account of the "tortuous evolution of the multinational corporation" (1969). He described multinationals as emerging through stages which could be described as "ethnocentric" (merely duplicating domestic operations abroad) or "polycentric" (merely operating a series of national subsidiaries without any connections). Few firms had attained what he called a "geocentric" outlook, namely, one which took the world as its focus. This remains a powerful concept, as captured in the current distinction between the "multinational enterprise" (which is ethnocentric or polycentric) and the "transnational enterprise" which is geocentric in outlook.

2. The concept of "latecomer" multinational refers to the fact that firms which emanate from latecomer industrializing nations start with clear disadvantages, but also benefit from certain advantages, among which is the absence of inertial organizational structures holding back development in incumbent firms. The concept of backwardness as a source of competitive advantage was introduced by Gerschenkron (1962) and has been applied to firms from East Asia by Hobday (1995) and by Mathews and Cho (1999).

3. As firms expand internationally, they are forced to find solutions to the problem of global integration but are also under pressure to enhance local responsiveness. This is the fundamental dilemma facing firms which aspire to operate multinationally. See Prahalad and Doz (1987) for the original formulation of the dilemma, and Bartlett and Ghoshal (1989) and Ghoshal and Bartlett (1997) for an extended elaboration.

4. The "Dragon dream" in Chinese symbolism stands for a noble ambition, one requiring great daring and courage to accomplish.

5. This degradation of (conventional) firm performance as it expands beyond a certain size is a well-recognized phenomenon. See Geringer, Beamish, and daCosta (1989) for a classic discussion of this theme. Acer's cellular organizational architecture attacks complexity at its source, so that the constituent business cells continue to operate as if they are small firms.

6. Documentary sources for Acer's business experiences include numerous magazine and newspaper articles over the years; a useful sketch of Acer's experiences up to the mid-1990s is *Made in Taiwan: The Story of Acer Computers*, by Robert Chen, first published in Chinese in 1996 and in English translation in

Taiwan in 1998 (Chen 1996/98); and Stan Shih's own account of his business philosophies in *Me Too Is Not My Style*, published in English translation by The Acer Foundation in Taiwan in 1998 (Shih 1998).

7. By "leverage" is meant the practice of finding ways to access technological knowledge outside the company and internalizing it, to enhance the company's core knowledge and competence. The term was introduced in its present form by Prahalad and Hamel (1990). This is the technological strategy that East Asian firms like Acer have been able to master to great effect. See Mathews and Cho (2000) for an extended discussion.

8. Acer encountered many intellectual property hurdles along the way, which are fascinating but not directly related to the firm's internationalization; see Chen (1998) and Shih (1998) for details.

9. Chen (1998): 177–184.

10. This dilemma is elaborated in chapter 5. See Doz and Prahalad (1991) or Bartlett, Doz and Hedlund (1990) for representative discussions.

11. At the time of finishing this book, in late 2000, Simon Lin had assumed the reins as CEO of Acer Inc. and president of Acer Information Products, while K.Y. Lee was president of Acer Peripherals (renamed Acer Communications and Multimedia in 2001). In the 2001 restructuring, Simon Lin moved to become President and CEO of Acer's design, manufacturing and services spinoff, Wistron Corporation, responsible for all Acer's OEM work, and moving immediately to a position as the world's top ICT contract manufacturer.

12. Personal interview in Taipei, March 1997.

13. The business literature on corporate spin-offs has exploded, under the impact of celebrated cases like Lucent (AT&T spin-off), Agilent (from HP), Lexmark from IBM, Unova from Litton Industries, and The Associates First Capital Corp. from the Ford Motor Company. A comparable Japanese approach is known as *bunsha* or corporate fission: see Sakai and Sekiyama (1985), as well as Sakai and Russell (1993) for a description and elaboration. Johnson, Brown, and Johnson (1994) provide a review of the economic evidence concerning corporate spin-offs and their performance effects. The issue is discussed below, in chapter 6.

14. See Birkinshaw (1997) and Birkinshaw and Hood (1998) for many examples of these conventional tussles between MNE headquarters and subsidiaries. Acer's organizational architecture completely bypasses such problems.

15. Acer retreated from management of its memory chip operations in mid-1999, handing over a major ownership share, and full management control, to the Taiwan semiconductor leader, Taiwan Semiconductor Manufacturing Corporation (TSMC). However, other parts of its cellular business units retained an active interest in semiconductors, such as Acer Laboratories Inc. (ALI).

16. This brought Acer's focus clearly on related groups of products and their customers—more or less as Sony's restructuring in 1999 into four worldwide product-related divisions achieved.

17. This is a major new strategic direction for Acer, and for Taiwan, bringing the Acer Communications and Multimedia Group into the most advanced global business of third-generation mobile telephony ground stations. Technology for the new venture is being transferred from the Computer and Communications Laboratories of Taiwan's Industrial Technology Research Institute, in a tried and

tested formula for Taiwan's technological enhancement through public-private technological cooperation.

18. Divisionalized firms faced this dilemma and solved it by incorporating as a single "holding company"; stock exchange requirements were doubtless an important factor in the evolution of this organizational form. This is a case of institutional shaping of an economic outcome.

19. Acer's global cluster is further elaborated and analyzed in chapter 6.

20. The strategic and organizational innovations developed by Acer are of such interest that they have attracted the attention of business schools around the world. Cases on Acer have been prepared at INSEAD, at the Ivey School of Business in Canada, and at Harvard Business School in the United States. See Deborah Clyde-Smith, 1997, "The Acer Group: Building an Asian Multinational," reproduced in De la Torre, Doz, and Devinney (2000), pp. 190–202; Prescott C. Ensign, "Acer in Canada," Teaching Note 8-97-MO4, Richard Ivey School of Business, University of Western Ontario, 1997; Christopher Bartlett and Anthony St. George, "Acer, Inc.: Taiwan's rampaging dragon," Case N9-399-010, Harvard Business School, December 30 1998; and ibid, "Acer America: Development of the Aspire," Case N9-399-011, Harvard Business School, December 30 1998. These are reproduced in Bartlett and Ghoshal (2000a).

21. Bartlett presented the new Acer cases at a Research meeting staged by the Harvard Business School in Hong Kong, early in January 1999, with comments offered by Acer chairman and founder, Stan Shih. On this occasion, Bartlett posed three questions to the Acer organizational experience:

- What management practices and organization processes are required to integrate and control emerging networks of loosely linked cross-border organizations?
- How can countercultural management norms and practices be effectively transplanted? How are "fusion models" affecting the quality of management?
- What management tools and change processes are most effective in executing radical transformation of embedded business models and organizational capabilities? How fast can such processes occur in large, cross-border organizations?

22. See, for example, the discussion of management context in Ghoshal and Bartlett (1997): 153.

23. See the description by Michael Dell himself in Dell and Fredman (1999).

Part II

CHARACTERISTICS OF THE GLOBAL LATECOMERS

4

INCREMENTAL EXPANSION WITH
RAPID GLOBAL COVERAGE

Contrary to popular wisdom, companies from
the fringes of the world economy can become
global players. What they need is organizational
confidence, a clear strategy, and a passion for
learning, and the leadership to bring these
factors together.

Christopher Bartlett and
Sumantra Ghoshal,
"Going Global"

Stan Shih knew from personal experience all about the hazards involved
in entering foreign markets as a new player—his own path to "going global"
as a late-mover.[1] Rather than emulate incumbent MNEs by entering markets
through large investments in wholly owned subsidiaries, he favored an approach that would reduce the risk by entering into partnerships with local
distributors. In this way, Acer could gradually acquire knowledge of the
market and gradually increase its commitment to that market, leaving room
to change course or adjust strategy if circumstances changed. Thus, Shih
stood up at the June 1992 Acer International Distributors' meeting, held that
year in Cancun, Mexico, and declared that, henceforth, Acer was to see
itself "as a Mexican company." He meant, of course, that Acer would be a
Mexican company in Mexico—just as it would be a Brazilian company in
Brazil or a Malaysian company in Malaysia. The basis of this pronounce-
ment was that Acer was entering into a new partnership with its Mexican
distributor, Computec.

The 500 distributors gathered in Cancun were shocked at this announcement. They were used to the rhetoric of "partnership" so easily used by
traditional multinationals in dealing with local firms. The reality frequently
turned out to be very different. But here was Acer's chairman, apparently
very serious about the suggestion that Acer expand worldwide on the basis
of genuine partnerships with key local distributors.

The goal for Acer was clear—achieve the *fastest possible coverage of
world markets for PCs and their components*. The point of Acer's initial

foray into the international domain in the second half of the 1980s, making use of acquisitions in Europe and the United States, had been to achieve a kick start in these advanced markets. But it had not worked. The companies chosen as acquisition targets had not performed to expectation; indeed, they proved to be a drain on resources. Market share remained stubbornly low. A different strategy targeted at achieving accelerated market coverage in Peripheral markets, via partnerships with local distributors, promised to be a more rewarding route. This was the thinking that lay behind Stan Shih's bold announcement at Cancun in 1992.

The key to partnership arrangements is credibility and trust. As Stan Shih put it:

> We had to convince our partners that we really meant what we said and the best way to do this was by practice and example. So we started with local decision-making, giving our partner companies responsibility for making critical decisions concerning the promotion and positioning of the Acer brand and Acer products in their local market. We then moved through the phases of local assembly, to finally offer the best distributors local ownership and eventual control.[2]

Take the case of Mexico as an example. The company Acer was dealing with in Mexico as its local distributor in the 1980s was Printaform, which "repackaged" Acer's machines and sold them through its own channels using the Printaform brand. This was an interim arrangement. In October 1989, a key manager who handled the Acer product line left the company to form his own company, called Computec, in partnership with other investors; thereafter, they specialized in importing Acer machines and made the promotion of the Acer brand one of their critical strategies. Acer's interests were looked after by a country manager, who reported to the then headquarters of Africa Latin America Asia-Pacific (ALAP) operations.[3] This was a successful operation and led Stan Shih to take the initiative in 1992 of forming a joint venture with Computec, with Acer taking a minority equity stake of 19 percent.[4] Shih went on to say:

> This was the context for my declaring in 1992 that Acer would become a Mexican company. And this too was the beginning of our new strategy of "local touch." Indeed things evolved to the point where we entered into a full 50:50 joint venture with Computec in 1994 called Acer Computec Latino America (ACLA). We sought to list this company publicly on the Mexico City stock exchange. We made it independent of the Miami office which formerly controlled Latin America, through a share swap, and then gave it expanded coverage of neighboring Latin American countries. ACLA's initial foray was into Chile, where it took a small equity stake in a promising local distributor. This prospered, and then further markets were entered.

Thus the partnership model proliferated itself through Latin America. This was the real test of the joint venture becoming a true local company and the real test of our local touch strategy. So it was our original channel partner or customer who became our joint venture partner in Mexico.[5]

Through the concept of local partnership as a means of gaining rapid entry, Acer spread rapidly in Latin America, with the initial joint venture, ACLA, master-minding the extension of the strategy throughout the subcontinent. In the 1990s, Acer achieved stunning market leadership in this region, rising to be the no. 1 brand in Mexico, as well as in Chile, Panama, and Uruguay, and a leading contender in others.

Exactly the same strategy was pursued by Acer to gain a rapid coverage of markets in Southeast Asia, another critical Peripheral region. Here the key instigator of accelerated regionalization was Acer Computer International (ACI), formed as a new RBU in 1992 out of Acer's original marketing division covering Africa, Latin America, and Asia-Pacific. In this split, ACI was given responsibility for over 60 countries in Africa, India, Russia, the Middle East, and Asia-Pacific, while ACLA was given a broadened responsibility in Latin America. ACI pursued a rapid market entry in these 60 countries through a variety of strategies, of which distributor partnership was again prominent. The switch in strategy in the 1990s paid off, as Acer secured the no.1 brand position in several Asia-Pacific markets, including Thailand, Indonesia, Malaysia, and The Philippines.

Take the case of Thailand. Since the early 1980s, Acer had worked with the distributor Sahaviriya OA Group (SVOA), an affiliate of the leading Thai industrial conglomerate, Sahaviriya (SV). The partnership prospered, so that SVOA elected to become Acer's exclusive agent in Thailand. It sold both IBM/"Wintel" PCs, for which Acer was its sole supplier, and Apple machines.[6] The relationship grew so well that by 1993 it was proposed to form a joint venture between ACI and SVOA, named "SV-Acer Co. Ltd." Acer took a 49 percent stake in the joint venture, giving SV a controlling 51 percent. This was a deliberate strategy on Acer's part, designed to show the partner firm that it was really in charge of the joint venture and would have to make business decisions accordingly—rather than wait for instructions from Acer Inc. The newly formed SV-Acer then took off and brought Acer to no. 2 brand position in the Thai market.

The SV-Acer joint venture in turn formed the nucleus for further rapid expansion into neighboring countries. Based in Bangkok, its operations were extended to cover Vietnam, Burma (Myanmar), Laos, and Cambodia, as well as Thailand, that is, five Indo-Chinese countries in all. Thus, the approach in Southeast Asia mirrored the approach pursued in Latin America: form an initial joint venture and then allow it to expand into neighboring markets, forming new joint ventures as they are deemed to be desirable. The joint venture then starts the process of getting closer to the market in these other countries, through building long-term relations with domestic distributors. In Vietnam, for example, a liaison office was established in 1996, and SV-Acer used the services of around ten distributors and dealers in the country. The intention was to narrow this down over time until a partnership would be formed with one of them, which may in turn become a new joint venture. This then is a self-propagating and self-sustaining strategy of market entry via partnership being replicated throughout a region.[7]

A different pathway again, but in keeping with the same partnership principle, has been followed in India. Here the PC market was relatively closed up until 1991, when it opened up under conditions that Acer, and other companies, found very difficult for two to three years. Indian technology firms like Wipro, which had followed the latecomer strategy of diversifying away from its traditional cooking oil business and licensing PC technology from incumbents, were keen to establish themselves as India's main players. Wipro allied with Acer, assembling its computers in kit form and selling them as Wipro-branded products. Acer sold its products under similar OEM arrangements to other Indian producers, in the absence of making much brand headway itself. Acer and Wipro went their separate ways for a while and then teamed up again in the early 1990s, by which time Wipro had emerged as India's second strongest IT company. Its strategy of self-reliance was not working, and so it sought a more permanent joint venture arrangement with Acer.[8] By the mid-1990s, Wipro was looking for a long-term relationship with an overseas technology partner, while Acer was looking for a long-term distributor partner.[9] At the end of 1994, the two companies struck a deal and formed a joint venture, Wipro Acer Ltd. (WAL). It marketed its products under the brand *Wipro Acer*. (This was the single exception to Acer's rule that its products always be marketed under the Acer brand—a concession to the Wipro founder, Mr Premji.) Again, the Acer partner company was ACI, based in Singapore. Wipro took a controlling 55 percent of the joint venture and Acer 45 percent, in keeping with the spirit of Acer providing sufficient incentive to the partner. This arrangement again proved to be extremely effective. Acer's market share shot up from a negligible level in 1993, to taking the no. 1 international brand position in India in 1996–97.[10]

These partnership arrangements do not have to last forever, and indeed they do not. They last as long as they serve the purposes of the partner firms. For Acer, the point of the partnership is to establish a strong presence in the target Peripheral market and a network of outlets through the chosen distributor. For the partner firm, the point is to build its retail strength through an alliance with a leading brand. If successful, the partner firms may elect to go separate ways, as has happened in Mexico, as well as in India, and as is likely to happen elsewhere. For Acer, the dissolution of a distribution partnership is the signal that it needs to translate its newly acquired market position into a wholly owned distribution arrangement—in other words, to upgrade its commitment of resources to that market.

Acer's partnership strategies can be generalized as a form of accelerated market entry or *accelerated internationalization*. The success of the strategy depends on the choice of partner. The upside of the partnership strategy is extremely rapid market coverage. The firm (in this case Acer) does not have to expend funds and resources in getting to know the market itself. Instead, it selects a partner—like Computec in Mexico or Wipro in India—which already has that knowledge and is looking to grow a business in partnership with an emerging multinational. The partnerships thus established then serve as a platform for expansion into neighboring countries, where new partnerships are nurtured—and so the process propagates itself, like a kind of chain reaction. The process is illustrated in Fig. 4.1.

The downside of the partnership strategy is revealed when partnerships turn sour or do not develop as expected—as some inevitably must. In Japan, for example, Acer must have felt it was a real coup to enter into a partnership with the Japanese giant Mitsubishi in the mid-1980s. But 10 years later, Acer's share of the Japanese PC market was still minuscule. The partnership with Mitsubishi took Acer right up a blind alley.

Acer's operations in Europe provide another such counterexample. Acer's presence in Europe began with exports from Taiwan, and demon-

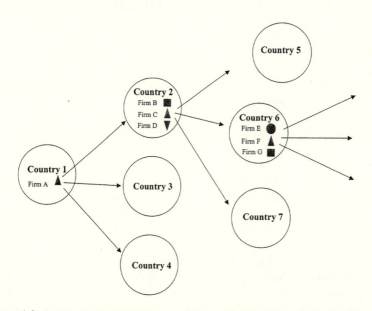

Figure 4.1 Acer's self-propagating partnership model. *Step 1:* Firm A searches for new markets, forming links with many firms in countries 2, 3, 4. *Step 2:* In country 2, firm A experiments with firms B, C, D for reliability. *Step 3:* Firm A selects partner firm C and forms JV in country 2. *Step 4:* Joint venture AC seeks new partnerships in countries 5, 6, 7. *Step 5:* JV AC experiments with firms E, F, G in country 6. *Step 6:* JV AC selects firm F to form new JV ACF in country 6 and then looks for partners in neighboring countries. Thus, the process of accelerated expansion is propagated from country to country.

strations of Acer products at trade fairs, through the 1980s. This led to the creation of a local office, termed (rather grandly) "Acer Europe," opened by Mr. Teddy Lu in Dusseldorf, with three employees, in 1985. In that first year, Acer's sales in Europe amounted to only $3 million. A year later the office was moved to a commercial site outside Dusseldorf, and a warehouse was built alongside. Mr. Lu and his staff worked to build relationships with efficient distributors in Europe and with OEM customers who put their brand on Acer's products (such as Philips). By the end of the 1980s, Acer Europe was contributing almost a third to group sales—a remarkable level of early success.

The next move was to establish national subsidiaries in various countries. This was done in the expectation that a national office would be closer to the domestic market and would be able to establish relations direct with dealers. By 1992, Acer had established national subsidiaries in six European countries: Denmark, France, Germany, Italy, The Netherlands, and the United Kingdom. These subsidiaries covered other countries as well; for example, Acer France, formed in 1989, looked after sales in neighboring Spain and Portugal.

Acer's strongest European performance was in Germany, where Acer managers developed a strong relationship with a national distributor, Cetec. The result was that Acer sales and brand awareness in Germany far exceeded the level anywhere else in Europe. Cetec looked for a long-term commitment from Acer, and in 1989, offered Acer a 50 percent share in the company (with an option to purchase the remaining 50 percent in 1991). It was run as a very independent operation. When, for example, Acer developed a worldwide advertising campaign in the early 1990s and wanted to run this campaign in Germany, the Cetec owners objected, on the grounds that the image presented was not compatible with the image of Acer they had been promoting. Stan Shih bowed to their request to run their own separate campaign in Germany. This provides an interesting insight into the workings of partnerships. In 1991, Acer exercised its option, and Cetec was fully acquired and integrated into the Acer Group as part of the German national subsidiary. Thus ended a troublesome partnership. In Italy, Acer was involved in protracted legal battles with its distributor-partner and again eventually created its own national subsidiary in Italy.[11] This too soured relations in Europe and placed the partnership model under stress.

In the wake of these experiences, the European RBU pursued a strategy of national subsidiaries and wholly owned regional headquarters, rather than partnerships with local distributors. There is great organizational flexibility involved here. While the partnership model was abandoned in Europe and the United States (and Japan as well), it was pursued with increasing thoroughness in Peripheral markets such as in Latin America, Asia, Africa, and the Middle East.[12] This pursuit revealed a strength of the RBU-SBU organizational model: RBUs could decide for themselves what mode of market entry they would pursue and what model of international expansion would work best for them. But as success in the partnership strategy of accelerated Peripheral internationalization was revealed, it became championed as a preferred strategy by Acer around the world.

Thus, Acer's worldwide expansion in marketing terms encompassed a conventional "establishment chain" moving from exports, through local distributors, to tied distributors becoming partners, to wholly owned subsidiaries.[13] It also encompassed the inheritance of distribution arrangements acquired with company takeovers. With its takeover of Altos in the United States, for example, Acer also acquired distribution subsidiaries in Europe. The headquarters of Altos Europe, in grand offices in Paris, were far more salubrious than Acer Europe's crowded offices—a source of much tension at the time. This was also a contributing factor in Shih and his senior managers embarking on a quite different strategy of expansion through partnerships in Peripheral markets, where such tensions would not arise.

Stan Shih felt comfortable with this partnership strategy because it was in a real sense a return to choices made very early in Acer's career. As Shih himself put it:

From the very beginning we relied on partnerships for our major expansions. For example, when we expanded our very early operations from Taipei to Taichung and Kaohsiung [in 1977], which at the time was a big step for our tiny firm, we relied on partnerships with local distributors or dealers.[14] We allowed these people to own a substantial portion of the business. The upside of this arrangement was that they would make more exertions to expand the market for our early Acer products (then known as Multitech) and they would reduce the risk of expansion. The downside, of course, was that we would have to share the benefits of growth. But for me it was self-evident that sharing in the benefits was a sound and reliable approach to expansion.

You see the same pattern in our approach to gaining distribution rights for U.S. microelectronic products at the very beginning of our business, when we did so by entering into a 60:40 venture with a Chinese-American based in Silicon Valley. Subsequently he did very well out of this deal—but so did we. (Later we bought him out—at great profit to himself—but his assistance at the beginning had been invaluable.) This is a strategy which has always seemed to me to provide the greatest benefits not just for the partners but for the company initiating the approach. The strategy is based on minimizing the risks of mistakes. It seems to me that risks are minimized by people who have a stake in the success of the business they are managing. These are the origins of our "local touch" approach.[15]

The market where partnership was not tried, and where acquisitions proved to be very troublesome, was that of the United States. Acer had enormous trouble making its U.S. operations profitable—partly through its choice of distributors and marketing strategy, and partly through its continuing reliance on retail market channels, where virtually no PC firm makes a profit. Its major competitors like Compaq and Dell focus their efforts on the corporate and educational customers rather than on the retail market, where profit margins are considered too low. As Shih put it:

> The difference lies in the strong presence of the manufacturers themselves in the U.S. market. In the U.S. it was manufacturers like IBM, Hewlett-Packard, Apple, and Compaq who were able to enforce control over the distribution channels and this formed an effective barrier against entry for newcomers like ourselves. These companies were able to promote their product direct to the dealers and to the consumer marketplace through heavy advertising which was beyond our resources at that time. A company like Dell could take this situation to its logical extreme and eliminate all the overheads entirely by distributing direct to customers through telephone ordering and assembling the PCs on demand from components sourced from the cheapest supplier. It was these kinds of operations that intensified the competition in the PC distribution channels in the U.S. and made life so difficult for us.

> But in the developing countries it was a very different situation. There, the major U.S. producers had no direct manufacturing presence. Or, if they did so, it was in manufacturing components as part of a global production system rather than manufacturing for local supply. This meant that we had the opportunity to develop a different kind of relationship with local distributors and were able to enter into exclusive distribution agreements in a way that was simply not possible in the U.S. These agreements from the late 1980s and early 1990s led to the rapid expansion of Acer's market share in many developing countries, in Latin America, South Asia, South East Asia, and the Middle East. This provided the background for the extension of the strategy which has become "local touch."[16]

Newcomers' and Latecomers' Internationalization Patterns

Acer is certainly not alone in developing an innovative approach to achieving accelerated internationalization. In this chapter, our concern is to probe the patterns of internationalization utilized by newcomers and latecomers, to look for the clues that help to explain their success in reaching global scale so quickly.

The key to grasping the sources of accelerated internationalization is to see that latecomers and newcomers are more interested in rapid coverage than with solidity of headquarters-subsidiary connections, as in the case of traditional MNEs. Thus, a latticelike international structure, with interim connections established between partner firms spanning the globe, is preferable to the solid masonry of traditional structures. Acquisitions and partnership arrangements alike serve the purpose of accelerating global coverage.

Take the steel industry, and Ispat International, as a case in point. The founder of the corporation, Lakshmi Mittal, was able to build a global network of steel mills so quickly because of his strategy of buying plants that were already in operation, even run-down, and turning them around, usually with an infusion of new investment—rather than pursuing the much more costly route of building greenfield operations. Industry insiders suggest that "by buying poorly run plants, Ispat has invested less for each ton of steel-making capacity than any other firm in the world—half of what has been spent by Nucor or Steel Dynamics, another American mini-mill firm that is reckoned to be the world's lowest cost builder of new steel plants."[17] But buying decrepit steel mills is only half the story. They then have to be turned around, with an infusion of investment. In Trinidad, for example, Ispat took over a loss-making steel mill in 1988, spent $10 million in modernizing the technology, doubled production within three months, and within a year had turned the plant into a profitable operation. At the other end of the scale, once Ispat's global strategy was in place and it was making headway in Europe, in 1997, Ispat bought a series of mills from a loss-making division of the German steel giant, Thyssen, and immediately announced investment plans in new technology amounting to $40 million. Again, these mills were soon making their contribution to Ispat's rapidly assembled global network.[18]

The faster Ispat was able to add mills to its network, the more it was able to generate economies due to its global reach. As soon as Mittal brings a new firm into the Ispat Group, he redirects sales and purchasing internationally in order to secure global economies. Such changes can be implemented swiftly in Ispat's minimill network structure, which does not depend on traditional scale economies for its effectiveness but on its flexibility and adaptability.

Likewise, the Hong Leong Group in Singapore started slowly in hotels in the 1980s and then accelerated in the 1990s through acquisition of existing chains. Kwek Leng Beng's interest in hotels dated back to the early 1970s, when City Developments Ltd. (CDL) acquired the King's Hotel in Singapore. Overseas expansion was initiated with the purchase of the Grand Hyatt Hotel in Taipei—the city's most magnificent hotel—and went on to include the famous Plaza Hotel in New York, the Hyatt Kingsgate in Sydney, and the Britannia Hotel and then the Gloucester Hotel in London. By 1989, there were enough hotel interests for them to be gathered into a separate company, CDL Hotels International, and floated on the Hong Kong Stock Exchange. Then in the 1990s, CDL Hotels International (CHIL) was used by Kwek Leng Beng as the vehicle for accelerated acquisition of hotels around the world. This was done not through the purchase of individual properties, but now by acquisition of existing hotel chains.

The first hotel chain purchased in this way was the Millennium chain, consisting of four-star hotels in Australia, New Zealand, Indonesia, The Philippines, as well as the United Kingdom and the United States, followed by the Copthorne chain of European business hotels, acquired in 1995 from the Irish airline, AerLingus. By the end of the 1990s, through these acquisitions and others, no fewer than 66 hotels had been gathered together, spread across 12 countries, including France, Germany, and the United Kingdom; the United States; Australia and New Zealand; and Hong Kong, Malaysia, Indonesia, and The Philippines. Group assets reached U.S.$2.6 billion by the end of the 1990s, with turnover of just U.S.$1 billion. CDL Hotels and its subsidiaries were listed on five stock exchanges around the world. The group was ranked as the world's eighth largest hotel management company.[19] The high point for Kwek Leng Beng was the public flotation of the group's U.S. and European hotels under the name "Millennium & Copthorne Hotels" on the London Stock Exchange in 1996. In early 1999, the global consolidation of the hotel business was all but complete, with M&C acquiring all of CHIL's hotel interests in Southeast Asia and Australasia.

Kwek Leng Beng's strategy has been to expand through acquisition, and as hotels under existing management companies like Hyatt or Hilton are acquired, to buy out the management contracts as they become available. The aim is to turn *Millennium & Copthorne* into a global brand as well recognized as Hyatt, Hilton, or Sheraton. For example, when the Hyatt Regency Hotel in Sydney was acquired in the mid-1990s, it was substantially refurbished, but there was no name change until the Hyatt management contract lapsed in 1997. Then it was renamed the "Millennium Sydney" and its management was taken over by CDL Hospitality Management Services, a hotel management subsidiary of CDL Hotels International (CHIL). Cost benefits are reaped as the group integrates its management operations, for example, through use of the Anasazi worldwide reservation system, linking the hotel management company globally to travel agents and airlines. Kwek's worldwide business strategy is to grow through the securing of more hotel management contracts (as Hyatt, Sheraton, et al. did in earlier decades), taking significant equity stakes where needed to secure the contract.

As a final example (out of dozens that could be chosen), Li & Fung from Hong Kong was able to achieve extremely rapid global coverage in its industrial contracting business, partly through its willingness to seek industrial customers anywhere they could be found, and partly through its adroit acquisition of rival operations when they became available. It thus accelerated its global expansion through its own partnership arrangements, with customer and supplier firms, as well as through strategic acquisition. Meanwhile Li & Fung expanded its enormous network of contract suppliers throughout the Asia-Pacific region, encompassing more than 5,000 contract manufacturing firms working to Li & Fung specifications. Li & Fung is a classic case of expanding rapidly through a "lattice" structure rather than through the solid masonry of headquarters and subsidiary relations.

Fundamentally, accelerated internationalization is a ticket of entry to the fast-moving global economy. Latecomers (and newcomers) cannot afford to choose a slow and steady internationalization approach—their strategic goal is to create a presence, to become a player, and from that position to draw on resources and strengths that would not otherwise be available. It is the multiply connected worldwide web of the international economy that ultimately underpins the success and plausibility of this strategy.

Striking parallels with these latecomer experiences have been provided by earlier international expansion strategies and patterns devised by Nordic and Scandinavian corporations, expanding abroad in the later years of the nineteenth century and early years of the twentieth century. These earlier patterns of international expansion also tended to gravitate to Peripheral markets rather than confronting major markets head-on—as investigated in a sustained series of empirical studies by Swedish researchers based at Uppsala University and elsewhere.[20] As latecomers in the European context, the Scandinavian countries, and Sweden in particular, sought to develop the competitive strengths of their firms through internationalization. This is the reverse of the standard model of international expansion, which is supposed to be driven by the firm's goal of exploiting and extending its existing advantages. The parallel with Scandinavia's multinationals, which in the context of Europe at the turn of the century were the latecomers of their time, is intriguing and worthy of closer examination.

Swedish MNEs as Counterpoint to East Asian Latecomers

Sweden (and to some extent the other Nordic countries, including Finland) provides a fascinating counterpoint to the postwar experience of East Asia. In the European context, Sweden was a latecomer industrializing nation and employed many of the same strategies of state involvement and strong financial centralization in supporting the development of industry that were later to be found in East Asia. Even more arrestingly, Sweden industrialized through the creation of several large MNEs, which expanded abroad in order to secure markets and enhance production and technological capabilities. They pursued this strategy out of necessity, since they did not have the option of simply exporting home-based assets, as in the case of typical U.S. MNEs, or of securing resources from colonies, as in the case of United Kingdom, French, or Dutch MNEs. While their expansion seems cautious and incremental by the standards of the 1990s, it was for their time exceedingly rapid. More to the point, it was driven by the same imperatives of achieving global reach as a strategic, competitive goal, in advance of having the resources needed to exploit such global reach fully. Remarkably, Sweden had one of the most internationalized economies in the world at the end of the nineteenth century—a direct outcome of its latecomer strategies.[21]

The internationalized Swedish firms survived the vicissitudes of two world wars and in the 1960s and 1970s grew rapidly, so that Sweden became the most internationalized economy in the world. Leading Swedish MNEs of the early years of the twentieth century, which emerged in Sweden's industrialization post-1870, included firms like ASEA (electrical machinery), Electrolux (domestic electrical appliances), L.M. Ericsson (telephone equipment), Alfa Laval (cream separators and dairy equipment), SKF (bearings), and Swedish Match (matches).[22]

L.M. Ericsson was one of the earliest Swedish MNEs to expand abroad, seeking markets in foreign countries for its telephone equipment before the domestic market in Sweden had grown to sufficient size. The firm traces its origins to 1875, and by the turn of the century was well established as a telephone equipment supplier, employing 1,000 workers at its plant in Stockholm and exporting around 50,000 telephone sets per year. In 1900, no less than 95 percent of its production was exported, half to the United Kingdom. Since its customers were mostly public sector telephone system operators, Ericsson was subjected to political pressures to build production facilities in its foreign markets. (This reveals that the pattern of international expansion by the MNE is not entirely a matter of choice.) The largest facilities built before World War I were in Beeston in the United Kingdom, and in St. Petersburg in Russia. Other Ericsson factories had been established in Paris, Vienna, Budapest, as well as in the United States, in Buffalo, N.Y. This initial foray into the United States never secured a foothold (against the dominance of the U.S. incumbent, Bell Telephone), and it was sold in 1923. In 1913, at least 50 percent of Ericsson's total sales were still outside Sweden. Its overseas sales were in a variety of countries, the largest of which was Russia. Ericsson actually had to have three quite separate efforts, spanning close to 100 years, before it successfully entered the U.S. market.[23]

Alfa-Laval started as the dairy equipment supplier Separator in the late nineteenth century. The relatively small size and lack of sophistication of the Swedish market compelled the firm to seek its major markets abroad, where the United States rapidly came to dominate. Indeed, Alfa-Laval built up its major R&D facilities within the United States, but later regretted this and sought to downsize the U.S. operation after the First World War to bring more of the basic R&D work back to Sweden. Relations between the Swedish and U.S. arms of Alfa-Laval were at times extremely tense. This pattern of expansion followed by contraction (as international circumstances dictated) led Zander and Zander (1997) to characterize Alfa-Laval as an "oscillating" MNE—that is, nonconforming to the general perception that MNEs pursued endless growth.

Svenska Kullager Fabriken (SKF) began operations in the metal industry in 1907 and had to build up markets for its ball and roller bearings in the

United States, as well as in the United Kingdom and France, before it could take on established German firms even in the domestic Swedish market, as well as the wider European market. SKF subsequently looked to stimulate its downstream business and to this end created an automotive firm as user of its bearings—Volvo. This proved to be a very successful spin-off that rapidly expanded internationally itself. Indeed, Volvo became much better known than its parent and built its competitive capabilities in Peripheral markets such as Argentina, prior to tackling the automotive majors in their own territory. This strategy turns out to be characteristic of latecomers that has been reinvented by East Asian latecomer multinationals like Acer.

The stimulus for such strategies was likewise a sense that the domestic market was not a sufficient training ground for international competitiveness. As Olsson (1993) put it, summarizing the early internationalization experience of these and other Swedish firms:

> The limited size and relative backwardness of the Swedish market thus seems to have been a blessing in disguise for Swedish firms. The difference in size of the home markets significantly influences the development of small country MNEs as compared to, for example, their American counterparts. The eventual victory of several of the Swedish MNEs on their domestic battleground was rather a result of the ongoing development of their products in stimulating international competition. (1993: 102)

Very much the same considerations apply today to the cases of latecomer MNEs expanding internationally from East Asia and elsewhere in the Periphery. These companies too, like their earlier Swedish counterparts, have had to build up their competitive capabilities abroad (rather than staying at home) and have then sought to establish a beachhead for themselves in the advanced markets of the United States, Europe, and Japan. This fascinating characteristic of latecomer globalization has been underremarked in the literature on globalization.

Scandinavian scholars such as Johanson and Vahlne, backed by others including Forsgren, Zander, Mattson, Andersson, Nordstrom, Lindqvist, and Andersen, have examined the incremental character of these firms' internationalization and likened it to a process of increasing resource commitment and accumulation of experience or learning.[24] Their studies have focused on the internationalization of Swedish firms, as well as related Nordic firms from Finland, Norway, and Denmark.[25] The insights gained, and their formulation as the so-called Uppsala model of incremental internationalization, have proven to be very influential in the field of international business studies.

Take the case of the Swedish firm Pharmacia, which expanded internationally rapidly in order to develop a defense against competitive attacks by incumbent U.S. or European pharmaceutical giants. Its pattern of expansion was characteristic of many Swedish MNEs. By the mid-1970s, it had operations in nine markets. In eight of these, the firm had pursued an incremental pathway through exporting initially, utilizing the services of an agent, and then after a few years of growth, taking the next step of creating a sales subsidiary. (In two cases, these sales subsidiaries had been expanded to encompass local manufacturing as well.) In the ninth country, a sales subsidiary had been opened almost immediately, indicating a degree of organizational learning regarding the internationalization process itself (as opposed to learning within any particular foreign market).

This pattern was reproduced, more or less, by other Swedish MNEs. Consider the cases of Sandvik and Atlas-Copco, both of which had started their expansion in the early years of the twentieth century, and Facit and Volvo, which saw expansion in the postwar era.[26] All four chose markets in a manner which seemed to be predicted better by a desire to minimize "psychic distance" between the home base and overseas operations rather than rational or strategic calculations of market size, while their "establishment chain" in each market was strongly incremental.[27] In the case of manufacturing subsidiaries, there was a difference observable between the earlier and the more recent internationalizers.[28] However in no case had a firm started production in a country without first having some experience of the country through export activity.[29]

These Swedish patterns of international expansion, particularly the focus on distant markets as a means of building strength prior to meeting strong competitors closer to home in Europe, provide a striking anticipation of strategies later to be followed by East Asian latecomers and newcomers to the global economy. What is missing in the Scandinavian experiences is the sense of urgency involved in more recent experiences. But that too is evident in more recent Swedish expansion patterns, such as by IT firms in the 1980s. Out of many such cases consider just Datatronic AB, which expanded rapidly abroad from Sweden on the basis of various collaborative alliances and strategic acquisitions, particularly of the U.S.-based firm, Victor Technology. It provides an interesting example, made more relevant in that it expanded in the IT industry, just as Acer did a decade later.[30]

An account of the success of Peripheral firms calls for a theoretical account of the process of internationalization—one that is adequate to account for the variety of experiences, including the experiences of newcomers and latecomers over the past decade. The "problem" with these cases of accelerated internationalization is that they cannot easily be fitted into the conventional accounts, whether they be "incremental" or economistic, that is, the "internalization" approach. To demonstrate this, we need to look briefly at the existing theoretical frameworks, before investigating how they might be extended or adapted to cope with, and help explain and predict, the new patterns of international expansion observable at century's end.

Theories and Frameworks of International Expansion

The patterns of international expansion can be discussed from two perspectives, namely, the organizational accommodation of the firm's operating in multiple markets, and the forms of commitment through which the firm builds a presence in foreign markets. The literature has tended to divide into a series of fragmented studies of issues such as forms of market entry, or organizational patterns of expansion, or "stages" through which the expanding firm might be expected to pass.

Take the issue of the organizational form of international expansion. Here we see a striking contrast between the patterns pursued by earlier MNEs and those pursued by latecomers. Conventional MNEs from the United States typically followed an expansion pattern where their overseas operations would be gathered together within a separate "international division." This was the major finding reported by Stopford and Wells in their classic study published in 1972.[31] It is only as firms acquire much more international experience that they initiate new organizational arrangements, such as worldwide product divisions or country-specific marketing divisions. European MNEs generally followed the same kind of pattern (Franko 1976) while Japanese MNEs did likewise, if they were large enough to sustain such expansion; otherwise, the small- and medium-sized Japanese firms that were active internationally utilized the services of Japan's unique global trading firms or *sogo shosha*.[32]

It is hardly surprising that the successful newcomers and latecomers almost *never* resort to the organizational device of an international division. If they did, it would be evidence that their international outlook is at best only partial. Rather, their entire business is oriented toward the world market from the moment of their first step outside their domestic operations. In the case of Acer, for example, the initial international forays were conducted by the major technology companies within the group, namely, Acer Inc. for PC assembly, and Acer Peripherals for production of components. Both had their own overseas operations; they never had to work through an Acer "international" division. Likewise, with Ispat International, its steel business was from the outset internationally oriented; there was never any question of "adding" an "international" side to a largely domestic business.

With regard to the forms of commitment taken by firms as they build up their resources in a given foreign market, the literature is full of paradoxical and conflicting claims and evidence. One dominant school, dubbed the "internalization" approach because of its insistence that MNEs expand by internalizing new operations (in common with the OLI framework, as discussed in chapter 7), holds that the firm makes a priori transaction cost-oriented calculations prior to entering each new market. There is little scope for capturing cumulative learning effects in such a model. By contrast, an alternative approach, dubbed "internationalization" by its critics, and the "stages approach" by its proponents, holds that the firm moves through a given sequence of stages in entering a new market, based on its need to gradually acquire knowledge and experience. This process is driven by two forces, namely, the gradual commitment of resources to the new market as the firm acquires experience in operating there, and the scope for expanding operations (e.g., into manufacturing) becoming enhanced as the firm builds its resource base in the new market. The stages observed, based largely on the early experiences of Scandinavian firms expanding abroad, are those of export through an agent; consolidation of export activities through a marketing subsidiary; and then a broadening of activities to encompass local production or other functions. A subsidiary issue concerns choice of new market; the Scandinavian researchers noted a definite propensity on the part of early expanding Swedish firms to move first to other Nordic countries, then to other markets in Europe, and only then to venture more widely abroad. This tendency was captured in a notion of "psychic distance" from the home market being a factor in determining choice of market—as opposed to the more obvious factor of choosing markets by their economic significance alone.[33]

Now again it is clear that many latecomers (and newcomers) depart from these recognized patterns in numerous ways. In terms of the internalization approach, the idea that firms venture abroad only when they have sufficient resources to invest in full-blown subsidiaries, for example, is wide of the mark in the case of many newcomers, especially the "born globals." It also fails to capture the earlier experiences of many Japanese MNEs that utilized initially the services of trading firms to make up for their own lack of international experience and resources. It completely fails to capture the experience of latecomers, who favor partnerships and alliances as a way of reducing the risks of new market entry, contrary to the dictum of "internalization."

Empirical work has demonstrated that this is a pattern common to many of the present incumbent MNEs as well. Notable U.S. examples include Caterpillar and Upjohn among others. Caterpillar still operates around the world through a network of independently owned dealers, whose origins go right back to the period at the end of the Second World War.[34] In the case of the pharmaceutical MNE, Upjohn, the company has been found to have utilized partnerships as its mode of entry just as frequently as the forms of entry predicted by either the "internalization" account or the Scandinavian "internationalization" account.[35] European examples include several firms internationalizing from Italy: a 1988 study found that almost all the firms studied considered international cooperation agreements to constitute the optimal internationalization route.[36] Such results are very hard to square with either of the dominant theoretical accounts of internationalization.

Newcomers and latecomers have little in common with the "stages" account, other than in their following an incremental approach to international expansion. Their pattern of market entry varies widely and certainly cannot be captured in the rigid sequence as outlined in the various versions of the "Uppsala" model; they are quick to learn, and as their international experience accumulates, they are able to effect very rapid and sudden market entries—as in the case of Ispat buying into national steel industries in a big way or a Li & Fung or Hong Leong buying international chains of operations, as in their purchases of the Inchcape Buying Services and the Millennium & Copthorne hotel chains, respectively.

Moreover, there is very mixed evidence that newcomers and latecomers have followed the predictions of minimizing "psychic distance" in their early explorations abroad. This factor certainly did apply in the case of Cemex, expanding from Mexico to neighboring Latin American countries and to Spain in Europe or to Texas in the United States. But then there are the numerous East Asian examples where the firm's expansion is dictated entirely by "market size" considerations, and not at all by any notion of "psychic distance." How else can the Chinese or Korean focus on the United States and Europe be explained, in advance of their subsequent focus on other countries in Asia?

Accounting for Latecomer Internationalization

The experience of latecomers and newcomers require us to go beyond the formulations of both the "internalization" approach (Reading school) and the "internationalization" account (Uppsala school). The Reading school's account is constrained by the fact that it does not move beyond the abstractions and a priori reasoning of transaction costs economics. It does not offer a defensible account of the *process* of internationalization at all. The problem with the Uppsala school's approach, realistic as it has been in posing a process view of international expansion, is that it fails to capture many of the significant features of more recent latecomer and newcomer expansion patterns. Granting the evolution of the model through several variants—as discussed below in chapter 8—and even hypothesizing a putative fifth variant, which further enlarges the range of options to be considered in the firm's international "establishment chain," for example, to include partnerships or IJVs, it remains incomplete as a means of highlighting the essential features of latecomer behavior. The reason being that it is locked into an account of the firm's own internal capability enhancement, based on experiential learning within a particular market, rather than encompassing overall learning in terms of internationalization itself (and thus allowing for speeding up of the process, or skipping of steps, at later stages of internationalization). More seriously, the Uppsala model continues to posit the importance of "psychic distance" as a factor in choice of market, despite the extreme subjectivity of such a construct, and despite the overwhelming evidence that more recent internationalizing firms are guided by strategic considerations of market significance rather than considerations as to whether the market is "close" in cultural or institutional terms.[37] Psychic proximity obviously has its appeal—as evident in many of the Scandinavian firms' experiences in earlier years or in the case of the Mexican cement MNE Cemex internationalizing in the 1990s initially to Spanish-speaking countries. But to pragmatic latecomers and newcomers in a global market, it takes second place to strategic considerations of market size and significance in determining overseas destinations.

We shall consider these issues in greater depth and in a more general setting, when we consider the impact that latecomer and newcomer internationalization has had—or needs to have—on the theories and frameworks of international business. In particular, in chapter 8 we shall develop a more general process-oriented account of internationalization that accommodates the various experiences and strategic options taken by the latecomer multinationals.

Concluding Remarks: Accelerated Internationalization and the Global Economy

Accelerated internationalization on the part of latecomer MNEs (and various other newcomers to the global economy) is partly a matter of necessity, in that latecomers will never establish themselves in the face of competitive resistance from incumbents by pursuing a steady, solid expansion pathway, and partly a matter of sound strategy. But the most fundamental feature of our depiction of the process is that it rides on novel features of the global economy itself. It is the newcomer and latecomer MNEs which appear to be best attuned to these new possibilities and are achieving astonishing rates of accelerated internationalization as a result.

In offering a definition of "internationalization" it is the network character of the international economy which has been emphasized, acting to "pull" firms into engagement with it—as opposed to the traditional view which sees firms having to overcome numerous obstacles as they "push" their way into the international domain. A more accurate view, and one which can make sense of the accelerated internationalization of the new kinds of MNEs, is that the international economy is a dynamic, constantly shifting structure of connections between firms—a network in the purest sense of the term—and that this is a permanent feature of the international economy, and one moreover that is becoming more pronounced as firms multiply their connections and the scope and scale of the global economy expands.

Thus, a view of the global economy as a network of networks helps us to make sense of a latecomer MNE strategy of accelerated expansion through partnership formation. The firm expands internationally in such a network environment by multiplying its linkages. This is a sensible strategy in such an environment. Thus, our aim here, as in the rest of the book, is to make

the actions of the latecomer MNE plausible, given the changing characteristics of the global economy.

Notes

1. I use the phrase "latecomer" rather than "late-mover." The reason is that
late-mover as a term is aligned with first-mover and implies a degree of strategic
choice (whether to go early or late into a given market). But latecomer implies
that to be late is not a question of strategic choice; it is a question of history.
Latecomers have to live with the fact of being late; this provides the starting
point for their strategic choices.

2. Interview with JM and Charles Snow, Taipei, 31 October, 1 November
1996. See Mathews and Snow (1998).

3. This was York Chen, who has since led a varied career within Acer and
explained all the background to JM.

4. The ACLA CEO was named as Juan Manuel Rojas, who originally started
Computec after leaving Printaform.

5. Stan Shih interview, ibid.

6. The founder and manager of SVOA was Jack Hu, a former Taiwanese
businessman, who emigrated to Thailand. In SEAsia, almost all Acer's partners
are Chinese—but not necessarily of Taiwanese origin.

7. The Asian financial crisis of 1997–98 played havoc with these arrangements. SVOA itself fell on hard times and has been through bankruptcy proceedings, while SV-Acer was restructured as Acer Thailand, effectively buying
out SVOA's interest. This was one of the few casualties Acer experienced as a
result of the financial crisis in Asia.

8. Wipro is an example of a latecomer IT firm utilizing leverage strategies
to catch up with incumbents—and in this case, Acer appears to it as an incumbent. On the strategies pursued by Wipro IT founder, Azim Hasham Premji, see
for example S. Chakravarty, "What's cooking at Wipro?" *Forbes*, 14 Dec. 1998,
pp. 74–75.

9. In fact, Wipro was on the point of signing a JV deal with Compaq or with
AT&T before Acer was added as third short-listed candidate. Stan Shih traveled
to Bangalore and formed a strong bond with Wipro founder Mr. Azim Hasham
Premji, and the JV with Acer resulted.

10. There were two local Indian firms, HCL and Zenith (a former Acer distributor), with higher market shares.

11. The Italian national subsidiary has since become a star performer for
Acer, with Acer Notebook machines being market leaders in Italy by a wide
margin.

12. Another interesting feature of Acer's market coverage arrangements, reflecting its bias toward Peripheral markets, was the fact that North African sales
were managed through ALAP, based in Singapore, rather than from Europe,
while Latin American sales were likewise managed through ALAP, rather than
through Acer America. I am indebted to York Chen for pointing this out.

13. The "establishment chain" is the term used in the incremental model of
international expansion dubbed the "Uppsala model," as first elaborated by Jo-

hanson and Vahlne (1977) and much elaborated since. The model is discussed at length in chapter 8.

14. Geographically, this involved an expansion from Taipei in the north of Taiwan to the second and third largest cities, Taichung in the center and Kaohsiung in the south.

15. Stan Shih interview, *ibid.*

16. *Ibid.*

17. "The Carnegie from Calcutta," *The Economist*, 10 Jan. 1998.

18. The international business literature refers to this phenomenon as "learning through acquisitions." See Håkanson (1995) for a discussion in the context of Swedish MNEs' acquisition of overseas R&D laboratories—a case that has important parallels with Peripheral firms' expansion through acquisition, as discussed below.

19. The ranking was provided by *Hotels* magazine in its 1997 listing of the world's top 100 hotel management companies.

20. See Johanson and Wiedersheim-Paul (1975) for representative case studies—which were later generalized in the "Uppsala model" of internationalization, as discussed below.

21. Sweden's industrialization when it occurred was very rapid, in a pattern later replicated by East Asian countries. In 1870, manufacturing and mining accounted for less than 15 percent of Sweden's output; in 1880, it was still less than 20 percent; but by 1910, it had surpassed 30 percent; see Carlson (1977). Rapid internationalization (comparatively speaking) accompanied this rapid latecomer industrialization.

22. See Olsson (1993); and Lundstrom (1986) for discussions of the history of Swedish MNEs. Hörnell and Vahlne (1986) provide a discussion of Swedish MNEs' contribution to the wider economy.

23. On the history of Ericsson, see the magisterial study by Olsson (1976) in Altman and Olsson (1976).

24. For representative studies, see Johanson and Vahlne (1977); Johanson and Mattsson (1988); Andersson, Johanson, and Vahlne (1997); Nordstrom (1991); Lindqvist (1991); Andersen (1993; 1997) and Zander (1994). Björkman and Forsgren (eds) (1997) provide an overview of Nordic research in this area.

25. On the specifically Swedish case, see for example Forsgren (1989; 1990) and Forsgren, Holm, and Johanson (1995); for Norwegian firms, see for example Juul and Walters (1987); for the case of Finland, see the studies by Luostarinen (1980), Luostarinen and Welch (1990), or Holmlund and Kock (1998); and for the case of Denmark, see for example Pedersen and Petersen (1998).

26. These four cases are discussed in Johanson and Wiedersheim-Paul (1975).

27. Of 63 sales subsidiaries operated by these four firms in the mid-1970s, no fewer than 56 had been preceded by export agents.

28. Sandvik and Atlas-Copco had 27 manufacturing subsidiaries, 22 of which had been preceded by sales subsidiaries in accordance with the establishment chain model. In the case of the later firms, there were seven manufacturing subsidiaries, and five of these had been created without any intervening sales subsidiary.

29. See Johanson and Wiedersheim-Paul (1975: 321). Earlier studies had been published in Swedish, by Johanson & Wiedersheim-Paul in 1974; and by

Hornell, Vahlne and Wiedersheim-Paul in 1973. For a full discussion of these earlier contributions, which are not available in English, see Nordström (1991).

30. On Datatronic, see Nordström (1991). The company's success did not last into the 1990s. In 1991, the firm's U.S. management bought back the assets of Victor technology.

31. See Stopford and Wells (1972) for their pathbreaking study of multinational organizational arrangements.

32. See Yoshino (1976) on Japanese experiences with the *sogo shosha*, as well as Kobayashi (1980), Kojima and Ozawa (1984), and Cho (1987).

33. On the Uppsala school, see the early studies by Johanson and Vahlne (1977) and more recent expositions by Forsgren and Johanson (1992) or Eriksson, Johanson, Majkgard, and Sharma (1997; 2000). For critical studies, see for example Turnbull (1987) and Clark, Pugh, and Mallory (1997).

34. See the case discussion of Caterpillar's worldwide network of partnerships, in Bartlett and Ghoshal (2000a).

35. See the study by Fina and Rugman (1996). Ironically, this study was conducted with a view to resolving the claims of the rival "internalization" and "internationalization" accounts.

36. See Viesti (1988: 82).

37. It is the absence of such strategic factors that has been criticized by many scholars, including Buckley (1991); Nordström (1991); Melin (1992); and Smith and Zeithaml (1999).

5

STRATEGIC INNOVATION
Leapfrogging through Linkage, Leverage, and Learning

The Integration-Responsiveness (IR) grid provides us with a way of capturing the pressures on a given business—pressures that make *strategic coordination* and *global integration* of activities critical, as well as the pressures that make being sensitive to the diverse demands of various national markets and achieving *local responsiveness* critical.

C.K. Prahalad and Yves L. Doz,
The Multinational Mission

In a world of forward-thinking competitors that change the rules of the game in support of ultimate strategic goals, historical patterns of competition provide little guidance. Executives must anticipate competitive moves by starting from new strategic intentions rather than from pre-cooked generic strategies.

Gary Hamel and C.K. Prahalad,
Do you really have a global strategy?
Harvard Business Review

"Starting from new strategic intentions" is exactly what many latecomers (and newcomers) have done. Merely following conventional approaches would have provided them with little leverage against incumbents' advantages. So entrepreneurs like Stan Shih of Acer and Lakshmi Mittal of Ispat have devised novel ways of resolving their strategic dilemmas, such as the dilemma of achieving global integration of operations without sacrificing local responsiveness, turning their disadvantages as latecomers into sources of global strength. While Hamel and Prahalad discussed stretch and leverage as concepts applying to any firm, it turns out that some of the best exponents in the global arena have been latecomer multinationals, which have been able to leapfrog over the incumbents, achieving rapid

107

global reach through innovative strategies based on linkage, leverage, and learning.

Stan Shih is a great practitioner and fan of the ancient game of GO. The game, which is played by two people placing stones on a board, is reputed to be older in origin than chess.[1] Shih argues that among the board games, it is GO which most closely resembles the competitive circumstances of business. In chess (both western and Chinese variants), the object is to engage in combat, utilizing various degrees of armed strength (pawns, knights, castles, reflecting feudal ranks); the winner is the one left standing at the end, capturing the enemy's king in a "checkmate."[2] In the game of GO, by contrast, the aim is to build up a position of strength as successive stones are placed on the board. Although stratagems of besieging and attacking the enemy are part of the game's strategic portfolio, a result does not call for the eradication of one player's forces by the other's. Both players have all their pieces (identical "stones") on the board at the end of the game, and the winner is the player who has surrounded the most territory. This has striking similarities to market penetration and competitive face-offs in business.

A treasury of strategies has been developed to inform the game of GO, many of which have application to comparable business situations faced by the latecomer MNE. One of the most important of GO strategies is that of *bu ji* (arrangement and layout) or the securing of remote territory, while waiting for the best opportunity to enter the main battle. In GO, the players start from the four corners of the board, securing territory there (and engaging in skirmishes to do so), before seeking to map out a defensible position in the center of the board. Likewise, the latecomer MNE seeks to build strength in Peripheral or emerging markets, or in certain sectors of advanced markets (such as contract supply), before engaging in full frontal, branded product assaults in highly contested markets of the Triad.[3]

A second GO strategy is to enhance the strategic layout of one's stones and extend the territory enclosed by them, by creating "living eyes" (*huo yen*) or arrangements that can resist enemy attack. The idea is to create as many as possible, but at least two—so that one's stones cannot be surrounded and killed by a single assault. This is a strategy that involves building strength through connectedness, rather than through solidity. It is essentially a network approach. The same principle carries over to the strategy of the latecomer MNE, which needs to build reinforcing positions as it encircles the most advanced positions of the incumbents. It develops its strength through a diversity of products, rather than having a single product which can be knocked out by a concentrated counterattack on the part of a market incumbent. The latecomer needs to develop a network of diversified businesses that support each other, through core competencies, rather than a single line of business which is very vulnerable to counterattack. Hence, it is no accident that latecomer MNEs are frequently to be found in group formation, with each business lending strength to the others, rather than as single, integrated, and atomistic entities.

Potential living eyes can be turned into "dead eyes" by one's opponent, unless they are sufficiently strengthened, which brings in the third GO strategy: take a long-term view, by building connections between scattered pieces of territory. This is called in Chinese "long breath," and it forces the GO player to keep an eye on long-term strategic goals while fighting tactical skirmishes—where the long-term goal is the securing of as much territory as possible. The best *bu ji*, that is, arrangement, is a set of scattered but interconnected spaces surrounding as much territory as possible and keeping the enemy at bay through the internal "living eyes" within the structure. The business counterpart is the strategy of the latecomer MNE in building as many alliances as possible—for the MNE draws strength and resources from each such alliance, enabling it to expand its reach and build its inner strengths without wasting resources in head-to-head battles too soon.

Latecomer Stratagems

Strategic calculations—such as those made in every game of GO—are central to the success of a multinational enterprise. Such enterprises are able to exploit global scale and scope as formidable competitive weapons, provided they can solve the organizational problems that are generated by multiplying complexities and can generate strategies that exploit potential synergies. They can bring their full force to bear on markets chosen for their strategic significance and coordinate their activities to achieve some degree of synergy. But for the latecomer the situation is quite different. The latecomer does not have global assets to exploit. It sees its international expansion as a means of gaining access to resources that would not otherwise be available.

Shih has been inspired by GO stratagems to develop unorthodox ways for Acer to expand and prosper internationally. He characterizes the conventional approach as one where the firm seeks a large market for a product in which to support volume production, in the quest for economies of scale and lower costs. But GO-thinking preaches a different approach, namely, one of securing a firm foothold in many small markets before tackling the big players in the large market. The logic behind this thinking is that resources are limited for the latecomer, and so entering a large market early will likely lead to premature hostilities and defeat for the latecomer, before getting a chance to become established. Better to grow in the Periphery, where the markets are less cluttered before tackling the highly reinforced center.

This most emphatically does not mean seeking an "easy" option, as in adopting second-best technology or producing second-best products. On the contrary, the strategy depends on the willingness of the firm to opt for the very latest product and process technology and the very best marketing and distribution systems, for only in this way can the Peripheral experience equip the firm for its decisive battles at the center.

Acer's expansion strategy through partnership in the Latin American and Southeast Asian markets in the late 1980s and early 1990s illustrates this approach. There were two parallels with the game of GO operating here. First, both were cases of building strength in Peripheral markets to complement the assaults in the more advanced markets; techniques of brand support and promotion could be tried out before being applied in the more demanding conditions of U.S., European, or Japanese markets. Second, positions in these Peripheral markets were built by expansion from a solid core. Initial market strength is established, in this case through vigorous partnerships in Mexico and Thailand, respectively, and then these operations expand their influence to neighboring countries. Such an approach works well in GO, and it appears to translate effectively across to global business as well.

In GO, the successful player sometimes has to be willing to concede some territory to the opponent in order to win greater territory elsewhere. These trade-offs, and the stakes involved, lie at the core of the game between experienced players. Likewise, the latecomer MNE has to know where to pick its battles, and where to retreat before losing too many resources. Of course, established players also use such stratagems, but they frequently have more at stake. A retreat from a particular PC segment by IBM or Compaq carries a stronger message than if Acer or Mitac makes such a retreat—and carries stronger penalties in terms of punishment by shareholders. So a latecomer MNE pushes ahead on many fronts, in order to "take positions" in emerging markets and product segments, but is willing to give up some of these positions as counterattacks occur, in order to keep its strategic connections and core competencies intact.[4]

Thinking according to the logic of GO gives insight into the strategic perspective of the latecomer MNE. It brings out a clear difference between the concept of strategy for the incumbent, the established MNE, and that of the newcomers and latecomers, which lack assets and resources but do not lack imagination, intelligence, and guile.

Our concern in this chapter is to develop a systematic account of the differences between the strategic frameworks employed by incumbent MNEs and those of latecomers and newcomers. We shall look first at the conventional framework as applied to the case of the incumbent international firm. We shall then probe this framework, to see to what extent it can be accommodated with newcomer and latecomer experience. We shall then propose a novel framework for latecomers, based on the degree to which firms employ strategies of linkage and leverage, which are the principal focus of the analysis offered. The chapter concludes by discussing latecomer (and newcomer) strategy from the resource-based view (RBV)—where the emphasis is placed not on how existing resources may be enhanced (so that existing advantages may be sustained), but on how external resources might be targeted for purposes of linkage and leverage. This brings in resource leverage as a principal strategic gambit of latecomer MNEs—and the RBV of the firm as a way of making sense of resource leverage. This is certainly an unconventional way of viewing the issue, but one that promises many advantages.

The Strategic Framework of the Incumbent MNE

The language of strategy, as conventionally discussed in the management and business literature, is concerned with how a firm may prolong and sustain the advantages that it has already acquired. The most obvious benefit for a firm of achieving global scale is that this provides the passport to the formulation and implementation of global strategies. These in turn depend for their implementation on global organizational processes.

Multinational firms can integrate operations across borders and standardize production, logistics, and R&D to achieve economies of scale not available to domestic competitors. They can spread their brand image over numerous geographic areas (economies of scope). They can share their core competencies across business units. They can exploit market imperfections, such as differences in national resources, and share resources between subsidiaries. Exploitation of common core competencies results in gains through synergies.[5]

The strategies of multinationals could be explained from a variety of perspectives, not always in agreement with each other. The pioneer of globalization discourse, Theodore Levitt, argued in his classic paper "Globalization of Markets" (1983) that the global firm seeks strategic advantage through standardizing a product and offering the same everywhere. Economies of scale are sufficiently powerful to drive out competitors when such a strategy is followed, he claimed. A different view is offered by Hout, Porter, and Rudden (1982), in another classic *Harvard Business Review* article, when they argue that global strategy calls for a variety of responses to novel situations. The key to multinational advantage, in their schema, is the capacity to achieve synergies across activities carried out in different countries. Kogut (1985a; b), by contrast, describes the global strategist as one who wins through flexibility and arbitrage, playing off one market against another and always exploiting advantages of information for competitive effect.

It was Ghoshal (1987) who first brought the differing conceptions of international strategy and the demands of international competition (as opposed to the simpler demands of domestic competition) into a coherent and systematic framework. Ghoshal set out the key issues to be resolved by every firm (efficiency, risk management, learning) and then postulated three sources of advantage in resolving them that were available to a multinational firm but not to a domestic rival. These three sources of strategic advantage are (1) national differences to be exploited; (2) scale economies to be captured; and (3) scope economies available to the MNE (such as sharing investments and costs across products, markets, and businesses). Ghoshal's framework is captured in Table 5.1.

For Ghoshal, the sources of competitive advantage could be translated into actual performance improvements to the extent that the MNE was clear in its strategic goals. These encompass: (1) achieving efficiency in current operations (taking into account differences in national markets); (2) managing risks involved in operating internationally; and (3) drawing on the global and multiple experiences in order to foster innovation, adaptation, and learning.

The advantages that potentially accrue to a firm which can produce and market its goods or services on a global scale are thus prodigious. But the key phrase is "potentially accrue." For these advantages can be reaped only by multinational firms that are able to overcome the greater costs of operating internationally with savings and efficiencies reflecting the global coordination of its operations, without sacrificing the local responsiveness in individual markets needed to match the customized offerings of domestic competitors. The real challenge for the MNE is not to be able to perform

Table 5.1   Organizing Framework for Analyzing Global Competitive Advantage and Competitive Strategy

	Sources of Competitive Advantage		
Strategic Objectives	National Differences	Scale Economies	Scope Economies
1. Achieving efficiency in current operations	Benefiting from differences in factor costs (e.g., wages and cost of capital)	Expanding and exploiting potential scale economies across countries	Sharing of investments and costs across products, markets, and businesses
2. Managing risks	Managing risks arising from differences between countries	Balancing scale with strategic and operational flexibility	Portfolio diversification of risks and creation of options and side-bets
3. Innovation, learning, and adaptation	Learning from societal differences in organizational and managerial processes and systems	Benefiting from experience—cost reduction and innovation	Shared learning across organizational components

Source: Based on Ghoshal (1987)

either one of these, admittedly demanding, operations. It is to be able to perform them *simultaneously*.

A remarkable group of scholars, all originating from Harvard, have captured this challenge in the so-called global integration–local responsiveness dilemma.[6] It is called a dilemma because MNEs have traditionally tended to favor the pursuit of one goal at the expense of the other. They have sought to overcome national differences through global standardization, which results in loss of local responsiveness. Alternatively, they have sought to emphasize their "national" character in each of their markets of operations, at the expense of securing any advantages from global coordination or standardization. It is only a handful of global companies in the 1980s and 1990s that have managed to resolve this dilemma and capture benefits over domestic rivals, and other global firms, by being able to satisfy both goals simultaneously.

Thus, Ghoshal's framework needs to be supplemented by the Bartlett/Ghoshal/Doz/Prahalad formulation of the fundamental dilemma facing any firm with global aspirations—that is, its capacity to resolve the demands of global integration and local responsiveness simultaneously. This is the GI-LR dilemma. It is widely seen to be one of the most demanding faced by any firm.

Now the point of identifying these issues was to argue the case that very few MNEs had the organizational capabilities to satisfy these demands simultaneously. The few that had were termed by Bartlett and Ghoshal *transnational corporations*, meaning that they had overcome the limitations of earlier "international" and "multinational" organizational forms (corresponding, roughly, to Perlmutter's ethnocentric and polycentric stages in management attitudes).[7]

There is some empirical verification of this point available. The difficulties of organizing activities internationally increase in a multiplicative fashion as international locations proliferate. Several studies have found that MNE performance improves with international expansion only up to a certain point and then degrades.[8] Expanding geographic spread multiplies transactions between subsidiaries and increases managerial information-processing demands (unless they are reduced at source by organizational innovations such as cellularity).

In the decade since these frameworks were offered, the IB scholarship has demonstrated that these are problems for large, incumbent firms—but not necessarily so for smaller, more nimble MNEs that have populated the international economy during the 1990s. The mini- and micro-MNEs, identified as newcomers, niche players, and latecomers in chapter 2, have been able to resolve these difficulties and dilemmas in innovative ways and thereby strengthen their own competitiveness.

In the meantime, the literature on competitiveness has moved on and focused more on the issue as to where the sources of advantage of the multinational come from. Do they stem from the character of the markets in which they are involved—with some markets being much more "globalized" than others? Or do they stem from the internal resources and capabilities of the firms, which are built up through their internationalizing experiences? Put this way, the issue is posed in starkly different terms for latecomers and newcomers as opposed to incumbents.

Sources of Competitive Advantage

Two clear and contrasting approaches have been developed to seek to account for the sources of firms' competitive advantage. One approach looks to the commercial, industrial, and technological environment *outside the firm*—to the influences of immediate competitors, customers, suppliers, prices, costs, and quality. The more the firm is exposed to demanding customers, leading-edge competitors, high quality suppliers, the more pressure it experiences to upgrade its capabilities and thereby broaden the base of its strategic options. In Porter's framework, these options are characterized in terms of generic strategies of cost minimization or product differentiation, and they are chosen within the pressures experienced through his famous "diamond" of external forces.[9]

The other approach looks to the *internal sources of advantage*, in the form of the resources which underpin the firm's basic capabilities. This is the approach now known as the resource-based view (RBV) of the firm. This theory was launched effectively by Wernerfelt (1984), drawing on earlier work, which argued that firms compete not just in terms of final products but in terms of the underlying "resources" that make production and product diversification possible. This has since turned into a most productive stream of research, which has been popularized in the form of the "core competence" view of competitive strategy.[10] Fundamental efforts have been expended to establish the criteria of firms' resources that lend long-lasting or "sustainable" competitive advantages.[11] Efforts to integrate the resource-based theory with economic accounts of firm behavior and with dynamic accounts of firms' capabilities enhancement show how the theory is becoming central to an understanding of firm competitive behavior.[12]

What is remarkable is that almost all of this theoretical effort has been expended in an effort to understand how firms prolong their competitive advantages, by extending or broadening their underlying resource base, rather than seeking an understanding of *how they create advantages in the first place*. From the first perspective, namely, the firm's external environment, theorists declare simply that the fount of competitive advantage is innovation.[13] This rules out of court any prospects for the latecomer MNE, which pursues a "fast follower" rather than an innovation strategy. Likewise, some resource-based theorists ruled out of order any examination of how firms acquire strategic resources in the first place. Dierickx and Cool (1989) declared that it might be a matter of "luck" or some other nonrational process and was therefore not amenable to analysis, while Barney (1986) made the point that firms could acquire resources without being able to anticipate their later strategic significance. This is a perfectly comprehensible and defensible position, if one's interest lies exclusively in accounting for how firms prolong their acquired competitive advantages. But it makes no sense if one is interested in how firms go about the business of acquiring resources, as a rational and calculated act that is a prelude to their securing a competitive position in a highly contested market. This understanding is, after all, the position of the latecomer firm and of a good many other firms that have aspirations to enter markets that appear to lie beyond their reach.

The strategic posture of latecomer MNEs is quite different from that which is portrayed in these conventional analyses. The latecomer is interested in acquiring resources in order to expand its capabilities—and the best way for it to do so is to expand internationally, by making linkages with other firms in other markets, and by leveraging resources from its collaborators and contractual partners.

Linkage and leverage then emerge as fundamental for the latecomer (and newcomer) MNE, as a way of constructing a competitive position that did not previously exist or was not previously supported by a resource or asset endowment. Can we reconcile this perspective with Ghoshal's overarching framework for conceptualizing global strategy?

The Strategic Framework of Latecomers and Newcomers

If resources are lacking, then their leverage from external sources is the obvious way to proceed. The concept of "resource leverage" matches the theoretical requirements of the latecomer firm exactly. The concept was introduced and has been used as a means of explaining how the best competitors in the world stay abreast of new developments, by ensuring that through alliances and various forms of joint ventures, they identify and secure access to the resources needed to keep diversifying their product portfolio.[14]

The same idea underpins the strategy of the latecomer firm. Whereas the economic development literature discusses its strategy in terms of technological diffusion and technology transfer, these are much weaker concepts than "resource leverage." They place the impetus for the transfer on firms in the advanced countries (rather than on the latecomer's own strategic calculations), and they ignore the issue as to how the latecomer can shape events so that business arrangements involving "transfer" can be turned into leverage and learning opportunities. So the first point is that we can appropriate the concept of "resource leverage" as the overarching strategic framework, in which to make sense of the successes of latecomers in breaking into advanced technological sectors. Acer, for example, was able to break into PC systems in the first place through OEM contracts with IBM and other leading players. It was able to break into production of memory chips through a joint venture with Texas Instruments. It was able to develop its own line of flat panel displays for laptop computers in the 1990s through licensing arrangements with Japanese firms.

Linkage is an outward-oriented concept. It refers to the ways in which the firm may extend its influence into new markets or new businesses. In the international setting, it refers to the capacity of the firm to extend into new cross-border activities via interfirm relations. The more dense these interfirm connections, the more opportunities there are for the firm to be drawn via such linkages into the international economy.

Leverage is both an outward- and inward-oriented concept. It refers to the outward reach by the firm for resources beyond it, which may be contained in firms and institutions "out there" in the global economy and with which it must form linkages of one kind or another, and to the inward process of capability enhancement that the firm engages in after absorption of new resources.

Learning is the enhancement of capabilities that results from the repeated application of linkage and leverage strategies. Linkage, leverage, and learning help to explain why a latecomer like Acer will go to such lengths to find partner firms to help it develop new international business lines like semiconductors or CD-ROMs or flat panel displays. In each of these cases, Acer firms found U.S., or European, or Japanese firms interested in establishing a relationship with a firm like Acer, with a view to having a reliable "second source" and contract (OEM) manufacturer or indeed a partner in a fabrication joint venture, as in the case of Acer's joint venture with Texas Instruments. They were able to offer these partner firms something valuable, namely, their manufacturing or fabrication expertise (low cost, timeliness, and high quality) and in return were able to leverage skills and knowledge through these various contractual linkages.

The same practices have continued into the 1990s. The biggest technological leap undertaken by Acer Peripherals (API) was its entry into CD-ROM production to become the largest producer in Taiwan. While other Taiwanese firms collaborated in an ITRI project to acquire the optical technologies involved, API went its own way through technology transfer from Philips in an agreement reached in 1994.[15] The key to producing CD-ROMs is manufacturing prowess, given the intensely short product cycle times (comparable to those in hard disc drive production, which even API has not yet attempted). API was able to bring all its manufacturing capabilities acquired through many years of running its monitors, keyboards, and printer production lines at maximum capacity. Thus, it was able to absorb the acquired technological resources and build a platform of internal capabilities that could allow API to subsequently keep up with the punishing pace of technological change in the CD-ROM industry.

API has been able to purse a similar kind of strategy to leverage its way into the flat panel displays industry—a critical industry for Acer which uses so many flat panel displays in its laptop computers. API decided to concentrate its process of acquiring expertise in this new sector by creating a dedicated subsidiary, Acer Display Technology (ADT). This company acquired initial capabilities through participating in ITRI-based innovation networks, but it took a giant leap forward in 1998 with the negotiation of a technology transfer agreement (technology leverage) with IBM Japan, for the acquisition of the leading thin-film transistor liquid crystal display technology (TFT-LCD) now used for all laptop PC screens. Again, this acquisition provided the initial resource base that could then be internalized to become a sustainable capability, utilized in a manufacturing operation for TFT-LCDs that was coming on stream in 1999 and by 2001, following the merger between ADT and Unipac, had emerged as third largest in the world.

Linkage and leverage also provide a clue to the means through which latecomers are able to satisfy the demands of the GILR dilemma simultaneously. If the firm is expanding abroad in order to follow a customer firm, for example, then it can maintain that customer affiliation only to the extent that it is able to achieve cost savings derived from integrating production or logistics activities. This is certainly what Ispat is able to achieve as it expands its global network. It is also what Acer is able to achieve following a different approach, through the tight interdependencies between its operating parts and the "scalability" of their organizational configuration. The local response side of the dilemma is satisfied because of the tight customer focus required to keep such corporate accounts.

The processes of linkage, leverage, and learning provide a generic account of newcomer and latecomer strategy but what is missing is the role played by the incumbents themselves. Why do they offer the opportunities seized by the latecomers and newcomers? Are incumbents making mistakes or are they behaving rationally?

Latecomer Strategy: The Search for Complementarities

The key to grasping the strategy of the latecomer firm is to see how it is crafted to *complement* the strategies or needs of incumbents (and start-ups). For every strategic goal or initiative taken by an incumbent, there is a latecomer willing to provide the service or resources that *complements* this goal. This is how the latecomer gets its start, how it secures its competitive foothold. Consider three such strategic shifts on the part of incumbents: outsourcing/OEM contracting; second sourcing; and technology licensing. Each of these strategic shifts on the part of incumbents, which serve their own strategic needs, creates opportunities for latecomers which they are quick to seize and turn into opportunities for leveraging and learning.

Outsourcing/OEM Contracting   Outsourcing began in the 1960s and 1970s as advanced firms in advanced countries exported their manufacturing of mature products to low-cost production platforms in Asia. This was in accord with classical "product cycle" considerations, as theorized by Vernon

(1966). Latecomer countries benefited from these decisions, in terms of the raising of their "social capital," and soon individual latecomer firms were bidding for parts of the manufacturing cycle, as in the case of testing and packaging activities in the semiconductor industry. OEM contracting can be considered as a form of outsourcing, where the activity contracted to a third party is a critical, high value-adding part of the process. Many IT companies like IBM, Apple, Compaq, and Dell have outsourced the production of entire products like PCs to latecomer firms in East Asia, thereby not only securing their own strategic advantages in terms of low-cost production, but also offering the latecomers valuable learning and leverage opportunities. Many Taiwanese PC firms like Acer, Mitac, and Tatung have established themselves with the help of such OEM contracting.

Second Sourcing   Second sourcing is a related concept, where a supplier of critical high technology products like memory chips or logic chips seeks an outside "second source" to back up its own supplies (in case of problems in meeting a customer's order) or to take over the more mature products as the innovator moves on to the newer products. Again, this strategy on the part of incumbents creates numerous opportunities for an agile latecomer to grasp a business opportunity and use it as a leveraging and learning experience.

Technology Licensing   For many start-ups, the dilemma is how to translate their innovative technology and product ideas into cash flow that will sustain the company. Licensing their technology to a third party is often the most attractive strategy, particularly if that third party undertakes to manufacture the new product as well. In this way, the start-up can stay small, innovative, and agile. It is latecomers which seek out these opportunities and turn them to their advantage.

These and many more such examples reveal how the latecomer fashions a rather different view of competition than that which informs the conventional approach. It is strategy which is infinitely adaptable, seeking to match the needs of incumbents or even meeting them before the incumbent has articulated them. The only strategic goal of the latecomer is to be adaptable in the overall pursuit of catch-up.

The principle of competition operating here bears description under its own name. Let us agree that it be called the *principle of competitive complementarity*. Simply stated, it refers to the fact that a challenger firm can do well to complement the strategies of incumbents rather than directly confronting them. Latecomers can gain a competitive foothold through interpreting the needs of incumbents and offering services to these incumbents as a way of leveraging the resources (skills, technologies, market access) that the latecomers need in order to initiate an upward spiral of capability enhancement. This principle differs from the conventional account, in that such a firm is competing not through a zero-sum clash of resources or assets or market deployment, but through complementing the needs of its adversaries. This description clearly applies to the case of the latecomer. In effect, the latecomer *turns its competitors into its customers—* at least initially. The point is for the latecomer to get started. Once launched on its career, it can rapidly evolve into a conventional competitor. But the key is to find the way to establish that competitive foothold in the first place.

The Complementarity Principle: A Resource-Based Framework for Accommodating Latecomer Global Strategies

It is the principle of complementarity that provides the key to reconciling the practices of latecomers and newcomers with the organizing framework for global strategy developed by Ghoshal. Through linkage, leverage, and learning, the newcomers and latecomers are able to exploit the sources of competitive advantage that would normally be available only to incumbents. For example, incumbents seek to enhance efficiency through exploiting differences in factor costs, for instance, by outsourcing; but this strategic initiative in itself creates the complementary opportunity that latecomers (and some newcomers) seize to bring them into relationships with global firms as OEM suppliers. Whereas incumbents can learn from the variety of experiences of their operations in different markets (provided they have the organizational capacity to do so, for example, through treating subsidiaries as equal partners and not just as agencies of implementation), latecomers can likewise learn directly from their linkage with these incumbents through second sourcing and technology licensing. While incumbents look to manage risks through portfolio diversification, latecomers likewise spread their risks by developing a variety of businesses so that they are not critically dependent on a single product or a single market. Even with their strong niche focus, newcomers and niche players tend to broaden their product range as they internationalize. There is therefore a powerful business insight contained in the notion that for every strategic initiative of an incumbent, there is a complementary business opportunity for another firm—with the successful firms being those that are fastest to identify and take advantage of such opportunities.

The principle of complementarity can be stated as follows:

In their quest for resources to enhance their competitive position, challenger firms look to complement rather than directly confront the strategies of incumbents. One avenue for doing so is to seek out forms of linkage and leverage with respect to incumbents that complement the strategic initiatives pursued by the incumbents for their own good reasons.

By framing strategy in terms of linkage and leverage, utilizing complementarities wherever they can be found, latecomers are able to reduce their
risks and magnify their impact, beyond what would be possible by working
on their own. It can be repeated over and over again, yielding learning. This
is a strategy of potentially enormous significance for newcomers and latecomers as much as for conventional firms looking to enhance their prospects by entering a new market or developing a new product. It is the principle that seems to underpin the success of a wide spectrum of collaborative
arrangements.

In terms of global competitiveness, the use of linkage and leverage is
exercized in the context of the international economy across borders and
without regard to specific national advantages. It can be contrasted with
Ghoshal's framework, as in Table 5.2.

Pursuing a strategy based on complementarity is certainly one strategic
advantage exploited by latecomers. Another is their capacity to resolve the
GI-LR dilemma at source and actually accelerate their internationalization
through this means. How is this done?

Latecomer Firms and the Resolution of the GI-LR Dilemma

All MNEs have to generate coordination mechanisms if they are to survive
as global entities—but the evidence of deteriorating performance as their
reach extends indicates that few are able to manage the organizational dif-

Table 5.2   Global Competitive Advantage for Latecomer and Newcomer
MNEs

	Sources of Competitive Advantage		
Strategic Objectives	National Differences	Scale Economies	Scope Economies
1. Achieving effi-ciency in current operations	Differences in fac-tor costs encourage OEM contracting	Product choice guided by possibil-ities of scale-efficient mass pro-duction	Sharing of invest-ments and costs across products, markets, and busi-nesses
2. Managing risks	Partnership ar-rangements to min-imize country risks	Balancing scale with strategic and operational flexi-bility	Diversification of businesses to spread risks
3. Innovation, learning, and ad-aptation	Learning from in-cumbent partners	Benefiting from ex-perience—cost re-duction and part-nership arrangements	Shared learning between businesses in network struc-ture

ficulties involved. Bartlett, Ghoshal, Doz, Prahalad, and colleagues have captured this organizational challenge in what they call the "global integration–local responsiveness dilemma." Few firms, they argue, are able to resolve this dilemma.

But latecomer and newcomer MNEs have the potential advantage that they can acquire such organizational capabilities as they expand. Indeed, it may well be the case that they can accelerate their expansion precisely by resolving the GI-LR dilemma as they grow. This potential advantage has to be turned into an actual performance advantage through the explicit steps taken. In the case of Acer, the local responsiveness is achieved through the cellular organizational innovation. Global integration is achieved, up to a point, through direct interaction between Acer business units. But incompatibilities crept into these BUs' operations in the absence of specific measures taken to coordinate operational standards. These steps were being taken, belatedly, within Acer in the wake of its reorganization into a set of global business units at the end of the 1990s. For the latecomer as much as for the established MNE, *global coordination* emerges as the critical issue in determining winners and losers in global competition. But for the latecomer, it turns out to be feasible to resolve the simultaneous demands of GI and LR *as it actually expands*, rather than through making expensive structural adjustments once it has arrived as a global player. Indeed, simultaneous satisfaction of GI and LR demands acts as a means of accelerating its expansion. This capability gives some insight into the power of the latecomer perspective.

Now using the resource-based view of the firm, we can go further in characterizing the resources that latecomers and newcomers will tend to target—and hence the kinds of industries in which they will seek to establish themselves—and compare the results of the analysis with the actual choices made by newcomers and latecomers. But to do so, we need to give the established theory a "twist"—in the same spirit as the latecomers themselves, who find novel ways to do what others do and do it better.

The Targeting of Resources for Leverage: the Latecomer as Challenger

If targeting of resources is the key to international expansion on the part of newcomers and latecomers, what can we say of theoretical significance concerning the kinds of resources they are likely to target? In other words, can the resource perspective provide insight into the kinds of industries targeted by newcomers and latecomers, and can it generate insight into the kinds of leverage and linkage strategies they pursue? Here we enter territory uncharted in the management and international business literature.

In the resource-based view of the firm, it is claimed that firms will seek to extend their competitive advantages by basing them on resources that are difficult to imitate or replicate by rivals or difficult to substitute through alternative technological channels. This leads authors such as Barney (1986) and Dierickx and Cool (1989) to develop a set of criteria characterizing those resources which, they claim, are most amenable to being sustained as a source of competitive advantage. These are that the resources should be:

- nonimitable—i.e., not easily imitated by rivals;
- nonsubstitutable—i.e., not easily substituted by others or rendered obsolete; and
- nontransferable—i.e., not easily bought or sold on markets but having some intrinsic connection to the firm.

Viewed from the perspective of the latecomer firm, these criteria characterize the challenge that it faces. How is the firm to overcome such a "resource position barrier" (Wernerfelt 1984)? One way to answer this is to twist the question. Thus, the latecomer asks not "How am I to overcome this insuperable barrier?" but *Where can I find the resources that are most amenable to leverage?*" In other words, it puts the focus on the sources from which strengths can be derived, rather than on the strengths of the rival incumbents. With this twist, the criteria utilized by the resource-based view turn out to be exceedingly useful.

In practice, we know that resources are never completely inimitable, durable, or nontransferable. If they were, there would be no diffusion of innovations, no high-technology competition, and certainly no latecomer firms. Indeed, we know that leading high-technology firms like Intel, Motorola, or Texas Instruments do *not* regard their resources as *nonimitable, nondurable*, and *nontransferable*. They exploit their resources for their own benefit, in the early stages of development of a new market, and then disseminate them for further profit through licensing to third parties and technology transfer to affiliates. In some cases, such as Intel's celebrated withdrawal from memory chips production in the mid-1980s, they formulate their strategies precisely on the understanding that resources have become imitable and have been transferred, in this case to Japanese competitors.[16] Why should the latecomer firm not draw similar conclusions?

This gives the clue as to how to reformulate the conditions specified in the resource-based theory of the firm, so as to render intelligible the strategy of the latecomer MNE. Let us turn these criteria into their positive variants. In this form, they clearly do not apply to the resources being developed or extended within the firm. But they certainly can be applied to the *types of resources that latecomers might wish to leverage* from external sources. Specifically, the latecomer MNE is likely to target those resources which are *most*:

- imitable—i.e., most easily imitated (through reverse engineering, e.g.);
- substitutable—i.e., most susceptible to technological overthrow and replacement (Schumpeterian competition); and

- transferable—i.e., most easily transferred as explicit technical knowledge (available through consultants) or on the open market in the form of specialized equipment.

These criteria thus provide us with a framework for characterizing the strategy of the latecomer MNE consistent with existing organization and management theory. *The latecomer targets resources for leverage which are most imitable, substitutable, and transferable.* Let us further probe these criteria, emphasizing the IT industry which Acer and other latecomers have been able to penetrate very successfully.

Imitability

Resources that are imitable are those that can be replicated by the latecomer, that is, where the latecomer can appropriate the resources in standardized form, such as through licensing a product design or reverse engineering a product technology which has become standardized. Resources become imitable through the strategies of leading firms themselves, as noted above in the case of Intel. Incumbent firms draw learning curve advantages only for as long as critical technologies remain proprietary. As they diffuse, they cease to become sources of advantage for incumbents. The "tacit knowledge" underpinning the advantages leaks out as well; it can be acquired as part of a technology transfer agreement or a contract manufacturing arrangement, for example. More formally, and again reversing the criteria usually advanced in the theory of the RBV of the firm, we may say that resources are most imitable when they are *least*:

- *path dependent*—i.e., not having a specific history which tends toward firms having highly specialized skills;
- *causally ambiguous*—i.e., resources where it is relatively straightforward to attribute the main factors involved in their successful practice; and
- *subject to "time compression diseconomies"*—i.e., they do not need long periods of prior apprenticeship in securing the tacit knowledge needed for their practice.[17]

In high technology industries, it is the availability of product designs under license, or the possibility of purchasing a stake in high technology start-ups, or of opening a "listening post" company in high technology areas such as Silicon Valley, that enables the latecomer MNE to replicate and imitate the products of advanced firms. Latecomer firms can counteract the effects of causal ambiguity and time compression diseconomies by such stratagems as utilizing the services of engineering consulting firms—which embody current best practice and can pass it on for a substantial fee—and through tapping into the knowledge of equipment vendors. These latter firms frequently embody a host of previous technological learning in their latest products and are prepared to pass this on as part of the equipment supply contract.

Substitutability

Resources are substitutable if they are subject to strong tendencies toward product and process technology turnover, such as in the case of rapid product cycles.[18] Each such change in product or process technology opens up new possibilities for the latecomer to enter the market; barriers to entry are turned into *windows of opportunity*. This is of course just another way of saying that resources, which are most susceptible to leverage through substitution, are those which are most subjected to Schumpeterian competition; it is "gales of destruction" that blow through the industry, destroying the advantages of incumbents, that open up opportunities for newcomers.[19]

Transferability

Resources are transferable if they can be bought in the form of product licenses or particularly in the form of transferable process technology from independent equipment vendors. In the early days of high technology industries such as semiconductors, firms such as Fairchild would develop their own process technology (fabrication equipment) in close consultation with equipment suppliers. But as the industry matured, these equipment vendors would look for wider markets, and latecomer firm new entrants could be important customers for this equipment. Resources could also be transferred through OEM fabrication contracts, where product and process specifications would be supplied as part of the contract. The commissioning firm might also insist on an exchange of engineers (and thus an exchange of tacit knowledge) in order to ensure the quality and reliability of chip supplies. From the perspective of the latecomer, these specifications and exchanges represent an unparalleled learning opportunity.

How are such criteria to be utilized in practice? It is feasible for a latecomer MNE to perform a study of potential resources (through consultancies, or through fact-finding missions, or simply through attending trade fairs) which analyzes potential resources in terms of the criteria of imitability, substitutability, and transferability. Indeed, in retrospect, we may see that this is precisely what latecomer firms have done in practice; they have formulated in an ad hoc way a strategy for breaking the grip of incumbents, in sectors where resources were available and where they were most imitable, substitutable, and transferable. The fact that technological change tends to follow pathways, or trajectories, is another factor that assists the latecomer in predicting and anticipating the overall direction of change—as emphasized in the dynamic capabilities paradigm.[20] The argument offered here provides a plausible and testable account of the acquisition of advanced capabilities by latecomer firms. The aim of these firms is not to stay as "fast followers" forever but to catch up with the world's best and to become leading players themselves—as Acer has arguably done already in the IT industry.[21]

Resource Targeting by Latecomer and Newcomer MNEs

There is abundant evidence that latecomer and newcomer MNEs have indeed targeted resources for leverage which are imitable, transferable, and substitutable. Consider the case of Ispat in the steel industry. This firm was able to purchase steel-making technology on the open market, from specialist suppliers; it did not have to invent the processes itself. Moreover, Ispat was able to take a risk in investing in a novel technology that promised great cost savings, namely, Direct Reduced Iron (DRI). Incumbent steel producers had already invested in plant that could not utilize this innovation, and in any case, it seemed to be on too small a scale for integrated steel producers. But for a latecomer looking to get a foothold in the industry, it offered a perfect way in with significant cost reductions. Thus, Ispat was able to leverage this novel DRI technology because it was transferable; and it was able to draw cost advantages because it acted as a viable substitute for the usual processing technology.

In the case of Acer, its linkage and leverage activities were firmly targeted on resources that were transferable and whose underlying processes were imitable. The examples above, where Acer Inc. and API developed CD-ROM products through technology leverage from European and Japanese firms or the case of flat panel displays, where API leveraged technology from Japanese partners, are simply two examples out of many where diversification into a new and technologically demanding international business has been accelerated through linkage and leverage.

In each case, the initial linkage and leverage is followed by strenuous efforts undertaken by the Acer firm to internalize the technology and integrate its requirements into the firm's existing capabilities, thereby extending them. And in each case, the Acer firm is careful to select a technology for leverage that has reached a degree of standardization (i.e., it is at the point of being substitutable, imitable, and transferable). Acer has learnt from its mistakes here. An early attempt to enter the memory chip business in the mid-1980s, without adequate technology transfer or existing knowledge base, ended in a costly failure.[22] Likewise, attempts to enter the flat panel display industry in the early 1990s ended in frustration. It was only when the knowledge of these technologies was sufficiently generalized and available through the public domain, as well as from incumbents, that Acer's entry as a latecomer became feasible.

Concluding Remarks: Linkage, Leverage, and Hypercompetition

The perspective developed in this chapter turns out to have much wider applicability than in the case of the latecomer or newcomer MNE. In fact, it turns out to be the orientation of firms caught up in conditions of "hypercompetition" (D'Aveni, 1994). They too seek to create competitive footholds, rather than seeking elusive "sustainable" competitive advantages, and they do so through discovering ways in which they might complement the activities of other firms. This provides the setting in which the strategy of the latecomer may be seen to have potentially much wider significance.

In global high-technology industries, the traditional approaches to maintenance of competitive advantages by incumbent firms are widely seen to be increasingly problematic. Many authors have sought to capture these conditions in descriptions such as "turbulent" or "hypercompetitive." D'Aveni (1994) postulates the emergence of new rules of competitive engagement, in that firms are being forced to destroy their own sources of competitive advantage and forced to create new ones; they cannibalize their own leading products or brands before they have run the full course of the traditional product life cycle. He claims that entry barriers have less salience as technological change sweeps aside such barriers through Schumpeterian substitution.[23] Finally, he claims that firms are increasingly adopting a strategy of acquiring competencies as "insurance" in order to deal with unpredictable events, as opposed to planning product and market sequences in logical progression.

It is claimed that these new rules of competition demand that firms behave in new ways. The conditions call into question established categories and strategies such as "first-mover" and "late-entrant," requiring firms to adopt a blend of both, innovating through fast imitation, for example. It is striking how these novel strategies recall the strategies and techniques of the latecomer MNE, as it seeks to enter new high-technology sectors. It is plausible, then, to argue that the conditions applying to firms engaged in "hypercompetition" are also the conditions faced by firms which seek to enter advanced technologies and markets through "linkage and leverage." Thus, the strategies employed by the latecomer may also be desirable strategies for firms engaging with each other in hypercompetitive conditions or for firms aspiring to enter markets that lie beyond their present reach. Such strategies include finding ways to complement the initiatives of incumbents; targeting resources for leverage which are most imitable, substitutable, and transferable; and iteratively applying these approaches in an upward spiral of enhancing levels of absorptive capacity and combinative capabilities. Such strategies are, fundamentally, concerned with questions of knowledge leverage and securing transient competitive advantages through the management of knowledge leading to learning.[24]

What is striking is that the latecomer or newcomer does not seek permanent "sustainable" competitive advantages but rather analyzes the world in terms of its potential for appropriability, imitation, and transfer. It sees the world as full of customers and potential resources for leverage rather than a world of zero-sum competitors. After all, the notion of *sustainability* of competitive advantage is grounded in the prolongation of nonequilibrium distribution of resources and profits, in the extraction over a prolonged period of monopoly rents. By contrast, the success of latecomers in high-technology industries, and of firms generally in conditions of hypercompetition, rests in an embrace of competition via the promotion of diffusion, as well as of collaborative advantage, through resource leverage and complementary activities. It is this combination of competitive and collaborative capabilities which appears, at the most fundamental level, to account for latecomer success. This strategic pathway of "linkage and leverage," practiced so ably by latecomer multinationals, is clearly a powerful model of wealth generation of potentially wide applicability.

In this chapter we have been concerned with the outward strategic orientation of internationalizing firms. But their organizational solutions to complexity and global reach are the means through which their strategic initiatives are implemented. Here too we find evidence of innovation, as in the creation of global cellular clusters, which resolve once and for all the problems of subsidiary—headquarters' relations that plague conventional MNEs. How such clusters are created and maintained is an issue we examine in the next chapter.

Notes

1. GO has a rich culture in the East, particularly in Japan, where it was imported from China; today the number of GO professionals in Japan playing tournaments is comparable to the number of golf professionals playing in the U.S. GO remains very popular also in China, Korea, and Taiwan, where Stan Shih learned its mysteries.

2. The Persian origins of chess as it arrived in the West are evident in this term, which came to us as "Shah-mat" or "king dead."

3. Chinese and other Asian guerrilla movements long ago took their strategic inspiration from such concepts, as in the Maoist slogan "Take the countryside first before assaulting the cities." Mao was said to play GO each evening while engaged in civil war with the Nationalist KMT forces in China.

4. Hence, familiar exhortations like "Sticking to the knitting"—meaning that firms should not engage in too many businesses at once—carry little salience for latecomers.

5. See Hamel and Prahalad (1985); Doz (1986); Kobrin (1991); Kogut (1985a; 1985b); Porter (1985; 1986a; 1986b; 1990) for representative discussions that emphasize how global strategies call for transborder calculations, and Ghoshal and Nohria (1993) for the impact of such strategic calculations on global organizational forms. Roos, von Krogh and Yip (1994) situate globalizing terms within connectionist and cognitivist perspectives.

6. The group includes Yves Doz, Chris Bartlett, Sumantra Ghoshal, and C.K. Prahalad. See for example Bartlett and Ghoshal (1989); Ghoshal and Bartlett (1997); and Prahalad and Doz (1987). For the original PhD work on which these studies were built, see Prahalad (1976); Prahalad and Doz (1981); Doz, Bartlett, and Prahalad (1981); Bartlett (1979; 1986); Ghoshal (1986; 1987); as well as Ghoshal and Bartlett (1988; 1990).

7. See Bartlett and Ghoshal (1989) for the most extensive description of the category of "transnational corporation." For studies of how firms strive for global and local focus simultaneously, see Sugiura (1990) and Mair (1994) for the case of Honda. For a recent synthesis and elaboration of the literature, see Harzing (2000).

8. The classic study is that by Geringer, Beamish, and daCosta (1989), where a cross-sectional study of MNEs demonstrated a curvilinear relationship between size (multinational extension) and performance. The findings were corroborated by Hitt, Hoskisson, and Kim (1997).

9. See Porter (1985; 1990) for an exposition of the diamond of forces shaping competitiveness.

10. See Prahalad and Hamel (1990) and Hamel and Prahalad (1994) for the initial exposition of the "core competence" perspective.

11. Dierickx and Cool (1989) and Barney (1991; 1995) provide representative cases.

12. See for example Peteraf (1993). On dynamic capabilities, see Teece, Pisano, and Shuen (1997).

13. Porter (1985; 1990) takes this to be axiomatic. Yet innovation involves the diffusion as well as generation of new knowledge—and latecomers can draw competitive benefits from managing the process of diffusion as much as incumbents seek to draw benefits from the generation of new knowledge in the first place.

14. See Prahalad and Hamel (1990) and Hamel and Prahalad (1994) for expositions of resource leverage.

15. In fact, API has very close links with Philips Components, based worldwide at Eindhoven in The Netherlands. API is PC's largest customer for optical components, while Philips is now one of API's largest customers for its CD-ROMs.

16. See Burgelman (1994) for a classic description of this episode.

17. See for example Reed and DeFillippi (1990) for a theoretical discussion of the term.

18. See Anderson and Tushman (1990) for a representative discussion of the technological dynamics involved.

19. There is by now a substantial literature on Schumpeterian competition. See Schumpeter (1934) for the original exposition. Mathews and Cho (1999) has an overview of the field.

20. See Teece, Pisano, and Shuen (1997) for an elaboration of the dynamic capabilities paradigm.

21. In this sense, the account offered here is consistent with that of Oliver (1997), where she proposes a blend of institutional and resource-based accounts of firms' strategic choices—the difference being that I am concerned with the creation of competitive advantages, not their maintenance and sustainability.

22. The firm involved in this abortive venture was called Quasel. See Mathews and Cho (2000) for an account of the episode.

23. See Makadok (1998) for a critical discussion of these claims.

24. See Leonard-Barton (1995) and Grant (1996) for representative discussions of knowledge management as a strategic priority for firms.

6

ORGANIZATIONAL INNOVATION
Building Global Reach through Cellular Clusters

In the global economy, businesses are increasingly forced to shift from being multinational to being transnational. The traditional multinational is a national company with foreign subsidiaries. . . . Most companies doing international business today are still organized as traditional multinationals. But the transformation into transnational companies has begun, and it is moving fast. The products or services may be the same, but the structure is fundamentally different. In a transnational company there is only one economic unit, the world. Selling, servicing, public relations, and legal affairs are local. But parts, machines, planning, research, finance, marketing, pricing, and management are conducted in contemplation of the world market.

> Peter F. Drucker, "The Global
> Economy and the Nation-State"

The ultimate goal of geocentrism is a worldwide approach in both headquarters and subsidiaries. The firm's subsidiaries are thus neither satellites nor independent city states, but parts of a whole whose focus is on worldwide objectives as well as local objectives, each part making its unique contribution with its unique competence. Geocentrism is expressed by function, product and geography. The question asked in headquarters and the subsidiaries is: "Where in the world shall we raise money, build our plant, conduct R&D, get and launch new ideas to serve our present and future customers?"

> Howard V. Perlmutter,
> "The tortuous evolution of the
> multinational corporation"
> *Columbia Journal of*
> *World Business*

Where in the world was the best place to build PCs, or computer peripherals, or the most advanced flat panel displays? How should they be marketed around the world with maximum attention to local conditions? These were the questions addressed by Stan Shih in thinking through a geocentric organizational foundation for Acer in the 1990s. He came up with an ingenious way of expressing the solution. Acer should think of itself as consisting of organizational "clients" and "servers" rather than a conventional headquarters structure with subsidiaries. This thinking appealed to the computer culture of his Acer senior managers in 1992, when he sought to explain his revolutionary organizational architecture. By client-server, Shih implied that Acer's business units (then being fashioned as RBUs and SBUs) would interact with each other more or less like client and server in a decentralized computer network. The metaphor captured perfectly Perlmutter's earlier appeal for a multinational structure that would dispense with seeing subsidiaries as slavishly implementing policy or else doing whatever they wanted, in favor of seeing them integrated in a tightly knit partnership of equals.

The client-server metaphor actually translated very well across to the situation of a multinational with complex interactions and dependencies. In client-server computer systems, processes are implemented in dispersed fashion on "clients" or "servers," depending on the task at hand, as opposed to the traditional, centralized model which operated through a single mainframe computer and a lot of "dumb" terminals connected to it. This centralized model had broken down in the 1980s under the weight of complexity and volume of transactions being forced through it—and with system crashes becoming the frequent symptoms of overload. The client-server architecture allowed complexity to be reduced at source, by allowing terminals to perform their own local processing and communicate with each other utilizing systemwide protocols.

Likewise, Acer's business units would be able to negotiate directly with each other, without the intermediation of a central headquarters or divisional headquarters, as opposed to the conventional model of a center and subsidiaries hanging off it like so many "dumb" terminals in the traditional computer network. The client-server metaphor also implied that Acer business units (unlike traditional subsidiaries) would be able to take initiatives and would be responsible for their own business operations. These were, and are still, radical organizational concepts for a global firm.

Conventional MNEs had looked to create solid, vertically integrated international structures whose organization was sufficiently robust to withstand the vagaries of international demands (such as different economic and institutional settings), as well as cross-cultural misunderstandings. Strong, centralized, and authoritarian structures were seen as essential to underpin coherence as the firm extended its reach. Ford in the early twentieth century was the prototypical example, but then General Motors developed a more sophisticated version through its divisional structure. But such structures do not serve the purposes of the latecomer MNE, which has to utilize novel forms of organization to hold together the rapidly assembled international operation and to support innovative strategies.

Latecomer, geocentric global corporations do not succeed in forging a place for themselves in the global economy by following the conventional multinational rules. As Perlmutter predicted in his classic article in 1969, the geocentric global corporation seeks out novel means of organizing worldwide to take advantage of ingenuity and initiative, wherever it might be found. The latecomer simply takes the geocentric mindset to its logical conclusion. In this way, it fashions an entry for itself into markets, uninvited. Incumbents in fact do all that is legally within their power to keep the latecomers away, at least from their home markets. One of the critical sources of advantage that latecomers can fashion for themselves is radical and unconventional organizational innovations, such as the rapid spread into new markets through partnership and growth along multiple dimensions through global cluster formation—what Stan Shih called "client-server" and I am calling the "global cellular" model.[1]

Latecomer MNEs expanding rapidly around the world have two clear options for organizing and managing their exploding complexity. They can operate in a highly centralized fashion, as an extension of the wishes of the founder-chairman, with a central headquarters staff growing even faster than the company overall, and coordinating all the intricacies that result from each new market intervention. Such an option works until the global spread of the corporation is such that a more devolved structure is needed, either along conventional business division lines or area division lines—as predicted by Stopford and Wells in their 1972 classic book.

The other option is to expand rapidly by devolving as much authority as possible to designated business units, putting capable and entrepreneurial managers in charge of them. The business then grows through the efforts of multiple founder-entrepreneurs rather than just one—with the original founder-entrepreneur orchestrating and coordinating their efforts. This is the Acer solution—a courageous and radical approach to organizing a rapidly growing multinational business enterprise. Acer has developed its worldwide coverage through the creation of a cluster of more than 40 independent businesses—rather than in the conventional form of a tightly integrated and centralized structure. It has done this quite deliberately in its search for competitive advantages as a latecomer based on strategic and organizational innovation.

Acer has had less than 10 years to learn how to make its client-server worldwide organizational model work. As described in chapter 3, it has already gone through several different implementations of the client-server architecture. Many more are likely to be tried in the future. Thus, when describing this architecture we are definitely not describing a "one best way" of approaching worldwide organization. Instead, the client-server metaphor represents an inspiration, a framework, a paradigm to be used in designing the optimal kind of interactive architecture between a cluster of business units—taking particular form at any particular stage of their own evolution and of the business conditions in which they are operating.

Through this initial decade, Acer managers have been learning how to function in such a radically new organizational environment (new for the rest of the world, but actually harking back to Acer's earliest principles of organization based on partnership in its first 10 years as a domestic firm). They have been learning how the client-server organizational architecture places quite different demands on them as managers, requiring them to manage *relationships* rather than *operations*. Indeed, continuing the computer metaphor, Stan Shih declared at the beginning of 1999 that Acer was now inventing the organizational "operating system" needed to drive the client-server architecture. This operating system consists of a series of rules or guidelines for managing in this novel environment and organizational system. In 2000, he shifted his metaphor again and declared that Acer was organized according to an *internet organizational architecture*, and that the relations between the operating parts of the cluster needed to develop a language of codes and principles equivalent to an Internet Organizational Protocol. In this chapter, we pursue the principles of Acer's operating system and organizational architecture. We start with Stan Shih's own metaphor of the client-server structure, and more recently the internet architecture, to examine what he means by it. I then seek to generalize, to introduce the terminology of the "cellular" organizational architecture, which in my view provides greater generality than these computer metaphors. Its relevance to the discussion of internationalization derives from its direct application to the well-known problem of "subsidiary initiative"—the absence of which (or suppression of which) is one of the principal issues faced by conventional MNEs. The cellular MNE resolves the subsidiary initiative problem at source.

It is important to emphasize that we are not here depicting cellularity as a "one best way" of organizing but as an inspiration or paradigm that shapes the particular organizational configuration. The cellular metaphor simply works to remind entrepreneurial organizational designers (like Stan Shih) that for best results they should be devolving as much authority and responsibility into their organization's operating parts (or business units in a global cluster) and looking to provide ways of coordinating the cluster entities rather than, as is the way in conventional organizations, looking to centralize control over operations. Coordination of relatively autonomous entities turns out to be much more demanding that simply imposing external control on subsidiaries. It is more demanding, more sophisticated—and vastly more profitable.

Client-Server Organizational Architecture in Acer

The workings of the client-server (C-S) organizational system in Acer were thrashed out in the early 1990s when the then-CEO, Leonard Liu, introduced the concept of the business unit (BU), and with it, the notion of a profit center. Previously, Acer departments enjoyed a great deal of autonomy but were not responsible for their own profit-and-loss statements. They could arrange their pricing according to the needs of the parties, sometimes overinflating a price in order to give the seller an advantage, sometimes undersetting it, in order to give the buying division a break. It all came out in the final Acer profit statement. But this was not a good way to run a company, let alone a company with global aspirations. By 1990–91, the tensions in Acer were reaching the breaking point.

As Stan Shih put it:

> Things were so bad in 1991 that we held a series of "renaissance" meetings of senior staff to probe the reasons for our problems and to search for solutions. The reorganization into SBUs and RBUs followed from these discussions. The catalyst for the reorganization was that some of the more profitable parts of the enterprise were starting to complain that their business was being undermined by the losses being made elsewhere. Acer Peripherals, for example, had a very profitable OEM business, and it did not like to see its profits propping up what it saw as poor management of the American operation. So there was pressure for reorganization coming from the operating units themselves, which were already partly detached and operating as separate entities.

> So we bit the bullet and "broke" Acer up into a series of semi-autonomous operating entities, allocating market responsibilities to some (called the RBUs) and production and technology responsibilities to others (called the SBUs). This was a surgical operation on Acer. It hurt a few people and it was not widely liked in the company at the time. But I and the new group of senior managers that were in place from mid-1992 saw it as an absolutely essential prelude to getting the organization back under control—without collapsing into a monolithic, authoritarian hierarchy which I saw as a pointless organizational model that could not possibly work in our fast-moving industry. In any case, there was already internal pressure from within Acer for such a reorganization, to give the operating entities a greater sense of control over their own business.[2]

With the creation of RBUs and SBUs and profit centers within them, the attitudes of the business unit managers changed. The key to the new system was direct contracting between BUs. This implied the charging of prices between BUs, and immediately the issue of what was "fair practice" became a heated source of contention. The difficulties derived from the fact that Acer business units were producing and marketing branded product, as well as selling direct to OEM customers. In such a situation, OEM customers expect and demand extremely good prices that carry no marketing or brand promotion overheads. Yet when supplying branded product to RBUs, the SBUs as profit centers had to take into account the costs associated with promotion of the Acer brand—and so the prices to RBUs would have to be higher than those charged to OEM customers for sometimes identical machines. This created ill-feeling in the group. The RBUs felt that they were getting a raw deal (particularly when combined with their grievance that SBUs appeared to respond to outside firms' OEM orders with greater alacrity than to internal RBU orders), while the SBUs felt that they were being expected to subsidize the operations of the RBUs. The SBUs wanted the highest prices for their products, while the RBUs wanted to pay the lowest prices possible. This produced some price bickering that was quite new to Acer.

Such travails were certainly not unique to Acer. They are the stuff of any decentralized organizational system, in which the parts interact directly with each other. The benefits are felt as an attack on complexity, at its source, but the demands are that some form of rule-based coordination be found to facilitate inter-BU negotiations. This is what Acer was struggling with in the early 1990s and was a necessary feature of making its new C-S organizational system *work*. Rather than succumb to a chaotic power-driven pricing system, as in the open marketplace, Stan Shih made enormous efforts to introduce some *principles* into the inter-BU charging systems.

Inter-BU Charging Principles

BUs that were watching their profits felt less inclined to do each other favors—one of the engaging features of the more easy-going management system that had grown up during Acer's domestic growth. So the C-S organizational system introduced more cut and thrust in relations between BUs. The RBUs that might formerly have taken on each others' excess inventory and tried to sell it, for the good of the organization as a whole, would no longer be willing to do so. This and many other small changes were the price to be paid for the efficiency that came with closer attention to BU profit and loss. They were, after all, greatly outweighed by the benefits. Cost-conscious BUs, for example, were keen to find ways in which they could collectively lower costs. Common purchasing to receive bulk discounts was one such strategy. Whereas in the divisionalized firm such bulk purchasing arrangements are common and are organized by the head office, in the devolved Acer structure, such an arrangement needed to evolve out of the

BUs' own business sense and capacity to work effectively together. And evolve they did.

Shih captured the issues involved in trying to operate the new C-S organizational system in a set of principles. In his pithy Chinese way, he devised characteristic slogans to express them. What emerged was: "No excess baggage"; "If it doesn't hurt, help"; and "Each man is lord of his castle."

No Excess Baggage   This meant that all BUs were to be responsible for minimizing their own costs and eliminating waste. It posed key performance measures, such as high productivity and reduced waste, to be the responsibility of each business unit. Overall, revenues per employee, and for each BU, value-added per employee, became critical corporate benchmarks. Indeed, Acer made great strides in this department. Revenues increased from around $400 million in 1989, generated by some 5,000 employees, to $5.8 billion in 1995, generated by 14,000 workers—an increase in revenues per head from $80,000 to $400,000, or 500 percent, in just six years. This was a remarkable achievement initiated at the very beginning of the reengineering process by Shih's insistence that sloppy procedures had to be eliminated, and through his making each BU responsible for minimizing its own costs as well as expanding its business.

If it Doesn't Hurt, Help   This implied that Acer BUs should work together where feasible. In particular, they should purchase preferentially from each other, but only so long as the price and quality being offered was competitive with outside suppliers. Thus, cooperation between BUs was made the focus of the C-S arrangements, but with a competitive edge and sharpness (recalling Acer's brand name) induced by constant testing against the best of outside suppliers. Indeed, Shih insisted that at least half of the components produced by the various SBUs, be they monitors, CD-ROMs, keyboards, or whatever, should be sold to firms outside the Acer Group. This ensured the openness of the Acer BUs and forced them to focus on the external customers, who would ultimately be the source of the profits of the group as a whole.

Each Man Is Lord of His Castle   This meant, as the slogan implies, that BUs would have as much autonomy as was compatible with their belonging to a wider group. They would have the power to take initiatives, where these would expand their business or improve their profits—but not at the expense of other members of the group. Thus again, initiative and competitive postures should be directed outside the group, where profits should be sourced. Indeed, they were expected to take such initiatives.

These simple slogans created an initial set of rules to guide and frame the direct contractual negotiations between the BUs, placing the onus on each to be mindful of its costs and productivity improvements; to foster cooperation between BUs, but not at the expense of competitive performance; and to give as much rein to BU initiative as would be consistent with overall group needs and policies.

Underpinning these principles was the more fundamental point that BUs would not seek to make profits from each other, but *only from their external customers.* This meant that Acer's focus would be on getting the best prices from customers and seeing these as the source of value-added, while charging each other cost-plus prices within the group. This extremely important principle has underpinned the successful working of the C-S system ever since. Various cost-plus formulas were eventually agreed on as part of the process of settling on fair internal transfer pricing. SBUs ended up charging RBUs a little more than their OEM customers, but not as much as they would have liked. The RBUs ended up paying an extra premium for their branded product, but more than they wanted.

These inter-BU charging negotiations were Acer's first experiences with this new "client-server" organizational model. Since then Acer has expanded its use, so that it is now seen to be routine for Acer to form new business units (cells) and to disband old ones, as the need arises or circumstances change. In the first decade of its implementation, Acer managers have become remarkably proficient at utilizing the autonomy and initiative released by the devolved authority in the C-S system, in launching new products, new businesses and in disseminating organizational learning. The need for equal attention to be paid to coordination and standardization, to preserve coherence in the face of so much autonomy, has perhaps not been so readily recognized, at least until recently.

The senior managers of Acer regard their client-server model of global organization as right for their corporation. They see it as providing the optimal blend of centralized authority and coordination, combined with autonomy and independence vested in the business units, whether they be acting at any one time as "clients" or "servers." They do not presume to make judgments as to the efficacy of their organizational model beyond this system.

Now, of course, Acer's utilization of this approach to organizational design has evolved through the 1990s, as described in chapter 3. The point to be made is that there is a consistency in organizational pattern here that has been instrumental in Acer's being able to cope with global reach and complexity with apparently minimal fuss. The key to this is to see Acer's client-server model as an instance of a wider class of organizational architecture that I and others have labeled "cellular." The major virtue of this organizational architecture is that it resolves at source the major tensions found in conventional MNEs, namely, conflicts generated between subsidiaries and headquarters over strategic directions, authority, and responsibility.

The Cellular Organizational Architecture

Acer is far from being the only latecomer MNE to develop a cellular solution to its organizational problems. The Chinese industrial MNE from Hong Kong, Li & Fung, has likewise successfully reduced complexity at source by devolving as much responsibility as possible to its operating entities and their managers. It consists of around 60 business cells (called divisions) which are customer-focused—usually on one customer or related group of customers. This is a remarkable organizational structure for a trading company, which traditionally has been organized exclusively along geographic lines, with branch offices in each country as the profit centers (and competing against each other). It is very difficult to optimize along the supply chain in such circumstances.

With Li & Fung, by contrast, the customer-centric cells—called divisions, just to confuse the issue—shape the supply chain according to the customer's specific needs, seeking maximum performance in terms of logistics and delivery as well as quality. The leader-entrepreneur operates the cell (division) just as she would her own small business—and it is frequently a she in Hong Kong's pragmatic and egalitarian approach to business. The cells are provided with the financial resources and administrative support of a large organization, but apart from that they have a great deal of autonomy in meeting the needs of their customer.

As Victor Fung puts it, for the creative side of the business (meeting customer needs, attracting new customers), they want as much entrepreneurial behavior as possible. They rely on very substantial performance bonuses, which have no upper cap—so the harder people work to make a customer satisfied, and the higher the profit, the greater their individual reward. The other side to this is the tight overall control needed to complement such autonomy within the operating parts.[3]

What the Acer and Li & Fung cases have in common, along with many more examples, is a concern to move away from the tightly controlled divisional structures that operate in most international firms, toward an organizational model that places maximum authority and responsibility in the operating parts, consistent with the need to secure cohesion and coherence across the whole. This study is far from being the first to point to the need for such structures or to give them a name. Terms have been used such as "network" organization, "differentiated network," or "heterarchy" to get at the same idea. "Chunking" is another graphic term to describe the concentration of autonomy in operating parts, thereby releasing corporate headquarters for coordination roles and management of the interbusiness unit relations rather than direct operational control.[4] Organizations utilizing these concepts have been described as exhibiting qualities of holograms, hypertext, and object-oriented engineering. All are useful descriptors, all capture some aspect of the nonhierarchical features of these organizational innovations. Elsewhere I have argued that these innovations result in the creation of small, highly focused, self-acting units (holons) that cooperate together to get a job done. Since they behave like cells in a biological organism, let us agree to call them "cells."[5]

Essentially, the cellular form has the characteristics that its operating parts are semiautonomous business entities termed cells; these relate directly with each other through network connections of business-to-business contracting and subcontracting; and the whole is held together by operating rules and constraints agreed on through a system of shared governance that is supplemented by an operating center that takes strategic initiatives on behalf of the system as a whole. It is the behavior of the whole, when its parts are fashioned with such independence and self-sufficiency, that is of compelling interest.

Acer has grown to become a global cluster of more than 40 such cells or business units, some of which have globalized in their own right—such as Acer Peripherals—and which are spinning off (or "budding") new cells as the circumstances permit. Acer's own term for its structure—apart from the "client-server" metaphor, is the Chinese expression: "Circle of dragons without head"—that is to say, a circular arrangement of noble, independent beasts without any one being paramount. This is a remarkably succinct and graphic way to describe a cellular organizational architecture. The term "dragon" in Chinese connotes a noble beast of good fortune—a fortunate connotation for an autonomous, independent business unit.[6] The Chinese characters are shown in Fig. 6.1.

Organizational Principles of Cellularity

From Acer and other examples, the outlines of a new organizational form have begun to take shape. The emphasis in all cases is on small entities (be they teams, plants, or firms) taking responsibility for their own entrepreneurial actions within an overall vision and system that defines the organization as a whole. The successful examples have achieved a balance between local autonomy and global accountability. It is in creating the structures that make such a balance an explicit organizational requirement, and then in finding ways to manage it, that these successful companies demonstrate their competitive superiority. It is because of this emphasis on local autonomy combined with global accountability that I and my colleagues choose to call this new form of organization the *cellular structure*. Alternative terms have been used, as noted above.[7] However, it is the cellular metaphor that best captures the idea of self-reliant parts responding quickly to opportunities or adapting to unforeseen events, but always within the interests and operating rules of the total organization. The cellular metaphor evokes biological images of growth, nurturing, and vitality— all attributes of "living companies."[8] The cellular concept leads away from the notion of externally imposed control toward the idea of *self-imposed order*. The managerial challenge is to preserve autonomy while providing

Figure 6.1 "Circle dragon no head." The characters mean "circle of dragons with no head (or 'leading') dragon"—a characterization of a group of semiautonomous firms interacting with each other as equals and without a firm exercising purely supervisory functions.

structures and processes within which autonomous entities can find common ground and work together.

The Cellular Organization

In the cellular organization, the basic system elements or operating parts are *cells* which are entire operating units equipped with all the necessary resources and responsibilities to maintain their existence. The cellular organization can be characterized in terms of its defining features as follows.

1. The operating entities are discrete cells which are quasi-autonomous and self-sufficient.
2. The relations between cells are direct business relations of contract and subcontract, forming a network.
3. The whole maintains its integrity through shared governance; strategic coordination is provided by a coordinating center which acts as the "brain" or nerve center of the organization. It has limited powers of intervention and initiative in order to maintain the organization's integrity and identity.

This triple description can apply at any level of the organization. The cells might be manufacturing cells, in which case the "total" organization is the plant where they are located (or the "virtual plant" if it includes, say, a computer-aided design center located elsewhere that sends computer-generated designs over the internet). Or the cells may be several plants within a manufacturing business. Or they may be several businesses, producing a variety of products, within a single corporation. Or they may form a cluster of separate businesses, where the "total organization" is the network which emerges through their cooperation.[9]

The concept of the cellular organization is illustrated in Fig. 6.2. This figure shows the total organization as a cluster of business units, tightly integrated through their interactions with each other, but each drawing in business from the outside world. This is the key to sustaining the collaboration between business cells within the same organization. If they were direct competitors, or sought to generate profits from their dealings with each other, then the basis of trust that provides the foundation for the group's coherence would be lost.

It is at the *global level* then that cellularity can prove its benefits most decisively. Divisionalized organizations have sought to cope with the complexities of global scale through all kinds of expedients, from the simplistic measure of creating a separate "international division" to complex matrix structures and global business divisions. Incumbent MNEs such as ABB and AT&T have developed patterns of global coverage which differ remarkably from their earlier kinds of solid, market-by-market penetration by wholly owned subsidiaries. ABB was completely restructured as a global network

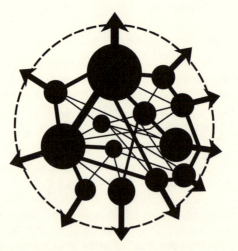

Figure 6.2 Cellular organizational architecture.

of profit centers in the 1990s. AT&T's Unisource worldwide joint venture business utilizes different service providers in each country, but provides the user with a seamless communications transition from one country to another. AT&T uses the slogan "The local company everywhere" to describe this organizational approach.[10] The similarities with Acer's approach of "global brand local touch" are indeed striking.

The cellular approach, by contrast, maintains the focus of each business cell and allows it to grow independently to global scale, while leveraging resources from its sister business cells and bringing its own global connections into the group for the benefit of all the cells. The counterpart that is required is global mechanisms of integration, to provide integrity and coherence to what would otherwise become a disorganized series of autonomous entities, competing with each other as much as with the outside world. The Acer Group illustrates these challenges, and the means tried for meeting them through various kinds of evolving cellular structures, in abundance.

Advantages of the Global Cellular Form

Considerable advantages can be expected to accrue to firms organized along cellular lines, by virtue of their being able to respond to changes in their environment through simple accommodations within cells, or through self-organized networks of cells, rather than through some major transformation of operations mandated by the corporate HQ. This cellular form gives them a flexibility, a responsiveness, and a resilience that is far in advance of even the most flexible divisionalized firm. There is a pronounced bias in cellular organizations toward entrepreneurship, self-organization, and common ownership—all characteristics that will likely be defining features of organizations in the twenty-first century.

An organization that exhibits features of cellular self-sufficiency, self-governance through network communication, and integration (which we take as definition of a cellular organization) derives potential advantages from this structure which are denied an organization that is structured along more conventional lines. The cellular organization is responsive and adaptive, because it is the cells themselves that respond or adapt quickly to new situations, without the necessity for central intervention. Groups of cells can self-organize a combined response to a new situation, through their direct, network communication with each other. The total cellular organization benefits from this devolved responsiveness, while maintaining its integrity, its identity, and its capacity for initiating strategic moves from the coordinating center. Thus, cellular organizations have an organizational architecture that biases them toward entrepreneurship, distributed ownership, learning, and mutual trust.

These innovations represent a fundamental break with the divisional form, even when corporations insist that their divisions are expected to take initiatives and operate as profit as well as cost centers.[11] The difference lies in the way that cells are conceived, as self-acting operating parts, empowered to raise their own finance, to seek out their own technological resources, and to integrate themselves in the existing cellular structures of the organization—rather than having all these things performed for them by a corporate headquarters. It is this overt reliance on a headquarters, willed or otherwise, that creates such tensions in conventional MNEs, and that are avoided in a cellular organizational structure.

Cellularity on a Global Scale: Beyond the Problem of Subsidiary Initiative

The management literature on MNEs recognizes that as they grow in scale and global coverage, so their management and organization presents more and more of a challenge. One of the critical problems addressed is that of subsidiary initiative. In the conventional MNE, with its solid structure made up of wholly owned subsidiaries formed in one market after another, each granted some specific charter and constrained to operate within certain financial guidelines (such as norms for monthly or quarterly returns on investment), the goal is control—and it is usually achieved, more or less. But the price paid is subsidiaries which lack initiative, or which are constantly at odds with the corporate headquarters, delaying the implementation of strategic initiatives and looking for ways of reducing what they see as the heavy hand of headquarters' bureaucratic control.

Thus, one of the biggest handicaps suffered by the conventional vertically integrated or divisionalized MNE is its failure to encourage, or capitalize on, subsidiary initiatives. Such initiatives are seen as a threat in the conventional corporation and are usually suppressed by the headquarters in the name of maintaining coherence and the existing division of labor between divisions and subsidiaries. This is particularly the case where subsidiaries are seen as "implementing" the current operations of the firm, while the ideas, programs, and initiatives emanate from headquarters.

There is by now a substantial literature on subsidiary-headquarters tensions. Birkinshaw and Ridderstråle (1999) were able to shed light on this process in their study of 26 initiatives launched from Canadian subsidiaries of seven U.S. MNEs in the 1990s. Of these, only 14 were actually adopted by the parent firm, while six were outright failures, blocked by headquarters, and a further six were drawn out to the point where they were no longer promoted by the initiating subsidiary. They documented prolonged attempts to defeat many of the initiatives by either U.S. headquarters or by rival divisions in the United States, who felt threatened by the subsidiary initiative. Such an initiative might be a bid by the Canadian subsidiary to manufacture an item currently brought in by the MNE, or a new product proposal that has to run the gamut of headquarter staffs as well as find a sponsoring product division.[12]

Most such initiatives in corporations are suppressed in one way or another by the "not invented here" (NIH) syndrome. But the headquarters-subsidiary relationship within an MNE adds a new level of complexity to the problems identified by Kanter with her "Ten rules for stifling innovation."[13] Birkinshaw and Ridderstråle (1999) refer to the MNE's "immune system" as acting to ward off such initiatives, seeing them as a "foreign body" to be attacked and devoured. But just as the body's immune system can make mistakes and view friendly tissues such as organ transplants as the enemy, so the conventional MNE loses the potential benefits of subsidiary initiatives by its action in suppressing them.

The cellular MNE, by contrast, draws its robustness from the fact that *initiatives are welcomed* wherever they emanate from, and there is no "hierarchy" of headquarters and subsidiaries to stifle threatening initiatives.[14] The idea of Acer's client-server structure is to leave such problems of "subsidiary initiative" behind, in the name of building an international organization that places a premium on innovation and initiative. It places senior managers in a context where they can exercise responsibility in pursuing such initiatives and be held accountable for their successes and failures.

Now the interesting feature of the management literature on subsidiary growth and initiatives, and the management issues raised by the voluntary or involuntary suppression of initiatives in conventional MNEs, is that *these matters are discussed without regard to organizational architecture*. From the perspective of the latecomer MNE, which sees organizational innovation as one of its principal competitive weapons, this makes no sense at all. In the context of the MNE, the cellular organizational form may be seen as *an organizational innovation which resolves the problem of subsidiary initiative*.

Let us take the case of Acer Netxus to illustrate the issues involved in a new business finding a "space" for itself in an existing global cellular cluster—in contrast with the process conventionally followed in establishing a new subsidiary. Acer Netxus was a spin-off from Acer Inc., launched to take advantage of new computer network opportunities as part of Acer's "budding process" of creating new enterprises. Because of the cells' autonomy, they cannot be forced to deal with the new business; it has to find its feet and demonstrate its efficacy to the existing cells. This is not always an easy task, as the newly installed manager of Acer Netxus, Dr. Lance Wu, discovered for himself.

Acer Netxus and Acceptance of a New Business Unit

As the field of data communications continues to expand, opening numerous business opportunities (computer networks; network communication products; data switches, etc.), Acer BUs have sought to keep up with this fast-moving field—and in the process have been placed in a potentially damaging competition with each other to develop incompatible lines of products. So Acer senior management took advantage of an opportunity to recruit a very experienced scientist and engineer in the communications sector, Dr. Lance Wu, to create a new, stand-alone BU, Acer Netxus, to address this expanding business area.[15]

Acer Netxus is one of the few "high technology" new businesses started by Acer other than through a joint venture with a well-known multinational.[16] Initial success was extraordinary; Acer Netxus had a staff of over 200 within its first year of operation and put a wide range of data communications products on the market. This successful experience threw up many organizational challenges. In a conventional divisionalized structure, a new business division can expect to meet with initial assistance and recognition, but in the Acer C-S organizational model the process is a little more complicated. A new business like Netxus has to forge relations with the existing BUs, and this has to be on the basis of mutual business interests. How does this process unfold?

The new business has to find a "space" for itself in the existing range of products marketed by BUs.[17] Two cases present themselves: either the new Acer business has products that duplicate those already secured by Acer from external suppliers, or they are new to the Acer portfolio.

Take the first case, where the new business supplies a product which BUs already obtain from third-party suppliers, for example, a Local Area Network data switching (Ethernet) card. Acer BUs provide PCs with third-party-supplied Ethernet cards installed as one of the options. Should they switch to purchase cards from Netxus, just because it has been established as an Acer business? Not necessarily. As independent business units, they make up their own minds as to whether to make the switch. But they can without too much disruption utilize the Acer Netxus product as a "second source," to build up an appreciation of the product's qualities and of the reliability of the new SBU as a supplier. If things go well, then some RBUs might switch to taking the Acer Netxus product as a primary source and switch their present third-party-supplied cards to "second sourcing." In other words, the new business unit has to prove itself, in business terms, before its products will be accepted by the existing BUs.

Take the second case, where Netxus produces a product which is new to the BUs, for example, an internet connection device such as the Acer-ISDN T30. In this case, the BUs have no customers for the new product, nor sales staff trained in its use. In a hierarchical firm, perhaps they would be ordered to take on the new product as one of their divisional responsibilities. Not so in the Acer structure. Again the newly established BU, Netxus, has to win the confidence of the BUs by finding a place for its new product. It will have to provide an initial specialized sales force of its own, making contact with potential customers in each of the markets covered by existing BUs, without being seen to get in the way of the BUs' activities. This could be a tricky situation. The aim is for the BU to take ownership of the product and sell it along with their existing Acer product line. But this will not happen before an existing customer base has been established, through the efforts of the new BU itself, and until the BU has proved itself in terms of quality and reliability of the product being supplied. (There were occasions in the past when RBUs had been persuaded to take up a product supplied by one of the SBUs, only to see support for the product drop off as the SBU switched attention to something else; this created bad blood between units, and an initial lack of enthusiasm by RBUs for new product offerings from SBUs. It was one of the triggering factors behind the 1998 reorganizations.)

Thus, much of the initial effort on the part of the new Acer business, such as Netxus, is devoted to making "space" within the existing Acer C-S BU structure for the new business and its product offerings. Netxus would have to make the initial investment in supporting a new product, for example, in creating new marketing channels and in establishing reliability of supply, in the expectation that the product would eventually be supported by the BUs involved. As Lance Wu put it, in explaining this strategy: "The BUs don't want to take on a burden—they want to take on a business." Accordingly, he sees it as his responsibility, within Netxus, to build up the business for the new product, to make it attractive for the BUs to take it on. In the meantime, he is content to pay the "brand name maintenance fee" as a means of offering recognition of the general brand promotion efforts of the BU.

Contrast this picture of business cells negotiating with each other and adapting to each other and to external circumstances, with the conventional picture of MNEs and their subsidiaries, as discussed above. This conventional picture is couched in terms of extreme levels of conflict between MNE headquarters and subsidiaries and between one subsidiary with another. Let us then summarize this discussion in the proposition that *the global cellular cluster organization, as implemented, for example, by Acer, provides a means of resolving the problem of subsidiary initiative.*

The Sustaining of a Global Cellular Cluster: Spinning Off New Ventures

New business development presents an important issue for every organizational model. This issue is magnified in a global corporation. Whether the company is a tightly integrated, hierarchical organization, or a loose-knit federation, the issue of new business development presents itself as a challenge to existing structures and relationships.

The fact is that most conventional businesses do not start "new businesses." They either stick with what they have; or, if they wish to diversify, they do so by purchasing a company as a going concern and take it over through merger or acquisition. This is the time-honored route to "diversification" in the conventional business world. On a global level, such a strategy runs into all kinds of problems of compatibility, from compatibilities of legal and accounting systems, to compatibility of cultures and operating styles (unless such acquisitions are themselves an organizational strategy, as in the case of Ispat).

The model of new business development within Acer is that each BU is expected to develop new business areas as the opportunity arises. The top management group within the company might also wish to enter a new business area (such as a communications product) and rather than authorize an existing business cell to develop this line, they may take the initiative to start such a new business as a global Acer initiative.

Acer has perfected a striking mechanism for maintaining and sustaining its global cellular cluster, namely, a process of spinning off—or "budding"— new ventures, thereby allowing individual business units to international-ize and grow to global dimensions in their own right. Acer's spin-off strategy sets it in a league of "lifelike" successful businesses that have employed the process to maintain and sustain the vitality and focus of their operating parts. A spin-off is defined by the case where a company distributes to its stockholders a portion of its assets, without extra charges being incurred. Typically, new stock is issued to represent ownership in the new business unit. The idea behind the spin-off is not philanthropy, but a hard-headed calculation that the spun-off entity will perform better as a focused business than inside a larger corporate parent. Within this structure, there are hidden some extremely interesting features that deserve special mention. Not the least of these is the financial transparency associated with Acer's devolved ownership.

Cellular clusters reproduce themselves through constant attention to spin-offs or "budding" of new enterprises. The spin-off of new ventures is practiced by a large number of firms originating around the world. In Europe, there are several famous examples, such as the Lanorossi Company in Italy, which has spawned a whole cluster of highly flexible and adaptive, high technology textiles and clothing firms. In Japan, there is the case of Taiyo Kogyo, which consistently splits existing businesses into smaller "daughter" businesses as they grow to a certain size, so that the business acquires the character of a global group of interlinked and coordinated firms. This process is christened by its author, Kuniyasu Sakai, as "bunsha" or "company fission."[18] In the United States, Thermo Electron spins off sub-sidiary companies in order to maintain closeness to the customer and clear accountability for profits and share price. The managers of the spin-off com-pany own stock in the enterprise, and if it performs well they receive ex-traordinary rewards.[19] Many studies demonstrate the efficacy of spin-offs, both in terms of market capitalization (where the combined capitalization of the parent and spin-off exceeds by a wide margin the capitalization of the previous integrated entity) and in terms of daughter firms' revenues and profits.[20] There have also been some attempts to model the effects, in order to generate more secure insight into the processes through which wealth is generated by spin-off enterprises.[21] Acer's experiences illuminate this field because of the very clear performance goals embodied in the Acer strategy and its repeated application.

Acer's Continuous "Budding" of New Business Ventures

Consider the case of the new businesses initiated by one of Acer's principal business cells, Acer Peripherals Inc. The API business unit has renewed and extended its operations through new business spin-offs, which now constitute a global cluster in their own right: the Acer Peripherals Group (APG). API raised considerable cash reserves from its IPO in the mid-1990s, and these enabled it to finance the spinning off of new ventures, together with supplementary finance from other members of the Acer Group and some strategic outside investors. (Acer's venture capital fund, Acer Capital, has been an important contributor to each of these new ventures.) API has created a group of firms with complementary but distinctive activities. Its strategy in doing so provides a fascinating counterpoint to the wider Acer Group's strategy of creating new businesses.

Darfon Electronics   The first spin-off was a company called "Darfon Electronics" (named in this way to make it quite distinct from Acer). The core business around which this venture was formed was flyback transformers (FBT), a key component in monitors. But the head of API, K.Y. Lee (one of the original collaborators with Stan Shih at the beginning), held back from initiating the venture with this product as its sole business and instead built up its core competencies through technology transfer from the parent API, until it could be launched with four product lines: flyback transformers; other specialized transformers such as SMD transformers for LCDs; spindle motors; and multilayer chip capacitors and inductors. It is still a small company with revenues in 1999 of around U.S.$50 million, growing to U.S.$80 million in the year 2000.

The interesting point about this new venture launch is that it was established with full regard to its sustainability. The parent company API has transferred all its initial technology; it has transferred almost 100 skilled staff across; it provided 100 percent of the initial finance (although the company is now owned 35 percent by its employees). In 1999, Darfon was doing around 60 percent of its business with API (supplying transformers etc.) and a further 10 percent with other Acer companies and around 30 percent with external companies, some of which are Acer competitors. API chief K.Y. Lee expected Darfon to soon do less than 50 percent of its business with API. This is further evidence of its being launched as a sustainable, stand-alone business.

The interest in this lies in the fact that the APG is replicating the new venture spin-off practices engaged in by the Acer Group as a whole, but with even greater attention to the details of sustainability and self-sufficiency. Thus, the APG, like the AIPG, can be viewed as a global group, following a similar trajectory to that of the Acer Group as a whole, but with some highly significant differences.

Acer Display Technologies   The second new venture was Acer Display Technologies (ADT). There is a long history to API's efforts to become self-sufficient in monitors and displays. As early as 1994, an attempt was made to launch a monitor-producing subsidiary, but these efforts were aborted. Further efforts led in 1996 to the launch of ADT as a small venture to get a foothold in flat panel display technology. It started as a pilot operation producing plasma display panels (suitable for wall TVs), using technology and skilled staff transferred across from the Electronic Research Service Organization (ERSO), the LCD-specialist laboratory at ITRI.[22]

ADT began commercial-scale production of TFT-LCDs in 1998, following its technology transfer agreement with IBM (Japan). Moving into production necessitated a huge level of investment, comparable to the levels needed to build semiconductor wafer fabs. Capital for the new venture was raised from Acer affiliates as well as from Taiwan sources.[23] Employees themselves account for around 15 percent of investment, and there are some outside investors—a Japanese fund and a U.S. firm, Capital Investment. The venture raised a credit facility on top of this.[24] The first LCD plant was being built by ADT in early 1999. It was thought unlikely to need the full amount of the funds raised. This is again an illustration of the cautious approach followed by Acer in its financial dealings, even at these very high levels of investment—an approach which makes it improbable that Acer could fall into the same indebtedness trap that snared Korean firms.

Again, API transferred skilled staff across to ADT, as well as its initial investment capital and technology. The CEO is H.B. Chen, who made his name within API as head of the Malaysian production facility at Penang.[25] The business model that drives ADT in its early years is to develop as a supplier to two customers only—API and IBM initially. External customers are likely to follow. Thus again it is evident that ADT has been established with careful attention being paid to ensure its sustainability. Given current projections for demand for flat panel displays worldwide, ADT could well become one of the largest operations within the Acer Group in the next few years.

Acer Media Technologies   A third spin-off has been Acer Media Technologies Inc. (AMTI). At the time of writing, this was still a very small venture, but again with big potential. It aims to take APG into the expanding area of optoelectronic storage media such as rewritable compact discs and digital video discs (DVDs)—based on API's growing sophistication and capabilities in production of CD-ROMs. AMTI was formed only in the latter half of 1998, with initial capital of U.S.$8 million provided by API itself (50 percent), outside investors (10 percent), and again employees taking up 40 percent of the equity. The small staff of around 20 engineers are highly skilled: no fewer than six have Ph.D.s! They were transferred across from API before the company was formally launched for 12 months of intensive training in the new optoelectronic technologies.

Comparable new businesses have been launched in other parts of Acer's global cluster. Acer Information Products Group, itself a global corporation, has also been active in launching new spin-offs. These include: *Acer Neweb*—a consumer communications company; *Nexcell*—an investment in a new business of potentially great interest to Acer (long-life batteries for portable PCs); and *Acer Netxus*.

New business creation provides the opportunity to focus on a new and promising line of business, undistracted by the wider concerns of the parent organization. This is its clear and tangible goal, but it also provides the intangible benefit of creating new avenues of advancement for management staff who might be held back by the Chinese norms of seniority, which make it difficult for younger, more talented managers to be given responsibilities over their seniors. But if they are transferred into a new business, then they can hire their own management staff and can be given every incentive to prove their excellence. This opportunity for advancement has been a powerful factor in the successful expansion and development of the Acer Peripherals Group and of Acer as a whole.

Financial Transparency Associated with Dispersed Ownership

Dispersed ownership of Acer not only underwrites its cellular character, but also plays an important role in enforcing operational transparency on the group. It has the interesting effect that it eliminates any tendency toward "transfer pricing" or tax evasion or any other of the unsavory deals in which traditional multinational enterprises have engaged in the past.[26]

Reference was made above to the financial sources of API's spin-offs. Acer is quite transparent about this matter—another feature that differentiates it strongly from divisionalized firms, where all capital budgets are approved by central headquarters and finance raised by the same headquarters. Acer, on the contrary, backs each new business cell with independent sources of finance, frequently raised from outside the group. This is seen not only as a smart way of raising finance and keeping a cap on the financial exposure of the group itself, but also as a way of involving external investors as quasi "auditors" of Acer's operations.

One of the features of the independence of Acer group members is that they are expected to raise capital for themselves, frequently through bringing in outside investors. This is not viewed within Acer as a dilution of control. One of the regular practices is for an Acer affiliate to start a new venture with financial backing from the parent, as well as other Acer group companies, plus one or two outside investors. This is how Acer Display

Technologies (ADT) was started by API, for example. The China marketing company, AMS, was also established as a new venture with investments from Acer Sertek, ACI, and Acer Inc.

The effect of this is that each Acer company needs to keep its own books—profit and loss accounts, balance sheet—and pay its investors a fair return on their shareholding. Thus, Acer is not only an unusual multinational enterprise (MNE) in its global cellular organizational structure but also in its financial transparency. It cannot afford to manipulate transfer prices to minimize tax liability, for example, because this would upset its financial responsibilities within each operating entity. The goal of public listing also constitutes in itself a financial discipline that would eliminate any possibility of manipulation of revenues, costs, or prices. This is a very important aspect of Acer's global structure which has been part of Stan Shih's vision all along.

As financial controller for the group as a whole, it is George Huang's responsibility to track the financial operations of the various constituent entities. His job is quite different from the kind of financial oversight affected by a corporate HQ in a divisionalized firm. There the HQ monitors financial aggregates with a view to enforcing certain performance norms. In Acer's case, by contrast, the relative autonomy of the different groups means that they monitor their own performance and maximize it to the extent of their own abilities. The financial oversight is to ensure that certain norms such as debt-equity ratios are not being exceeded, and that fair returns on shareholdings are being paid. In each case, Acer is not imposing rigid rules but ensuring that performance falls within the ballpark for that segment of the industry.

In operational terms, the most important aggregates tracked by the corporate HQ of Acer in Taipei are lines of credit being extended and inventory levels, since in the PC industry, these are the critical variables that can mean the difference between profit and loss. These are operational variables, where the corporate HQ is interested in ensuring that they fall within reasonable guidelines which are known to all. Again, this financial accountability is a very different kind of exercise from the familiar "managing by the numbers" that one encounters in the typical divisionalized firm.

The minicase histories of new business formation within Acer illustrate the dynamic responsiveness of the cellular process. They reveal a corporation that is juggling organizational and technological demands, keeping some operations in-house, when they require extensive manufacturing capabilities (such as in the case of CD-ROMs), but budding them off when they call for technological and market exploration best performed by a small, dedicated team. The management demands of this sort of process are formidable—and quite different from those associated with managing a division or traditional functional organization.

Management Difficulties Encountered in Global Cellular Clusters

We have been looking at the positive features of the cellular structure, in terms of adaptability, initiative, and responsiveness. But there are costs to be set against these. Teece (1998: 149) captures the essential difference when he makes the point that the "managerial functions in these inter-organizational networks are quite different from the authority relationship which commonly exists in hierarchies. Managers have to perform boundary-spanning roles, and learn to manage in circumstances that involve mutual dependency." The most obvious issue is difficulty of *coordination* between such highly devolved and autonomous entities. But surprisingly, provided sufficient resources and attention is paid to the mechanism of coordination, then coordination is not the insuperable problem that it might appear to be. The fact is that managers who are given as much discretion as they are in Acer actually welcome the imposition of coordinating devices like standards and rules. They provide guidelines applying to all, and the managers can see their clear benefits overall.

The real costs of the cellular system emerge in the sometimes unfettered rivalry it can engender and in the difficulties involved in setting new strategic directions for the group as a whole which might cut against the interests of an individual BU. These are issues with which Acer has had to constantly struggle. Competitive product development within the global cluster is one such issue.

Competitive Product Development

It is a fact of life within the cellular structure (no matter who is implementing it) that cells or business units will bump up against each other in the course of developing products and extending their business.

The divisionalized firm usually has a functional division called "new product development," and so ideas for new products tend to be channeled through this division. The case of Acer is very different. In Acer's cellular structure, all the cells are on the lookout for ways in which they might extend their business through developing, or extending, aspects of their product lines or services. This constant search by business units is one of the ways in which Acer's cellular structure can lend superior innovative performance over the traditional divisional structure. All of Acer's cells might simultaneously be developing new products, whereas in the divisional structure most of the operations pass over perceived opportunities in silence (because it is not their functional responsibility to develop new things) and those who do have the responsibility, both lack the market and production experience to be really effective and can handle only a few parallel product development projects at a time.

The drawback is that some of these development efforts might conflict with each other. Indeed, this is at times certainly going to be the case, given the close relations between the BUs and the rapid spawning of new products in the IT industry which span traditional areas, such as multimedia. This is precisely what happened to Acer in the case of CD-ROMs.

The Case of CD-ROMs   At the beginning of the 1990s, CD-ROMs were becoming essential components not just in desktop PCs but increasingly in mobile (laptop) PCs as well. Yet Acer had no internal capability in the manufacture of CD-ROMs. Accordingly, Acer Peripherals initiated a project (based on technology transferred from the European multinational, Philips) to develop the new products. But at the same time, the Information Products business unit of Acer Inc. separately and independently initiated its own project, utilizing Japanese technology. Both BUs within Acer could claim a legitimate right to extend their product ranges in this way, and both saw it as being in their own interests, as business cells within Acer, to have their own CD-ROM product.

For Acer Peripherals, the CD-ROM was seen as a core component for which there would be increasing demand both within Acer and from OEM customers outside. For the Informational Products BU, the CD-ROM was seen as a key storage device, not only for the PC but for evolving consumer products as well. The CD-ROM would evolve into the Digital Video Disc (DVD) and then into the DVD player, and the IPB unit wanted to be a world class supplier of this family of electronic storage devices.

Each BU knew about the other BU's product development initiative—and each persevered with its own efforts, believing it to be the better project. Thus, the race was on within Acer to develop the "Acer" CD-ROM system. In a more hierarchical company than Acer, the chief executive might have stepped in and allocated responsibilities, thus nipping this internal product development competition in the bud. This would secure a more formal and "tidy" organizational arrangement—but at the cost of curbing product development zeal—and reinforce the impression that initiatives are not to be taken by business units because they lead to problems later on.

In the Acer case, by contrast, by allowing the twin development efforts to proceed (once they had spontaneously arisen), the organization as a whole could benefit from the internal rivalry between the two groups, as they sought to develop their product faster and with superior features to match the Acer product line-up. This is a kind of "natural" competition that can develop spontaneously within the Acer cellular organizational structure—whereas in other structures, such parallel development efforts need to be artificially created and sustained (e.g., the setting up of parallel competitive product development teams by Japanese and Korean semiconductor firms). It is the strong market-orientation of the BUs, and the fact that they view the world as a business rather than as a division with certain circumscribed responsibilities, that drives this natural competition.

The competitive development could be tolerated by Acer for some time, partly because it gave tangible benefits of accelerated development and market testing, and partly also because in a growing market there was room for two suppliers within the company, both of which were compatible across the Acer range of products. It was actually safer for the marketing BUs to have two sources of supply within the company, than to have to rely on one source as it was ramping up. However, as only one of the products could carry the "Acer" brand, there had to come a point where a decision would have to be taken between the two competing developments. The twin development efforts could be allowed to proceed only so far before some decision had to be made as to which of the products would be branded as the "Acer" product. It would not be healthy for Acer as a whole to have two rival CD-ROM products being actively manufactured and sold as "Acer" products in competition with each other in the open marketplace.

The CD-ROM case turned out to involve Acer senior management in more than a year of agonizing before a decision was reached. This was partly because it was the first such experience in Acer of parallel development efforts, and partly because both camps pursued their projects with such vigor. In market acceptance terms, the API initiative performed much better—both in terms of sales to Acer RBUs and to external customers such as OEMs. But the IPB product also had very good features, and Acer Inc., as the "parent" entity, pressed strongly for recognition of its product offering. In the end, the issue went all the way to the Acer summit, where it was finally resolved in 1997. The decision was that the API product would carry the "Acer" brand. This meant that the IPB product would have to carry a separate brand. In fact, it is now sold under the brand "AOpen," and the group producing it within IPB has its own corporate identity and was indeed spun off as a separate entity in 1998. In the GBU reorganization, AOpen ended up as one of XBUs.

Such a result is probably the inevitable outcome of the process of resolving an internal product development "race." The winning product and the group producing it will take its place within the Acer cellular structure; the losing product and the group producing it will either give up at that point or pursue a separate existence that will probably take it into a new orbit outside the Acer structure, maintaining only tenuous ties to it. This is again a "natural" process in a loosely structured cellular organizational model like Acer's, with its emphasis on dynamic initiatives.

The "Messy" Weblike Character of Acer's Cellular Expansion

Acer's pattern of growth is strikingly lifelike, or "weblike," in its patterns of parallel and redundant activities, all of which taken together lend resilience and robustness to the total business. Whereas in a divisionalized firm, any hint of duplication is ruthlessly eliminated in the name of "efficiency," in Acer it is tolerated in the name of devolution. All that is imposed—but imposed strongly—is a set of guidelines, setting the limits to parallel or duplicative efforts, and since 1998, a set of global standards concerning such matters as IT infrastructure, customer service, brand focus, and logistics. Within these guidelines, Acer managers and their business cells can tolerate ambiguity and "fuzziness." As noted above, this organizational model can only work where managers have a high degree of commitment and confidence that their initiatives, if successful, will be rewarded, while their failures (within reason) will be tolerated. As the scale and pace of change within the entity called "Acer" increases, no other organizational model seems to come close in terms of adaptability and effectiveness.

Acer then maintains "control" over its dispersed operations without resorting to the usual administrative means for doing so, namely, centralized authority and divisional subservience. This has the interesting implication that many of the "global" competitive strategies discussed in the management literature, which call for subsidiaries to make sacrifices on behalf of the organization as a whole (e.g., underselling a global competitor in one market in order to dissuade it from entering another market), thus appear to be beyond the reach of Acer, with its global financial accountability and transparency. Whether this is indeed the case (or whether, alternatively, many of these strategies are in practice less important than they are claimed to be) is a matter of the greatest interest.

Concluding Remarks

Cellularity is a powerful organizational innovation. It leads firms to internationalize not only with a single, highly centralized corporate focus, but also in the direction of a cluster of firms, each of which can aspire to be global. Acer has demonstrated how effectively this organizational design can work to support a strategy of rapid internationalization. Li & Fung likewise shows that it is able to put such an organizational architecture to good use in promoting entrepreneurship and customer focus.

At the global level, cellularity provides a powerful means for firms to resolve, at source, the perennial problem of encouraging (or suppressing) subsidiary initiative. The conventional multinational structure, with its assumptions of hierarchical control by a headquarters over subsidiaries, proves to be less and less serviceable as firms expand their global reach and formulate strategies that call for local initiative and responsiveness. The conventional organizational architecture has no answer to this problem, and so incumbent MNEs have been searching for new forms, such as differentiated networks, worldwide matrix structures, and various kinds of "heterarchies." But the cellular solution is at once more radical (in the sense of getting at the root of the problem) and more effective. It is more radical because it establishes "subsidiaries" as full-fledged businesses that are expected to take initiatives to enhance their growth and profitability, within an overall business strategy that holds the group together. It is more effective because it starts with an assumption of local autonomy and builds coordination through its global organizational processes, rather than starting with an assumption of uniformity and trying to build diversity as an afterthought.

As a global organizational architecture, cellularity offers firms which can master it decided advantages in a multiply connected world economy. The cellular organization's network character, with business cells contracting directly with each other and with external customers, matches or complements exactly the netlike character of the emergent global economy. Cellular organizations can "grow" within the medium of this emergent economy, creating new cells and new connections, in a weblike pattern that replicates the most resilient and adaptable features of life forms.

While the cellular form offers considerable advantages in terms of flexibility and initiative, it calls for great organizational and management ingenuity in holding it all together—achieving global integration without sacrifice of local responsiveness. This is the management challenge for the global cellular firm—to produce managers who are comfortable with diversity, with a degree of ambiguity, and with the initiatives of their colleagues. It has been Stan Shih's greatest challenge within Acer to inculcate such a management style.

Notes

1. See Miles, Snow, Mathews, et al. (1997) for an exposition of this concept, and Mathews and Snow (1998) for an interview with Stan Shih that elaborates on the client-server metaphor.

2. Interview with JM and C. Snow, Taipei, October 31 and November 1, 1996, See Matthews and Snow (1998).

3. See Magretta (1998) for further insights into the thinking of Victor Fung.

4. See Mathews (1996a) for an elaboration of these terms.

5. See Miles, Snow, Mathews et al. (1997) for further elaboration.

6. The Chinese expression is "chun-long-wu-soh." Its original Chinese connotation was somewhat negative, implying an unorganized group of dragons with no leader, but Stan Shih has turned this into a positive, giving a graphic illustration of how the absence of an authoritarian leader can be a source of efficiency.

7. Miles and Snow (1995) used the phrase "spherical structure" to convey the idea that the organization could rotate its operating parts to meet any customer's requirements. Fairtlough (1995) referred to the small but powerful building blocks of a larger organization as "creative compartments." Mathews (1996a) used the phrase "holonic organization" after the terminology introduced by Arthur Koestler (*The Ghost in the Machine*, London: Hutchinson, 1967). A "holon" is an organizational entity that is both a part (-*on*) and a whole (*hol-*). Thus, it captures the idea that in a cellular organization, the cells are "wholes" in that they have self-acting capability, but they are also "parts" because they cannot act completely without obtaining resources from the rest of the organization.

8. According to Arie de Geus (1997), *living companies* have traits and abilities that allow them to renew themselves over many generations.

9. See Ostroff (1999) and Halal (1994) for similar notions of "horizontal" or "network" organizational architectures. Martinez and Jarillo (1991) discuss the coordination demands of such global approach. Yeung et al. (1999) discuss many of the organizational learning issues that need to be faced in new organizational architectures. Snow, Mathews and Miles (1999) discuss the organizational architecture of the cellular firm.

10. On ABB and its globally connected character, see Barham and Heimer (1998), as well as Belanger, Berggren, Bjorkman, and Kohler (1999). For a description of the AT&T system, see Warwick (1998).

11. See Miles, Snow, Mathews, et al. (1997).

12. See Birkinshaw (1997), Birkinshaw, Hood, and Jonsson (1998), or Forsgren, Pedersen, and Foss (1999) for further empirical work on this theme, and Pearce (1999) for the link between creative subsidiaries and technological development. Birkinshaw and Hood (1998b), Holm and Pedersen (2000), and Kristensen and Zeitlin (2001) provide a theoretical account of the factors that drive subsidiary initiative and how it is frequently blocked in conventional MNE structures. Birkinshaw and Hood (eds) (1998a) brings together some of the current work on this topic.

13. See Kanter (1985), p. 101.

14. This point finds corroboration in discussions of subsidiary initiative within a "network" model of the MNE. See Holm, Johanson, and Thilenius (1995) for a discussion in the context of differential acquisition of competences by subsidiaries.

15. Dr. Wu was former head of ITRI's CCL Laboratory; he brought with him a group of over 20 experienced engineers who now form the core of Netxus.

16. Another earlier case was that of Acer Laboratories Inc. (ALI), founded in 1986.

17. The general case, of a firm finding a place for itself in a tightly structured network, is analyzed by Kinch (1992).

18. See the description by Sakai and Sekiyama (1985) which remains to date the only account of the process known to me.

19. On Thermo Electron, see Slywotzky and Morrison (1997).

20. For a review of the evidence, which is by now substantial, see Johnson, Brown and Johnson (1994) and Miles and Woolridge (1999). Sadtler, Campbell, and Koch (1997) provide an interesting book-length survey of the issues—but in a typically Eurocentric fashion, without apparently being aware of the use of spinoff strategies in East Asia.

21. See Aron (1991) for such an economic model, where corporate spin-offs are a feature of incentive contracts for product managers in diversified firms.

22. The financing was initially 100 percent from API, until the ITRI investment arm put up a 10 percent equity contribution to help the venture get started. Then in 1997, ADT, along with other Taiwanese firms, engaged in serious discussions with Japanese firms to transfer the key TFT–LCD technology needed to produce flat panel screens for Notebook PCs. By March 1998, ADT had reached agreement with IBM (Japan) for the transfer of the required technology.

23. Capital of U.S.$380 million was raised from API itself (48%) and from

Acer Inc. (8%), together with 8 percent from Taiwan investment agencies such as the China Development Corporation (which also invested earlier in the TI-Acer DRAM joint venture).

24. This credit facility amounted to U.S.$220 million, from a syndicate of 20 banks, giving total up-front investment (debt plus equity) of U.S.$600 million. This was beyond the level of "start-up" finance and indicated how far and how fast API's involvement in display technology had moved.

25. The author visited this facility in 1995 during a visit to Penang.

26. One of Stan Shih's overriding objectives has always been to keep debt levels for the Acer Group as low as possible, consistent with desired global expansion. It is of interest that Acer in its first years in Taiwan got by without any bank loans at all, because of its ability to raise capital from its own employees who became shareholders.

Part III

COMPREHENDING THE IMPACT OF GLOBAL LATECOMERS

7

AN ALTERNATIVE OLI FRAMEWORK FOR LATECOMERS

The principal hypothesis on which the eclectic paradigm of international production is based is that the level and structure of a firm's foreign value-adding activities will depend on four conditions being satisfied. These are:

(1) The extent to which it possesses sustainable ownership-specific (O) advantages vis-à-vis firms of other nationalities in the particular markets it serves or is contemplating serving. . . .

(2) . . . the extent to which the enterprise perceives it to be in its best interest to add value to its O advantages rather than to sell them, or their right of use, to foreign firms. These advantages are called market internalization (I) advantages. . . .

(3) . . . the extent to which the global interests of the enterprise are served by creating, or utilizing, its O advantages in a foreign location (L) . . .

(4) Given the configuration of the ownership, location and internalization (OLI) advantages facing a particular firm, the extent to which a firm believes that foreign production is consistent with its long-term management strategy.

> John Dunning,
> *Multinational Enterprises*
> *and the Global Economy*

The international business literature has by now developed a sophisticated conceptual and theoretical framework that seeks to account for the phenomena of multinational corporations, foreign direct investment, foreign production, and other firm activities such as R&D, and the organizational and management issues associated with the growth and administration of such enterprises.[1] The question is: How well does it cope with, or shed light on, the phenomena of the new "species" of multinational, and in particular with a "Dragon Multinational" like Acer? There are two aspects of this issue to be explored: the extent to which we can make sense of the activities of the newcomers and latecomers in terms of the established frameworks, and the extent to which the experiences of the newcomers and latecomers suggest new avenues of conceptualization and new frameworks that might have wider applicability.

Existing frameworks that discuss internationalization—the definitions of the term, the impulse to internationalization, the process itself, as well as the sources of advantage of being international—were all formulated two or three decades ago, at a time when internationalization was seen as a major barrier and available only to the largest and strongest firms. To cross foreign borders was to enter dangerous territory, where the risks and costs of doing business multiplied, and the conceptual frameworks reflected this. But the new developments registered over the past decade, and in particular the new "zoology" of the international economy, call for a reconsideration and reformulation of many of these existing frameworks along the lines of some of the new directions discerned in the literature.[2]

The world has been discussing the concept of the multinational corporation for 40 years.[3] During the 1980s, the concept of the "transnational" corporation or enterprise (TNC or TNE) emerged, as a description of a firm which was overcoming traditional barriers to global integration and global outlook.[4] In the early 1990s, it was still the case that most MNEs were in fact national firms with international operations.[5] By the latter years of the decade, the transition from MNEs to TNEs was underway—as described by Drucker (1997). In his words, the "transformation into transnational companies has begun, and it is moving fast. The products or services may be the same, but the structure is fundamentally different. In a transnational company there is only one economic unit, the world. Selling, servicing, public relations, and legal affairs are local. But parts, machines, planning, research, finance, marketing, pricing, and management are conducted in contemplation of the world market."[6] To this one might add that it is not just structure but strategy and outlook as well. It is the transnational that is finally realizing Perlmutter's original concept of the "geocentric" management outlook.

The argument of this book has been that it is the outsiders from the Periphery—the latecomers as well as the newcomers—which have been setting the pace in this world-historic transformation. They have been playing the role of "outriders," experimenting with new strategic and organizational approaches to globalizing their operations. Some of these have worked very well, as described in the previous chapters; some have been complete failures. This is no more than to be expected as the world economy evolves to new forms. The evolutionary process throws up variations which are then subject to the ruthless selection pressures of the market—in this case, the global economy. It is the integrating tendencies within this emergent global economy that have created openings for the newcomers and latecomers; they would otherwise have had to struggle much harder to establish themselves against incumbent hostility and opposition.

In this chapter, the aim is to set the experiences of the newcomers and latecomers in the general context of the prevailing theories of the multinational enterprise (MNE): What motivates it, and what drives it to seek and sustain global coverage? Our task is to review the story of internationalization, however briefly, to build a picture of the forces that have driven firms to run the risks and endure the costs of globalizing their operations. It is out of this experience that theoretical accounts of the advantages of global firms have emerged. To what extent then do these accounts help us to understand the strategies and organizational gambits of latecomers and newcomers? In complementary fashion, how do the experiences of the latecomers and newcomers, in achieving global scale and global concentration so completely and rapidly, help us to extend or deepen the theoretical frameworks used? The goal is to fashion an account of incumbent advantage and latecomer and newcomer strategy in terms of the resources they own or the resources they seek to access—a resource-based view of internationalization.

Internationalization: Historical Evidence

Firms internationalized from the major industrialized countries in waves, depending on the historical circumstances.[7] Motives differed according to the period and country of origin of the major international firms of the twentieth century. European investment abroad in the late nineteenth and early twentieth centuries was frequently driven by the search for raw materials, and colonial or ex-colonial possessions were the obvious locations for such investment.[8] U.S. industrial firms like Ford, General Motors, and General Electric, by contrast, were investing in production facilities in European markets prior to the First World War, and then in a wave of foreign direct investment (FDI) that followed the conclusion of the war.[9] This investment in productive activities through subsidiaries, that is, through the formation of MNEs, was focused not on the acquisition of raw materials but on the exploitation of superior productive efficiencies in locations close to final markets. Likewise, Japanese investment abroad in the post-World War II period was driven not by the search for raw materials but by the strategic goal of market penetration. Investment in production facilities was dictated partly by considerations of costs and partly by strategic location of production facilities behind tariff barriers.[10]

All this kind of international activity called for advanced organizational and managerial competencies—which were available earlier in the twentieth century only in the largest firms.[11] These firms' appearance could be accounted for economically in terms of explanations having to do with locational advantages, organizational advantages, or internalization advantages—although it took some time for this to be formulated systematically, as described in a moment. But such a framework could not make much sense of other kinds of internationalization that preceded our present period of interest. Pioneers of latecomer development could be found, for example, in Sweden and the Scandinavian countries, which were late industrial developers relative to the rest of Europe. Lacking any colonial possessions, Sweden, for example, made extraordinary efforts in the late nineteenth and early twentieth centuries to develop international firms with global reach—and was very successful in doing so—as names like L.M. Ericsson, Sandvik, Alfa Laval, or SKF testify.[12]

Some European firms tried to internationalize too fast and as a consequence overreached themselves. Take Olivetti as an example. This was a relative latecomer in the European computer industry in the 1980s. In order to accelerate its catch-up, Olivetti went so far as to enter into two world-encompassing joint ventures in the mid-1980s, with AT&T (giving Olivetti instant access to the entire U.S. market) and with Toshiba (likewise giving Olivetti instant access to the closed Japanese market). However, Olivetti had to pay dearly for these joint ventures, giving up a substantial proportion of its equity, and in effect losing control of its own destiny. The company went into a steep decline in the 1990s. So this was a case of "overrapid" international coverage.

Other European countries with small domestic markets developed (and actively promoted) foreign direct investment by MNEs as a deliberate competitive strategy. Franko (1976) argued that this strategy was designed to compensate for their small domestic markets; spreading their activities overseas provided a means of spreading risks and accessing greater opportunities.[13] It was this latter point that most nearly anticipated the range of factors that can be seen to drive accelerated internationalization by latecomers and newcomers during the 1990s and into the twenty-first century.

Such a line of argument, however, remained marginalized, while international productive activity and foreign investment was discussed in terms of MNEs exploiting their superior assets and capabilities (what we would now call their "resources") in foreign markets. How then have the motives for foreign operations been theorized in the economics and strategic management literatures?

Theory of the International Firm—Improbable Beginnings

It was a struggle to achieve any kind of theory of the MNE at all. Traditional economic theory of foreign trade and foreign direct investment had no role for international firms to play. Movements of goods and of capital had traditionally been explained in terms of responses to changes in price signals, such as interest rates and exchange rates. Countries traded according to their comparative advantages. Firms as such played no part in the theoretical treatments of the international economy. It was only in the 1960s that scholars, such as Stephen Hymer and Charles Kindleberger at MIT, Edith Penrose at SOAS in London, and Raymond Vernon at Harvard, began to put together novel concepts of international economic expansion that depended on the part played by international firms themselves. They were able to demonstrate that postwar FDI differed from prewar portfolio investment, in that *it was firms themselves* which transferred attributes of ownership and control across borders, as well as the capital and goods measured by economics.[14]

Stephen Hymer pioneered the new approach in his 1960 Ph.D. thesis.[15] Hymer introduced concepts from industrial organization theory into trade theory to argue a case for the international firm being able to hold its own against domestic competitors in each of its host markets. Domestic competitors would be expected to have superior local market information, and so the international firm must be able to rely on its internal advantages, such as technology and marketing, to overcome these disadvantages and achieve competitive superiority. Indeed, Hymer was concerned that the multinational enterprise (MNE) would generate such advantages through these means that it would create barriers to entry for domestic firms in their own markets (i.e., in the MNE's host markets). He saw his work as creating a counterpart in the international dimension to the work of Bain (1956) in the domestic setting, where incumbents were seen as pooling their assets and capabilities to keep out competitors. As Hymer put it, Bain was "interested in the advantages which established firms have relative to new firms insofar as these advantages determine profits. We are interested in the advantages possessed by firms of one country relative to firms of another country insofar as these determine the nationality of the firm conducting a certain enterprise. That is, we are interested in the barriers to entry, not as they apply to new firms, but as they apply to firms of a different nationality" (1976: 42–43).

In delineating the advantages that might, in principle, be enjoyed by the MNE over its domestic rivals, Hymer opened the way to developing a theory of the multinational based on market imperfections and the capacity of firms to extend their advantages through their own internal organizational procedures. As Hymer himself put it, "Firms are by no means equal in their ability to operate in an industry. Certain firms have considerable advantages in particular activities. The possession of these advantages may cause them to have extensive international operations of one type or another. . . . There are as many kinds of advantages as there are functions in making and selling a product" (1976: 41).

Hymer enumerated these advantages as being of three kinds. The MNE's advantage might lie in its ability to acquire factors of production at a lower cost than other firms (e.g., locating labor-intensive production activities in low-cost areas or purchasing raw materials where they are cheapest). The MNE's advantage might lie in its being able to deploy advanced production technology and thus achieve efficiencies superior to those available to domestic competitors. Or lastly, the MNE's advantage might lie in its having better distribution facilities or a more differentiated product (e.g., taking advantage of global logistics or purchasing arrangements, and utilizing a common product platform to generate variations adapted to separate domestic markets). These were advantages quite different from those traced to economies of scale or scope, which later writers came to focus on. They were advantages that stemmed directly from the very reasons that provoked firms to expand internationally in the first place.

Kindleberger generalized these insights and identified four kinds of cases of market imperfections which could account for the activities of MNEs. These were imperfections in goods markets (leading firms to engage in arbitrage between countries, buying cheap to sell dear); factor imperfections (allowing firms to locate labor-intensive operations in low-wage countries); scale economies (enabling firms to pool activities across borders); and government-imposed disruptions (leading firms to locate production activities, for example, behind tariff barriers without any compensating efficiency gains).[16]

By contrast, Vernon (1966; 1971) linked firms' international expansion to technological (product life cycle) factors. Based on empirical observations that many U.S. firms were outsourcing labor-intensive parts of their production systems to low-wage countries, particularly in Asia, Vernon postulated a general model to explain this behavior, based on the phases in a product life cycle. He was not concerned to account for such firms' advantages over domestic competitors, as they frequently were not active in host markets at all other than as producers. But he was concerned to account for how such internationalized firms might draw advantages over firms that were not similarly international in their logistics and operations.

These approaches to developing an account of the advantages that might be enjoyed by the MNE over noninternational competitors (at home or abroad) were in keeping with the dominant experience of MNEs, which were expanding abroad from their strong domestic bases, either in the United States or Europe or, increasingly in the 1960s and 1970s, from Japan as well. They were seen to be taking with them abroad the advantages and assets built up at home.[17]

The next step was to link these arguments for advantage, based on market imperfections with the ideas of transaction cost economics, to create an integrated theory of the MNE based on its capacity to "internalize" activities that would otherwise be conducted externally through market relations. This was the step taken by the British economists Peter Buckley and Mark Casson (1976).[18] Thus, the international firm was accommodated with the view of the firm as an "island of organization" in a sea of market-mediated transactions, where the firm's international boundaries would be determined by the point where transactions costs of maintaining processes internal to the firm equaled the costs of outsourcing those activities to external suppliers. In this view, they brought the international firm within the ambit of the transaction cost economics (TCE) reasoning pioneered by Coase and generalized by Williamson.

In the case of international expansion, the transactions costs involved in operating in foreign markets multiplied, according to Buckley and Casson, while the opportunities for gaining advantage from internalizing activities multiplied as well. Firms could take advantage of differences in regulations and taxation requirements, for example, to engage in favorable transfer pricing arrangements that would minimize taxation liabilities. This was the "ugly face" of the MNE that gave rise to so much controversy in the 1960s and 1970s.[19]

By the end of the 1970s, this predominantly Anglo-American approach to theorizing the MNE was consolidated in the "internalization" view, cast by John Dunning (of Reading University, like Buckley and Casson) in terms of an "eclectic" theory of multinational advantage. Dunning brought together the advantages that international firms drew from extending their operations abroad, in terms of three characteristics or sources. First, there was the potential advantage derived from extending their proprietary assets abroad, such as brands or proprietary technologies, bringing greater fire power to bear on their domestic competitors in host markets (the "ownership" advantage). Second, there was the potential advantage of being able to integrate activities across sectors of the world with very different factor costs and resource costs (the "location" advantage). Finally, there were the potential advantages derived from building economies of scale and scope through internalizing activities spread across borders that would otherwise be dispersed between numerous firms (the "internalization" advantage).

The early multinational enterprises were forced to operate within a regime of relatively closed markets and found themselves constrained to produce miniversions of themselves as more or less self-contained national subsidiaries, each conceived as a means of implementing head office thinking and decisions in the host country. In such an environment it was inevitable that early theorizing concerning the sources of multinational advantage should focus on the firm's ability to exploit domestic assets abroad.

The eclectic "ownership-location-internalization" (OLI) theory of multinational activity, which was built on the solid foundations established by Hymer and Kindleberger, became the dominant view in the 1970s and 1980s. Few firms could, in practice, aspire to reaping all these potential advantages, given the formidable organizational demands they made on a firm—but why should this small matter bother the economists? In the 1980s, the whole question of the MNE's advantages was in a sense overtaken by the more general theory of competitive advantage—as formulated by Porter and others—but this latter theory does not engage with the specifics of international competition and global strategy. The OLI paradigm lives on as the dominant, indeed the only, theoretical account of the existence of MNEs as such and the sources of their advantages over domestic rivals.[20]

Motives for International Expansion

While the OLI framework sought to account for the sources of advantage of MNEs over domestically focused firms, another line of inquiry sought to generalize the motives that drove firms to expand internationally. Again, based on the experiences of MNEs up to and including the 1960s, four broad categories of motive emerged, namely that firms were resource seekers, market seekers, efficiency seekers, or strategic asset (or strategic capability) seekers.[21]

Resource seekers referred to firms expanding abroad in order to capture sources of supply of raw materials (typically in former colonial possessions) or to capture sources of low-cost labor. It was the latter factor that drove so many U.S. and later European and Japanese MNEs to East Asian production locations in the 1960s and 1970s, in a pattern captured by Vernon in the famous product cycle theory (Vernon 1966). *Market seekers* were interested in expanding the range of markets for goods which had proved to be competitive either at home or in earlier phases of international expansion. *Efficiency seekers* were driven by the steady internationalization of markets and increasing possibilities of capturing economies of scale in serving these markets; their motives were captured by Levitt so well in his 1983 article. *Strategic asset or capability seekers* were firms responding to global strategic imperatives, often forced on them by globalizing competitors.

It is this latter motive that brings the story of multinational expansion from the 1960s and 1970s into the global-oriented 1980s and 1990s. The literature has recognized—slowly—what managers in MNEs quietly became aware of in these years. It was not enough for firms to seek involvement in foreign markets. The winners were the ones that adopted a global perspective on their operations and restructured to achieve synergies between related activities. They made further moves—such as expansion into another market or entering into another global alliance—according to how they perceived the global imperatives. They made these calculations not in terms of a decision to enter one new market, but in terms of an integrated global framework and how this new activity would fit within such a framework.

Such a global perspective represents a fundamental departure in outlook, as foreseen by such pioneer scholars as Perlmutter (1969), Levitt (1983), and many others. It is captured in various phrases—from the multinational to the "global" corporation; or to the "heterarchical" corporation; or to the "transnational corporation."[22] In each case, what is at issue is the capacity of the firm to develop and act on a *global strategy*—a strategy that takes into effect what competitors are doing in any part of the world, and what possibilities exist for leveraging advantage from collaborators anywhere in the world. Such a global strategy works, of course, only in an industry that has global characteristics. As Porter (1986a: 18) put it, a global industry is not merely a collection of domestic industries "but a series of linked domestic industries in which the rivals compete against each other on a truly worldwide basis." Leading MNEs like ABB, AT&T, and HP all responded to these considerations and developed, and implemented, global strategies in global industries in the 1980s and 1990s.[23]

Now this is where the latecomers and newcomers enter the picture. They are of interest precisely because *they skip all the previous phases of motives for internationalization* and *they bypass all the previous phases of sources of multinational advantage*. There is little point in trying to read the motives of latecomers like Acer or Ispat or Li & Fung in terms of seeking access to raw materials or cheap labor. Likewise, there is little insight to be gained by looking at these companies in terms of OLI factors. Certainly, they pursue organizational advantages in multiple locations and internalize much of their technology and knowledge flow. But this is to say no more than the obvious. It doesn't really capture what is distinctive about these latecomer MNEs, and what makes them different from incumbents—and successful.

The same considerations apply to the newcomers like Fresenius, CMS Energy, or Gemplus. Their international expansion does not seem to be guided by the same kinds of considerations as motivated the larger and earlier MNEs, nor do their sources of advantage as they acquire global reach. They seem to be motivated much more by a sense of what it takes to be a global player in a global industry—or a global industrial niche—and then go about the task of becoming such a player in determined fashion.

It is clear that the OLI theory is based squarely on the experiences of large, successful international firms and continues to apply to these cases. It simply assumes that if the firm wants to move internationally, it does so: it has the resources and the capabilities at hand. The actual process of the firm's internationalization—the steps it goes through, the learning involved, and the strategic frameworks adopted—are of little interest to the theory. Thus, it has little dynamic content, or dynamic content of an indirect kind, and thus little explanatory purchase on novel ways of implementing an internationalization approach. There is little room in this theoretical account for the firm that moves internationally in order to acquire resources or to enhance its resources and capabilities.[24] There is little room in the theory for the firm's expansion internationally being seen as a way of building its competitive position—in a way that would not be possible in the firm's domestic market, which may be too small, or too undeveloped, to serve such a purpose.

It is striking that this is exactly what the newcomers and latecomers in the global economy have been doing. The most salient feature of their starting position is the *absence* of vast resources and capabilities. Firms like Acer, Ispat, Cemex, Li & Fung, or the Hong Leong Group expand abroad, or rather may be said to become *integrated* in the world economy, in order to tap into resources and markets that would otherwise be unavailable—such as through OEM contracting, or industrial supply contracts, or through involvement in international alliances. Global reach brings with it the fundamental advantage that it enables firms to deal with other global players, as both customers and suppliers. Global reach enables firms to insert themselves in global supply chains or value chains. They are motivated to integrate themselves in these international activities for reasons that have little to do with those discussed in the OLI "eclectic" paradigm.

The international business literature provides many more such examples of latecomer multinationals going abroad in search of new resources in the form of connections, partnerships, alliances, as well as customers and suppliers. Chinese firms expanding abroad from Taiwan, Hong Kong, and Singapore certainly fit such a pattern. For example, Yeung (1999a) surveyed firms internationalizing from Hong Kong and found a pattern of "horizontal integration" to be important, while the same scholar surveying firms expanding abroad from Singapore found that their most common motive was "market reach"—meaning their desire to encompass the leading markets and the assets within them in their field.[25] Likewise, Chen and Chen (1998a; b) found that Taiwanese firms expanding abroad did so for the pursuit of assets available only in advanced foreign countries.

We may summarize our discussion to this point as follows. Latecomers are attracted to global industries and seek to become global players. They utilize a range of strategic and organizational innovations to make up for their initial disadvantages. Their motivation is to have access to the greater opportunities and potential advantages that come from being a global rather than a domestic or slightly internationalized player. Latecomers have the outstanding advantage that they possess a global perspective (a "geocentric" outlook) from the outset; they do not have to evolve such a perspective slowly and painfully as they encounter global competitive forces. Instead, they shape their expansion (which may be incremental) in accordance with global competitive and collaborative considerations. Latecomers overcome their lack of initial resources by seeking to leverage resources externally, from international partners, through various institutional forms of linkage. They are "resource seekers"—where "resources" refer to strategic assets and capabilities needed by the firm to enhance its competitive position. The third point clarifies how it is possible to make a clear distinction between incumbent global strategies and those of newcomers and latecomers. It involves shifting to the modern "resource-based view" (RBV) of competitive and collaborative advantage. For some reason the RBV of the firm has not been extended in a significant way by its protagonists to cover the international firm.[26]

Ownership, Locational, and Internalization Advantages from a Resource-Based Perspective

As elaborated by Dunning, the OLI account of the competitive advantages of international firms, vis-à-vis their domestic competitors in host countries (rather than with respect to each other, which is the topic of global strategy), revolved around three quite different sources of advantage: ownership, location, and internalization.[27]

Ownership advantages were originally conceived as being of three kinds. First, there are those that stem from "the exclusive privileged possession of or access to particular income generating assets" (Dunning 1988: 2). These are the MNE's core resources, its assets and capabilities, in the language of the RBV. Second, there are the ownership advantages enjoyed by a branch plant compared with a newly established firm, in terms of the resources and capabilities transferred along with the plant. Third, there are those advantages that are "a consequence of geographical diversification or multinationality *per se*" (Dunning 1988: 2). In all cases, the MNE has resources, owned or accessible, that are greater than the resources available to domestic competitors and that account for the advantages enjoyed by the MNE. Dunning also distinguished between ownership advantages that drew on assets and those that drew on transactions. The former are the resources that are held to be superior; the latter stem from an international network that can lower transaction costs—provided of course the firm has the organizational capacity to affect such savings.

Second, these ownership advantages had to be transferable through institutional pathways internal to the organization, that is, they had to be advantages of internalization. The point of comparison here is that the resources underpinning international advantage had to be capable of internal transfer rather than made available through licensing from a third party, or through use of foreign-based enterprises, or through some other source external to the firm. This is an important point, for it clearly delimits the OLI theory that applies to incumbents from any potential application to newcomers and latecomers. As we have seen, newcomers and latecomers frequently expand abroad and derive advantages from their expansion, through linkage and leverage arrangements that explicitly depart from this internalization principle. Insofar as it applies at all to international firms (and Dunning was insisting up to the end of the 1980s, at least, that it was a key component of the OLI eclectic framework), it clearly applies only to firms not looking to expand by linkage and leverage with incumbents. From the RBV perspective, the internalization principle is a statement that MNEs derive advantages only from resources which are internal to the firm and which can be transferred through internal channels.

The third strand of the OLI "eclectic" paradigm is concerned with locational advantages, that is, advantages which accrue to the MNE by virtue of its ability to choose where to engage in production activities and to derive maximum advantages from this choice. Thus, the international production system can be crafted to take advantage of low-labor costs in some areas or high availability of skilled staff in other areas. It is this capacity that enables MNEs to evade various forms of protective barriers by locating production activities behind tariff barriers, for example. Again the link with the modern RBV is readily apparent: the MNE derives advantages from the resource of locational choice. This is a resource that domestic firms too are able to exploit, but only to a limited degree within their own country (choosing to locate near a city or close to a source of raw materials); it is a much more powerful strategic resource when deployed across the world.

Now the manifold changes in the international economy in the 1990s have led many international business (IB) theorists to develop different emphases within this framework. Over the course of the past decade, as the pace of globalization has quickened, the source of multinational advantage has been discerned to arise not so much through the exploitation of existing advantages, as in the tapping of resources that would otherwise not be available to a firm competing solely at home and seeking to sustain an international presence through exports.[28] As the global economy becomes more and more closely interlinked, so scholars have noted that MNEs have been seeking hitherto untapped advantages through the creation of global value chains, where production, logistics, product development, and other functions are distributed around the world in terms of considerations of cost (e.g., labor-intensive operations being located in low-cost countries) or considerations of knowledge and resources (e.g., locating R&D operations in knowledge-intensive regions).[29] The case of Japanese firms investing heavily in U.S.-based R&D facilities, particularly in the pharmaceutical industry, is a case in point.[30] Likewise, even well-established MNEs like Swedish firms, which have been internationally active for over a century, now seem to be locating their highest value-adding activities abroad, in the search for global advantages that are divorced from host country considerations.[31]

Proponents of the OLI framework have sought in the 1990s to enlarge the scope of the framework in various directions, to accommodate striking new developments such as the rise of international mergers and acquisitions, the rise of international joint ventures and collaborative alliances, and not least the rise of fast-expanding "newcomers" that appear to lack all the trappings traditionally associated with the MNE.[32] These are welcome extensions, but they do not change the fundamental fact that the OLI framework is one that sees the MNE as deriving advantages from overcoming market failures through use and transfer abroad of its superior resources.

From the OLI perspective, modified or otherwise, the MNE exists because of its possession of superior resources, that is, superior to those available to a domestic competitor. It is in this sense a strong statement of the RBV as applied to incumbents and the sustaining of existing advantages. It makes it as clear as possible that the prevailing view applies only to incumbent MNEs which have created their international empires and are seeking to derive maximum advantage from them. Through the internalization principle, OLI rules out of consideration cases where a firm can derive advantages by expanding abroad in order to access a resource that is otherwise not available. This is, as I argue here, the case that fits many of the latecomers and newcomers. To make sense of their internationalization, we clearly have to go *beyond* the framework established by OLI.[33]

An Alternative OLI* Framework that Fits the Experiences of Latecomers

The considerations that apply to international expansion in the pursuit of resources (and customers), not otherwise available, are quite different from those that apply to expansion which is designed to exploit existing resources. Three such considerations immediately present themselves. These are that the firms' international expansion is (1) outward-oriented (rather than fashioned by its internal resources); (2) dependent on linkage with and leverage from incumbents; and (3) based on high levels of organizational integration if it is to succeed. This then constitutes our alternative "OLI" framework that applies not to incumbent MNEs but to many latecomers and newcomers.

O: Outward-Oriented

The critical starting point for the latecomer and newcomer is that it is focused not on its own advantages, but on the advantages which can be acquired externally, that is, on resources that can be accessed outside of itself. Thus, a global orientation becomes a source of advantage—since the opportunities through which it can expand are likely to be found in the global market rather than in its domestic environment. The global outlook, which is an unnecessary luxury for the incumbent, is a necessity for the latecomer and newcomer.[34]

An outward orientation carries higher risks and uncertainties than a more conservative inward focus. The firm seeking to acquire resources and complementary assets in foreign markets has to overcome problems of market intelligence and uncertainty regarding the quality of knowledge potentially available. Small- and medium-sized firms in particular have to find ways to offset these risks or face bankruptcy if anything goes wrong. Thus, joint ventures and other forms of collaborative partnership, as a means of gaining entry to the foreign market, figure overwhelmingly as options of choice and indeed are observed as options of choice in practice.

As long ago as the 1970s, Lou Wells made precisely the same point in his discussion of multinationals from the Third World: they tend to expand abroad through partnerships and joint ventures rather than through wholly owned subsidiaries.[35] Partnerships and joint ventures are seen by the incumbent, generally speaking, as sources of leakage of proprietary assets and knowledge. They are seen by the aspiring MNE, by contrast, as principal vehicles for reducing the risks involved in international expansion.[36]

L: Linkage (and leverage)

Secondly, the focus of analysis will be on the ways that links can be established with incumbents or partners so that resources can be leveraged. The focus will be directed toward the resources themselves and their leverage potential. It will be concerned with how accessible such resources are—with their imitability, or transferability, or substitutability. This kind of analysis contrasts sharply with the conventional approach of the RBV of the firm. In the conventional approach, the object of analysis is the barriers to diffusion, seen from the perspective of the incumbent looking to delay the entry by competitors, that is, looking to sustain incumbent advantages. By contrast, from the perspective of the newcomers and latecomers, the object of analysis is how such barriers may be overcome.

I: Integration

The very fact that the latecomer and newcomer look to expand through various kinds of linkage and leverage arrangements means that it must counterbalance its dispersion with a tight integration of its core operating assets and capabilities. While incumbent MNEs can sometimes pay less than maximum attention to their global integration, deriving advantages as they do from simply having a presence in certain markets, this is a luxury that the latecomer and newcomer cannot afford. Ispat, for example, brings each new steel mill acquisition into its global network and immediately restructures all the supply linkages in light of the new addition.

Acer utilized its RBU-SBU structure of dispersed responsibilities to create a tightly integrated global logistics system, based on the famous "fast food" model. It derived its efficiency from the fact that it devolved responsibilities for placing orders with the RBUs, but required both RBUs and SBUs to coordinate their activities in tight orchestration; otherwise, the system would fail.

The latecomers (and newcomers) address the dilemma of achieving global integration and local responsiveness simultaneously from a different perspective than that informing the incumbent's approach. For the incumbent, it is generally the case that its global integration is built as it expands, but local responsiveness is hard to achieve—it is seen as a "problem" to vary codes and standards that operate globally. The problem for the latecomer and newcomer, by contrast, is generally that it easily accommodates local responsiveness (e.g., through partnership arrangements as in the case of Acer, or closeness to its customers as in the case of Ispat), but it has to make a supreme effort to achieve integration—given its limited resources and its dispersed operations.

The Alternative OLI* Framework and Organizational Learning   The 1990s have seen numerous attempts to move beyond the constraints of the traditional OLI framework toward something that is more amenable to alternative strategic goals and to dynamic, cumulative learning considerations. Kogut and Zander (1993) opened the way toward a quite different account of the internationalization process and of the sources of advantage of the international firm, conceived as an alternative to the conventional OLI framework. They state quite explicitly at the outset that firms "are social communities that specialize in the creation and internal transfer of knowledge. The multinational corporation arises not out of the failure of markets for the buying and selling of knowledge, but out of its superior efficiency as an organizational vehicle by which to transfer this knowledge across borders" (1993: 625). Thus, Kogut and Zander shift the emphasis and focus of analysis of the MNE. They argue that it is the presumed efficiency of market exchange which enforces a view of the MNE as deriving its rationale from the overcoming of market failures. If instead the evidence indicates that MNEs change their transfer practices in accordance with the knowledge characteristics of technologies and markets, then the case can be constructed that links their advantages to their own intrinsic properties as generators and diffusers of knowledge.[37] The alternative OLI framework (OLI*) is entirely consistent with Kogut and Zander's approach. It is consistent because the OLI* framework is concerned with the acquisition and integration of resources of all kinds, particularly knowledge resources. It is consistent at a deeper level because the OLI* framework sees the capacity of the multinational firm to integrate its resources across national borders and divisional boundaries as the critical capability underpinning success.

The alternative OLI* framework is also entirely consistent with the work of scholars who have discussed foreign direct investment by latecomer and newcomer firms as being motivated by "resource access"—not in the sense of access to raw materials, but access to knowledge and market resources. These motives apply to any firm in any country where local resources are seen to be deficient. They can apply to a NIC like Taiwan. As two scholars from Taiwan, Homin Chen and Tain-jy Chen put it, the "resource access" motive can be interpreted as "an attempt to access external resources in order to offset the weaknesses of the investor" (Chen and Chen 1998b: 446). They can apply to a European nation like Italy. As two scholars, Marco Mutinelli and Lucia Piscitello, put it, referring to perceived weaknesses in the Italian national system of innovation, there is a probability "that Italian firms in high-tech industries will resort to cross-border joint ventures and other cooperative agreements to access and/or jointly develop tangible and intangible complementary assets which are not available in the home country" (Mutinelli and Piscitello 1998: 494). They can apply to advanced technology firms expanding from an advanced home base in the United States in the search for new customers (Bloodgood, Sapienza, and Almeida 1996). These are all ways of expressing international expansion as a search for resources that are otherwise not available.

Links with the Network View of the Economy   The alternative OLI* framework offered here also provides the needed link between the characteristics of the newcomers and latecomers and those of the emergent global economy to which they seem so well adapted. The OLI* framework emphasizes the outward orientation of newcomers and latecomers, that is, toward resource access externally rather than through reliance on internal resources. The access is sought through linkage with and leverage from incumbents, who are prepared for their own reasons to enter into such arrangements. (We discussed this feature of the problem in chapter 5 on strategy, where we formulated a "principle of complementarity" between incumbent strategies and those formulated by newcomers and latecomers.) The wider context for the success of the alternative OLI* framework is that the world economy within which these newcomers and latecomers operate is so rich in existing interfirm interconnections. It is thus feasible for firms to formulate an internationalization strategy in terms of "global strategic linkages."[38]

Some reflection reveals that this argument is dependent on two underlying assumptions, namely, that resources are genuinely "available" in the wider global economy, through forming attachments of various kinds to incumbents, and that linkage and leverage arrangements are consistent with networking trends within the wider international sphere. Both assumptions appear to be well founded and supported by the evidence.

Resource mobility has been addressed by many scholars, but notably for the purposes of our present exposition by Dunning himself. In his later work he has singled out features of the emerging global economy which are highly relevant to our argument—such as the increasing mobility of firm-specific resources and the rising frequency of cross-border transactions.[39]

These features may be summarized in the claim that resources are becoming more mobile in an increasingly interconnected world. Internationally active firms are able to attract the custom of other internationally active firms and through this mobility share in resources that are denied firms that retain their exclusively domestic focus. Internationally active firms are those that are able to best make use of the expanding opportunities for inserting themselves in worldwide networks. In this sense, our description of the emergent global economy as a worldwide web of interfirm connections finds its exact counterpart in the emphasis of the alternative OLI* framework on outward orientation and linkage forms of contractual connection.

This approach helps to make sense of the organizational and strategic innovations developed by the newcomers and latecomers. If the incumbent MNE is like an army, moving its massive firepower in formation across borders, then the newcomers and latecomers are like guerrilla forces, darting and weaving and striking like lightning, trying to make up for their lack of substance with speed and surprise. This approach works in wars of national liberation—and the same kind of approach works in the battle to achieve a place in the global economy, albeit from an unpromising start.

Concluding Remarks

The argument developed so far may be summarized as follows. In this study, I have chosen a set of newcomers, latecomers, and niche players as representative of the new kinds of multinational players evident in the emerging global economy. They are a small sample, but a reasonable case can be made that they capture many of the most striking and original features of the new "species" of firm in the changing "zoology" of the international economy. The aim has been to demonstrate how the motives and the patterns of expansion to be found among these firms differ substantially from those identified in the case of incumbents. This can then be used to fashion an argument that it is indeed these characteristics of the newcomers and latecomers that accounts for their sudden appearance and success in the world economy.

The alternative OLI* framework then is a first fruit of our examination of the novel practices and experiences of latecomer MNEs internationalizing from the Periphery. It provides us with a framework that accommodates a wider class of experiences and enables us to highlight the specificity and novelty of the latecomers' strategic choices. Let us pursue this line of thinking and examine the process of internationalization itself, with a view to likewise establishing a framework that is adequate to the novel experiences and practices of the latecomers from the Periphery.

Notes

1. See Dunning (1993a; 1993b) for an encyclopaedic treatment of these issues, and Caves (1996) for a recently updated analysis of multinational phenomena from the perspective of economic analysis. For cases on which much of this theory is based, see for example Bartlett and Ghoshal (1992/1995/2000a) or De La Torre, Doz, and Devinney (2000).

2. See for example Andersen (1993); Cavusgil (1998); or Eriksson, Johanson, Majkgard, and Sharma (1997; 2000).

3. Credit for coining the term "multinational enterprise" in 1960 is given to David Lilienthal, former director of the Tennessee Valley Authority and of the Atomic Energy Commission in the U.S. See Fieldhouse (1986) for a discussion. Hymer (1960), writing in the same year, used the term "international operations of national firms."

4. Use of the term TNC/TNE was popularized by the United Nations Center for Transnational Corporations, and the mammoth 20-volume set of compilations, the United Nations Library on Transnational Corporations (Dunning 1994). It was Bartlett and Ghoshal (1989) who established the usage that sees the TNE as organizationally superior to the MNE, in that it strives for genuine global integration of strategy, organization, and management.

5. The phrase, which comes from Hymer (1960/1976), was used by Hu (1992) in his penetrating critique of MNE processes and organizational structures.

6. See Drucker (1997): 167–168.

7. See the historical treatments offered by contributors to Hertner and Jones (eds) (1986); Jones and Schroeter (eds) (1993); Jones (ed) (1993); Teichova et al. (eds) (1986; 1989) and Wilkins (ed) (1991) as representative examples. Okuchi and Inoue (eds) (1984) provide historical treatments of Japanese firms' internationalization. Jones (1996) provides a comprehensive historical introduction to international business, while Cantwell (1989) reviews the changing forms of MNE expansion in the twentieth century.

8. See Franko (1974a;-b; 1976) for an early representative discussion, and Wilkins (1986a), Hertner (1986), and Jones (1996) for later scholarly contributions. Onida and Viesti (eds) (1988) focus on the specific experience of Italian MNEs, while Jarillo and Martinez (1991) discuss the contrasting case of Spanish MNEs.

9. See the definitive studies on U.S. investment abroad by Wilkins (1970; 1974). She provided comparisons with European experience in Wilkins (1988) and with Japanese experiences in Wilkins (1986b). Yoshino (1984) considered the experience of U.S. MNEs abroad in comparison with Japanese experiences. The Harvard Multinational Enterprise Project, which consisted of an enormous database on U.S. multinationals, collected and managed over many years by Raymond Vernon, provided an important source for historical studies and overviews, notably those by Vernon (1971; 1977) and Stopford and Wells (1972). The Harvard record stops in the year 1975.

10. After a slow start, the literature on Japanese MNEs has developed rapidly. See Yoshino (1974; 1976); Tsurumi (1976; 1983); Kojima (1978); Ozawa (1979); Yoshida (1987); Nonaka (1990); Itami (1994) and Ohishi (1994) as representative examples. Several full-length case histories have now been published, such as Kinugasa (1984) on Matsushita and others; Chang and Rosenzweig (1998) on Sony; Yates (1998) on Kikkoman; and Craig (1997) on Matsushita. A Japanese data set on MNE expansion has been maintained over many years by the commercial publishing firm, Toyo Keizai. See Beamish, Delios, and Lecraw (1997) for an initial reception of this source in the international business literature.

11. In a masterly survey, Chandler (1986) argues historically that industrial enterprises in advanced economies internationalized as part of a common sequence that involved, first, combining production with distribution; next, by diversifying in terms of functions and internationally; and then by diversifying in terms of products produced. Such a sequence accounts for the common organizational patterns observable in incumbent MNEs.

12. Several historical and longitudinal accounts of these Swedish MNEs' internationalization experiences are now available. On the Swedish experience generally, see Carlson (1977; 1979); Lundström (1986) and Olsson (1993) for representative studies of earlier experiences, and Lindqvist (1991) for more recent accelerated internationalization by small, high-tech Swedish enterprises. Several excellent longitudinal studies of Swedish MNEs, spanning a century and more, are now available. For L.M. Ericsson, see the magisterial study by Attman, Kuuse, and Olsson (Vol 1) and Attman and Olsson (Vol 2) (1976); on Alfa Laval, see Zander (1994) as well as Zander and Zander (1997); on SKF and Sandvik, see Johanson and Wiedersheim-Paul (1975); on ABB and Electrolux, see Ridderstråle (1996). These and other cases are discussed above in chapter 4.

13. See the contributions to Agmon and Kindleberger (eds) (1977) for an early discussion of the phenomenon of MNEs originating from small countries.

14. As Edith Penrose (1968) put it so well, "Economic theory has never comfortably digested the large diversified firm. The theoretical system which provides the economic justification of a competitive economy takes grossly inadequate account of these great administrative organizations, and the theory of international trade and investment virtually ignores them, in spite of the fact that a very important part of both is carried on within the compass of their administrative framework" (1968: 25).

15. Hymer's thesis was published by MIT Press in 1976: see Hymer (1976). Hymer's later work was devoted to developing a Marxian critique of multinational enterprise; see Hymer (1979) for a collection of papers on this theme.

16. See Kindleberger (1969; 1970) for representative discussions, and Kindleberger and Audretsch (eds) (1983) for later evaluations.

17. This has remained the dominant point of view, in theory as much as in practice, with the exception of the Scandinavian/Nordic school, which was concerned to account for the quite different behavior of Scandinavian MNEs. This remained an "isolated" case until the arrival of the latecomer MNEs from East Asia in the 1980s and 1990s turned the conventional assumptions on their head.

18. See Buckley and Casson (1976) for their definitive treatment; and Casson (1982; 1986; 1987), Buckley (1988), and Buckley and Casson (1985) for further elaboration of the "internalization" theory of the MNE.

19. Vernon's 1977 study, *Storm Over the Multinationals*, provides a comprehensive treatment of both the positive side of MNEs' activities and the negative features, as viewed in the 1970s. See Vernon (1998) for an updated view from the 1990s.

20. Dunning (1993) himself has made no secret of the limitations of the OLI framework, emphasizing that its generality precludes it from explaining or predicting particular kinds of international production; and even less, the behavior of individual enterprises; see also Cantwell (1991) for an overview of these issues.

21. See Bartlett and Ghoshal (2000a): 5–9. For the case of Japanese MNEs' motives, derived from the annually published Toyo Keizai database, see for example Yamawaki (1994) and Padmanabhan and Cho (1996).

22. On the "global" corporation vs the multinational, see Levitt (1983) for an early exposition; on the "heterarchical" organization, see Hedlund (1986; 1993) and Hedlund and Rolander (1990); on the "transnational" corporation, see Bartlett and Ghoshal (1989).

23. The literature on "global industries" and the demands of global competition took definitive form in the 1980s. See Hout, Porter, and Rudden (1982); Hamel and Prahalad (1985); Kogut (1985a;-b); Ghoshal (1987); and Egelhoff (1993) for representative examples.

24. The absence of a strategic element to the OLI framework is the focus of several recent studies. Melin (1992) initiated a discussion of internationalization as driven by strategic motives, while Randøy (1997) discussed the issue from the perspective of case studies of the internationalization of Norwegian firms and divisions. Dunning himself (Dunning 1993a), and Dunning and Narula (1995), in the context of internationalization of R&D activities, discussed such strategic issues in the form of "strategic asset seeking" FDI.

25. See Yeung (1999b). The survey was based on interviews with 204 Singapore-based MNEs and 56 of their subsidiaries in Hong Kong and China.

26. This has not stopped some scholarly pioneers from investigating ways of applying RBV insights to international aspects of the firm's operation. See Andersen and Kheam (1998) for an exploratory study, and Fahy (1996) for an application of the RBV to the internationalization of services.

27. See Dunning (1980; 1981; 1988) for the most pertinent discussions of the OLI framework. Afterthoughts were added in Dunning (1995), but these did not change the basic framework.

28. For a review of this literature, see for example Forsgren (1999).

29. See for example Zander (1999a; 1999b) for a discussion of the dispersion of MNEs' R&D operations according to such criteria and Cantwell and Iammarino (1998) and Cantwell and Santangelo (1999) for further empirical demonstration.

30. See for example the analyses by Kogut and Chang (1991); Chang (1995); or Geringer, Tallman, and Olsen (2000).

31. See Blomstrom (2000) for an analysis of this trend.

32. See Dunning (1995) for such a discussion, in the context of what he calls "alliance capitalism." Related contributions have been made by Rugman, D'Cruz, and Verbeke (1995) and by Buckley and Casson (1998).

33. The OLI framework has been subjected to lengthy scholarly debate and evaluation; the critiques by Buckley and Casson (1985) and Itaki (1991) are representative examples. However, these critiques take the basic position that the firm has assets to exploit abroad, as a given; they are concerned with the logical consistency of the three "sources" of advantage. A different approach is being taken here, in that the resource base of the firm is in question, and what is being investigated is the dynamics of international expansion, rather than a priori, static calculations of comparative advantage.

34. The claim is strengthened by research which indicates the same kind of considerations lie behind Japanese FDI in U.S. manufacturing industry. Kogut and Chang (1991) found that host-country technological assets were determinants of cross-industry patterns of Japanese FDI; in other words, Japanese MNEs were looking to acquire technological resources as a result of their investments in addition to exploiting their own resources. These results were extended to the case of marketing assets by Pugel, Kragas, and Kimura (1996). If accessing both technological and market resources (e.g., knowledge of market trends and emerging technologies) has guided Japanese MNEs' investment in the United States, then it is a small extension to claim the same kinds of considerations have guided the investments of latecomer MNEs following in Japan's footsteps.

35. See Wells (1977; 1981; 1983) for successive elaborations of this theme, and Wells (1998) for a postscript on the experience of developing countries with MNEs.

36. See Kogut and Singh (1988); Geringer (1991); and Larimo (1995) for discussions of the strategic role that international joint ventures play in reducing risks.

37. Kogut and Zander therefore make the bold claim that the "notion of the firm as specializing in the transfer and recombination of knowledge is the foundation to an evolutionary theory of the multinational corporation" (1993: 625). This paper is part of a trilogy (Kogut and Zander 1992; 1993; Zander and Kogut

1995) which has the ambitious aim of establishing a new knowledge-based theory of the firm.

38. The phrase is used by Nohria and Garcia-Pont (1991) and elaborated further in the form of the "differentiated network" model of the MNE in Nohria and Ghoshal (1997).

39. The four features mentioned by Dunning (1997: 57) are:

1. the increasing mobility of firm-specific resources and capabilities—especially knowledge-related assets—across national boundaries;
2. the growing significance of cross-border transactions which are either intra-firm, or between firms with ongoing cooperative agreements;
3. the dramatic reduction in long-distance transportation and communication costs and of the psychic and cultural barriers between countries;
4. the growing importance of location-bound assets, notably an educated labour force and a sophisticated physical infrastructure, in influencing the siting of the value-added activities by MNEs.

8

A PROCESS-ORIENTED ACCOUNT
OF ACCELERATED
INTERNATIONALIZATION

Several studies of international business have
indicated that internationalization of firms is a
process in which the firms gradually increase
their international involvement. . . . We develop
a model of the internationalization process of
the firm that focuses on the development of the
individual firm, and particularly on its gradual
acquisition, integration, and use of knowledge
about foreign markets and operations, and on
its successively increasing commitment to
foreign markets.

Jan Johanson and Jan-Erik Vahlne,
"The Internationalization Process
of the Firm"

Early attempts to develop a theory of international expansion coincided
with attempts to come to grips with the phenomenon of the multinational
enterprise (MNE)—both as an important business development calling for
new economic evaluation and as a potential threat to states and firms in
host countries. Neoclassical trade theory, which dominated international
economics in the 1960 and 1970s, had no way of accounting for the existence of the MNE.[1] Since then, in keeping with the dominant MNE experience, the literature has emphasized either a solid process of extension
overseas from an asset-rich home base (extending competitive advantages
abroad) or, in the case of the so-called Uppsala school, a slow, incremental
pathway of expansion driven by the firm's experiential learning, market by
market. Scholars such as Perlmutter (1969) were concerned with management attitudes within the MNE (distinguishing between ethnocentric, polycentric, and finally geocentric outlooks); others were concerned to develop an economic theory of the MNE which could account for its potential
superiority and for its pattern of evolution.[2] But such studies were not con-

cerned with the process of international expansion and its organizational foundations.

The benchmark for studies of the organizational dimensions of the internationalization process itself was provided by Stopford and Wells (1972), with their research into the processes through which a sample of 187 MNEs, originating from the United States, adapted their organizational structures and processes as they expanded internationally.

Stopford and Wells identified three stages of expansion that have remained widely regarded as definitive. First, there is the establishment of foreign activities, function by function, such as through the creation of manufacturing or marketing subsidiaries. Second, these proliferating functional activities are brought under some central coordination and control through being incorporated in a separate international division or some other organizational device. Third, there might be further evolution toward the point when the activities contained in the international division are redistributed to newly focused worldwide product divisions or geographic area divisions. This was actually the dominant organizational solution to coordinating international activities through the 1970s and 1980s.[3] Stopford and Wells actually foresaw a fourth organizational stage that might encompass a grid, or matrix, tying together business areas and geographical areas—in a way which was a remarkable anticipation of the very kind of structures utilized in the 1990s by firms such as ABB, Sony, Matsushita, and many others.

The early work on patterns of expansion of U.S. MNEs was followed up by work which looked for distinctive patterns of expansion on the part of European and Japanese MNEs. This search was rewarded in studies such as that of Franko (1976) which looked at the "collegial management" patterns evident in the expansion abroad of European MNEs, resulting in a decentralized matrix as contrasted with the U.S. centralized approach. The Japanese expansion patterns, involving distinctive institutional forms such as trading companies preceding the expansion abroad of manufacturing activities, and the location of subsidiaries in each market served, were documented by numerous scholars.[4] These were patterns of expansion as revealed up to the end of the 1970s by North American, European, and Japanese MNEs.

What accounted for these patterns remained the subject of lively debate in the 1980s, with two theoretical camps forming in opposition to each other. The dominant view was based on a model of the appearance of the MNE as an alternative to arm's length export contracting between firms. The core consideration here is that the firm expands abroad in order to exploit some advantage that it possesses, either in terms of location or of assets owned by the firm. Because of market imperfections, it is led to internalize these transactions within itself, through various kinds of institutional forms (ranging from a wholly owned subsidiary, through joint ventures, to use of an agent). Dunning (1981) caught the flavor of this reasoning, based as it is on a priori transactions costs and market imperfections arguments, in what he called the eclectic theory of the MNE, meaning that it incorporated ownership (O), locational (L), and internalization (I) factors as driving the firm's internationalization.[5] As elaborated in the previous chapter, the OLI framework fails to accommodate the "resource-acquiring" approach to internationalization of the latecomer, and an alternative OLI* framework applicable to the latecomer case was offered as a way of remedying this.

A quite different approach to internationalization is behavioral and process-oriented, in that it seeks to account for the firm's international expansion as an incremental, organizational learning experience. This is the analysis of the actual process through which the firm internationalized, theorized in terms of the decision processes of the managers involved and the learning by the firm. Such an approach was grounded in the behavioral theory of the firm (Cyert and March 1963) and the theory of the growth of the firm (Penrose 1959), which has blossomed in the 1990s as the resource-based view (RBV) of the firm.

An initial implementation of this behavioral approach was studied at Harvard, in the work of Aharoni (1966), who examined the management *decision processes* involved in firms' international expansion, using a sample of 38 U.S. MNEs. What exactly did these managers do, and what factors were consistently important in their decisions to expand abroad or to expand a foreign operation? In fact, far from the economics world of rational calculation, Aharoni found that international expansion decisions were frequently made out of coincidence, hazard, or chance encounters. The process of increasing the firm's extension abroad was conceived very much in terms of a learning process. In Aharoni's words:

> There is a strong feeling that one should begin an investment program on a very small scale, learn from one's experience, and only after much more experience and expertise is gained increase the size of the operations. If possible, the firm would prefer to "test the market" by exporting to it before any investment program begins. The investment itself often starts with assembly or packaging operations, or in product lines in which the size of the capital investment is low. (1966: 150–51)

Other studies at this time focused on the process through which a firm embarked on export activities as an early form of international involvement. This led to the formulation of a "stages" theory of export development as a process.[6] This line of research was subsequently taken up and elaborated most thoroughly in the Scandinavian countries, where scholars felt that the dominant economic mode of reasoning shed little light on the alternative experiences of internationalization of Nordic firms. As we have seen, Scandinavian firms expanded abroad in patterns that strikingly anticipated those to be used much later by firms from East Asia—seeing the world as their market and expanding rapidly into new markets to build competitive strength rather than to exploit existing assets or advantages. A group of scholars based at Uppsala University in Sweden began to develop a "process"-oriented account of Swedish and Finnish firms' international expansion, based on the notion of the firms' experiential learning in foreign markets and the cultural factors involved in choice of markets.[7]

The first feature focused on by these Uppsala scholars was the choice of foreign markets, where they developed a behavioral alternative to the economic rationalist view. The idea stemmed from the sense that Scandinavian firms expanding abroad had sought to secure early advantage by locating their foreign activities, at least initially, in countries with which they had cultural affiliations. This was seen to be a sensible risk-reduction procedure, which was theorized by Hornell, Johanson, and Wiedersheim-Paul in terms of a foreign market's "psychic distance" from the firm's home market.[8] A rough scale of "psychic distance" of countries from a Scandinavian origin was constructed, and patterns of foreign expansion of Scandinavian firms shown to follow it remarkably closely.

A second feature of this behavioral approach was to focus on the actual sequence of activities and their institutional form as a firm increased its scale of activity in a chosen foreign market. This approach was what the Uppsala scholars called the "establishment chain" and again, based on Scandinavian experiences, they posited a four-stage sequence as being: a null-stage of zero foreign exposure; foreign involvement through exports, utilizing the services of an agent; establishment of a foreign sales subsidiary; and expansion of the subsidiary's activities to encompass production, as well as sales and marketing (and eventually other functions as well, such as R&D and customer service). This sequence was driven by the firm's accumulation of experiential knowledge within the foreign market, starting tentatively and with little exposure, and then incrementally increasing its commitment as its knowledge of the market grew.

Rugman (1980) dubbed this "internationalization" approach the "Uppsala school," since this is where much of the early work on process theory was developed, and the mainstream alternative to it, based on "internalization" considerations, as the "Reading school," since this is where Dunning and his colleagues worked. This dichotomy set the scene for internationalization studies through the 1980s. The differences between the two approaches are encapsulated in Table 8.1. Rugman's influential 1980 paper has set the terms of debate more or less ever since, with research being conducted within the twin schools seeking to validate one or the other point of view.[9] Without wishing to minimize in any way these contributions, it must be admitted that the difficulties involved in substantiating either one of these polarized views are by now so substantial that it would be better to start with a new and more generalized framework to make sense of the internationalization process.

Table 8.1   The "Internalization" and "Internationalization" Accounts of International Expansion

	Internalization	Internationalization
Reference structure	Expansion abroad through "internalization" of existing resources	Expansion into new markets through learning process
Institutional options	Export; subsidiary formation (FDI); agent/licensing	Export/agent; wholly owned subsidiary
Sequence predicted	Export → subsidiary → agent	Agent → sales subsidiary → production/sales subsidiary
Market choice: influences Underlying theory	Resources to be deployed Transaction cost economics	Psychic distance Market/organizational learning

The Uppsala school's approach has been refined over the years and subjected to a great deal of empirical testing—which is more than one can say for its supposed competitor, the "internalization" approach, or "Reading school" account. Early demonstration by Scandinavian scholars of a correspondence between the experiences of Swedish (and other Nordic) firms and their framework, with its twin notions of psychic distance as an explanatory variable in choice of market, and its positing of a deterministic sequence of stages in the establishment chain of the firm's operations in each foreign market, was followed by mixed results. The model has been subjected to much further refinement and testing and found to fit the experiences of several cases of Scandinavian expansion and of smaller firm overseas expansion, in general (e.g., small firms from the UK and elsewhere).[10] But there were also numerous counterexamples—so many that by 1991, when Nordstrom published a comprehensive review, it was clear that the framework was losing its explanatory salience. By the mid-1990s, when Andersen (1993; 1997) published further reviews, there was more contrary empirical evidence than supportive.[11] One of the original contributors, Johanson, himself contributed to the critique, by noting that the "stages" view would be more likely to hold in early years of the firm's international activity and in less internationalized markets, and that it would have less salience as the firm's international experience grew or as it expanded into more internationalized markets or industries.[12]

The Uppsala model of the firm's internationalization can be said to have evolved through four versions in its more than two-decades existence.[13] First, the original four-step establishment chain was modified to encompass more cases, with the driving mechanism no longer being seen as coming solely from the firm itself and its "experiential knowledge" but also from potential partner firms in the wider "networks economy." This was an important elaboration. Then in the 1990s, Uppsala scholars broadened the framework again to encompass alternative market entry strategies (such as acquisition rather than greenfield entry) and to bring in costs as a decision variable (where perceived cost is made to depend on experiential knowledge). The advantages in terms of broader coverage and realism are offset in this case by lack of empirical testing of the later elaborations. These four versions and the differences between them are illustrated in Table 8.2.

The underlying strengths of the Uppsala approach, whether considered in its first formulation or in terms of its evolution through subsequent variants, remain its insistence that the process of internationalization is a dynamic, learning process that cannot be captured by static considerations or by establishment options that are confined to wholly owned or controlled subsidiary arrangements.[14] This has also come to be the view of many of the contributors to the early development of the theory of international expansion. Buckley and Casson (1998a), for example, in reviewing the economics of multinational business, made some telling points regarding the theoretical treatment of foreign market entry. In place of the conventional

Table 8.2   Four Versions of the "Uppsala" Internationalization Process Theory

Uppsala Model	Forms of International Expansion: Establishment Chain	Factors/Driving Influences	Source(s)
Mark I	(1) no exports; (2) exports via agent; (3) marketing subsidiary; (4) marketing and production subsidiary	Choice of market: "psychic distance"; Establishment chain: sequential learning	Johanson and Vahlne (1977; 1990)
Mark II	Expansion via network linkages	Network partnerships	Johanson and Mattsson (1988); Axelsson and Johanson (1992); Forsgren and Johanson (1992)
Mark III	Expansion via organic acquisitions	Previous relations between acquiring and acquired firms; psychic distance	Andersson, Johanson, and Vahlne (1997)
Mark IV	[no change]	Perceived costs and risks, depending on prior experience	Eriksson, Johanson, Majkgard, and Sharma (1997)

static treatment, which is concerned with a priori analyses of one market entry decision after another without allowance for any dynamic learning effects or flexibility in response to changing conditions (e.g., market shrinkage in place of market growth), they call for a more dynamic framework of analysis.[15] They mention explicitly the possibility of market entry being fashioned through various forms of partnership arrangements, such as international joint ventures and partnership alliances.[16] Other leading scholars, such as Rugman et al. (1995) and Dunning (1995), now see international cooperative arrangements as increasingly the norm and potentially displacing the conventional model of the multinational enterprise.

The prelude to developing a framework that goes beyond the "internalization-internationalization" dichotomy is to consider the dimensions of the process of internationalization in a systematic way. This paves the way for a consideration of the strategic options available to firms as they contemplate their internationalization and for a consideration of the different choices made by incumbent MNEs and the newcomers and latecomers.

The Dimensions of the Process of Internationalization

The process of the firm's expansion internationally is an aspect of its growth or development or diversification that happens to take the firm's activities across national borders. Thus, fundamentally to discuss the firm's internationalization is to discuss its growth and development, its diversification into new markets or new businesses, its growing complexity and how it manages and organizes that complexity. The firm's internationalization can then be captured from several different perspectives. There is the growing number of countries it is involved in—a measure of its international expansion. There is the value-added dimension in different national settings or the linkages with global customers—a measure of its integration in the international economy. There is the chain of establishments in foreign markets, indicating greater (or lesser) degrees of commitment—such as the sequence from exports via an agent, to a sales subsidiary, to a production and sales subsidiary (highlighted as a typical sequence by the Uppsala school of internationalization)—a measure of the firm's involvement in or commitment to a foreign market. There are the international collaborative alliances that the firm might be involved in, from one to a few to in some cases dozens simultaneously—a measure again of the firm's integration in the world economy.

Attempts to capture this complex, multidimensional process, using just one or two of the dimensions, are bound to provide at best a partial view of the firm's internationalization. Yet this is what we find in the management literature. The issue of internationalization is discussed purely in terms of strategic aspects without regard to organization; or in terms of choices between market entry modes (e.g., greenfield site versus acquisition); or in terms of market choice and the factors that impinge on it. In fact, these are some of the aspects or dimensions of international expansion. But their partial delineation makes discussion of strategic goals or the interpretation of empirical results hazardous.

A little reflection indicates that there are three dimensions to the process of internationalization that are susceptible to strategic choice and that have an evolutionary or cumulative effect over time. They are:

1. Coverage by the firm of the international sphere
2. Commitment by the firm of resources to the international sphere (or degree of integration within the international economy)
3. The organizational resources committed by the firm to its international activities

Coverage implies extension, a spreading of activities across several different countries or markets. In terms of network terminology, it is the creation by the firm of new linkages with firms operating across borders in other parts of the world. Coverage is a measure of extension, or spread of activities, without taking into consideration the depth of involvement by the firm.

Commitment implies a deepening of activities or involvement, such as in moving from simply an export operation to one where production and marketing operations are distributed around the world, perhaps encompassing logistics and R&D operations as well. A convenient measure of such commitment, or penetration, is that of the share of value-added by the firm in the international sphere as compared with its domestic base. This gives a measure of "depth" to the initial dimension of extension.

Organizational resources committed to international activities describe the degree of "integration" achieved by the firm across its spread of international activities, such as in enhancing horizontal linkages between activities, as well as their vertical, product-focused linkages. This third dimension is a measure of the firm's own adaptation to its international activities and of its commitment to sustaining and developing them. It captures the spread of options available to the firm at any point in its process of international expansion.

These dimensions capture all strategically significant features of the firm's expansion. Various contributions to the International Business (IB) literature have sought to model the process of internationalization utilizing some or all of these dimensions. The network aspect was captured by Johanson and Mattsson (1988). They introduced a model of the firm's internationalization as a process that grows or expands along three dimensions:

1. International extension—making links with firms across borders
2. Penetration—deepening the commitment to links which have been established

3. International integration—enhancing the coordination across the firm as it internationalizes

A fourth dimension of time is implied, although not stated explicitly, in that the dynamics of the firm's expansion along these dimensions is the point of the analysis offered. This is discussed against the backdrop (in the context of) the degree of internationalization of the industry or markets in which the firm is involved. Four cases are identified, depending on the degree of internationalization of the industry/markets, and of the firm itself, as follows: early starter; lonely MNE; late starter; and the MNE among others. The two axes are the degree of internationalization of the market/industry (horizontal) and the degree of internationalization of the firm. The "early starter," for example, is more of a nineteenth-century case, where a firm internationalizes slowly in an industry that has only few international features, while the "lonely MNE" is a case of a well-internationalized firm within a poorly internationalized industry. These are the cases that best fit the "Uppsala" process model of internationalization.

An extension of this approach was developed by Nordström (1991), who blended industrial organization notions with internationalization processes to generate multiple patterns for the firm's international expansion. Based on the joint influences on the firm of its own characteristics, the host country characteristics, and the industry characteristics, three patterns of expansion into the international economy are identified as being:

1. The sequence of countries (foreign markets) entered
2. The depth of involvement in each market (and sequence followed, viz., the "establishment chain")
3. The pattern of establishment mode of national subsidiaries (e.g., greenfield developments vs. acquisitions)

Nordström was seeking with this framework to provide a broader setting for consideration of the process of internationalization than provided in, for example, the Uppsala model, which considers only the first two of these dimensions, and not in the context of firm characteristics or industry characteristics (and with only a single feature of the market entered, namely, its "psychic distance").[17]

Our approach is consistent with these scholars' frameworks, in that our dimensions capture the essential features of the firm's expansion within a context of an economy viewed as a network of networks. Consistent with Johanson and Mattsson, we see the international economy as a preexisting entity in which firms are constantly creating, breaking, and renewing linkages with each other, as customers or suppliers, as collaborators within various kinds of alliances, and simply as competitors which are connected to each other within a single industry through various "degrees of separation."

The key to developing an account of the multiple dimensions of internationalization is to create a space for strategic decision-making. This is in agreement with Melin (1992), who argued that much of the internationalization literature is deterministic; it does not provide such a strategic space. Bearing this in mind, our proposed framework allows for strategic variation along each of the dimensions, as we now demonstrate.

Coverage of the International Sphere and Involvement Internationally

A primary dimension must encompass the actual extent of involvement by the firm in the international economy, in terms of the multiplication of its links with firms which are already international or which operate in other countries.[18] At the most superficial level, this can be measured in terms of indices such as foreign sales as a proportion of total sales; or foreign production as a proportion of total production (perhaps broken down by product division); or, looking to the future, foreign investment as a proportion of total investment. Clearly, we have a sense that a firm which has a higher proportion of investment, or sales, or production, or employment in the foreign sphere (i.e., international sphere) as a proportion of total activity, is a "more internationalized" firm than one which has a greater bulk of activities in its domestic market.[19]

Such indices have to be treated with caution. A high level of foreign sales as a proportion of total sales indicates that the firm is active as an exporter—but it may not have much presence in overseas markets beyond this. A high proportion of employment in the international sphere as a proportion of total employment indicates a high degree of activity overseas—but it may be through subcontracting production to low-cost locations, a footloose strategy, or it may mean locating production and customer service inside key markets such as North American, European, and East Asian markets—a truly global strategy. Thus, the index on its own does not tell us much about the quality of the firm's international engagement.

A second aspect to the dimension of international coverage is provided by the number of countries in which the firm is engaged and their importance. Clearly, we have a sense that a firm that is engaged in 40 countries is "more internationalized" than one engaged in 20. But it may be that the first firm is Dutch, and 15 of the 40 countries are European, while the other 25 are in Latin America, Africa, and central Asia. Whereas the second firm is Taiwanese, and it has subsidiaries in the United States, Germany, Japan, and the other leading economies of the world, in that order. By criteria of market importance, we would then judge the second firm as actually being more thoroughly "internationalized" than the first firm, in terms of its strategic commitment to the international economy.

The importance of countries may be measured by the size and significance of their markets or the significance of firms within the country for the kinds of networks of interest to the focal firm. Along this dimension countries vary in terms of a number of criteria, any one of which may be more important than others in guiding or shaping the strategic choices made by firms as they expand from one country to another. The Uppsala school which emerged in the 1970s to describe the expansion patterns of Nordic MNEs posited "psychic distance" as one such factor, that is, firms would tend to expand first to countries with which they had a sense of cultural contiguity, through language, customs, institutions, or whatever.

All these aspects of the dimension of extension or coverage are susceptible to objective measurement quite separately from the firm's own internal management and organizational data and activities.

Commitment of Resources by the Firm to the International Sphere

The "depth" of coverage by the firm or involvement in international activities is the second dimension of interest. Again, we have an intuitive sense that a firm that is active in 35 countries is more internationalized than one active in only 25—subject again to qualifications. For example, if the first firm has only export activities through the use of agents in 30 of these countries, and small sales subsidiaries in the other five, while the second firm actually has built substantial subsidiaries encompassing sales, marketing, and production in 20 of the countries in which it is active, including the United States, Germany, and Japan, then we would change our opinion and declare that the second firm is more "internationalized." The second dimension of "commitment of resources" seeks to capture this intuitive sense.

As noted by Kutschker and Baurle (1997), international activities can extend from mere export to completely self-sustaining subsidiaries. Like them, I seek to capture this range of options and degrees of involvement (or penetration) in the international economy in terms of value-added. It is convenient and helpful to conceive of the firm as engaged in a sequence of activities captured by Porter (1980; 1985) as the "value chain"—namely, the value-added measure at each step of the process from receipt of raw materials or components to final assembly, delivery, marketing, and follow-up customer service. Porter introduced this concept as an aid in evaluating the firm's strategy—in what markets it sought to add value and thereby become a competitive player. In our case, we are interested in the extent to which the firm's value chain spans many countries or markets. The more countries it traverses or "covers," the more one can say that the firm is "internationalized."

Thus, a first aspect of the second dimension can be captured in measures such as value-added within any particular market (such that an increased commitment to the market, from sales subsidiary to production and sales, will entail an increase in value-added within that market). A second aspect can be captured in terms of the steps involved in the value-chain encompassed by the firm's activities, and determining how much of the value-added at each step is accomplished internationally, compared with domestically. A third aspect can be captured in the overall measure of value-added abroad, that is, within the international economy, as compared with value-added at home. This measure will quickly discriminate between firms which are strong exporters, but actually add most value in their home operations, and those which truly spread their value-adding activities around the world.

It is worth noting that this second dimension captures in a more abstract form the superficial shifts in depth of commitment that the Uppsala school captures, for example, in its "establishment chain." This refers to the actual sequence of operations established in a foreign market. The Uppsala school first proposed a sequence of such operations as being "typical" of MNEs expanding from Scandinavian countries at the turn of the century, that is, exports to a foreign market via an agent, through sales subsidiary formation, to sales and production subsidiary enhancement, to regional headquarters—which is designated as an "establishment chain" in the Uppsala model. Now there is no reason in principle why the establishment chain need conform to this rather prescriptive model. Indeed, the empirical record reveals plenty of variation from this sequence even among Scandinavian MNEs, not to mention MNEs expanding from other parts of the world. But some form of establishment chain has to be created as the firm expands, and its pattern does reveal something about the strategic choices being made by the firm as it broadens its activities.

The second dimension of "depth" of international involvement can only be measured by the firm itself, based on its own internal value-adding data. It is not accessible from external, objective data alone. Indeed, it is an important management exercise for any internationalizing firm to seek to capture measures along this second dimension, as a means of providing important strategic data which are not captured in standard profit-and-loss (income) or balance-sheet statements. Acer, for example, has found it to be extraordinarily interesting to plot its own activities along such a value-adding dimension, both as a global organization as a whole and within the component parts and by individual product. It was turning its attention to capturing such data and subjecting it to competitive analysis only in the late 1990s, after over a decade of international experience and evolution.

Organizational Commitment to the International Sphere

The most subtle, because intangible, aspect of the firm's international expansion involves consideration of the change in organizational structures and processes and thus the strategic resources which underpin the firm's options at any point in its international development. This dimension is captured by previous authors in terms of "integration." This is confusing, since we use the term "integration" to capture the involvement or multiplicity of linkages that draw the firm into the global economy. But the sense in which other authors use "integration" is in the commitment of organizational resources, such as in coordinating disparate activities across global value chains. We make the point explicit in our choice of term.

Now the conventional view of organizational commitment can be captured in some measure of "control" by a firm over its disparate national subsidiaries. Indeed, a firm which expands abroad purely in terms of a series of wholly owned subsidiaries (whether these are greenfield operations or acquisitions) is maximizing its "control"—but to what extent is it expanding its "integration" within the international economy? Consider the case of firm X expanding production operations abroad. It might set up a new production operation in country Y, but supply that operation from its existing supply base, or require its existing suppliers to establish local supply points adjacent to the new production operation in country Y. Now consider firm Z which is also expanding to country Y, but in this case it establishes a production operation and creates new links with local suppliers. This entails extending its standards of components or service supply to these new suppliers, which is a cost, but it is also a commitment to country Y, which is in some real sense superior to that made by firm X. It is a higher level of internationalization, in the sense that it multiplies the links that bind the firm to its international operations. It is this higher degree of integration within the international economy, achieved and sustained through organizational commitments, that we seek to capture along this third dimension.

One aspect of this dimension is the choice of market entry modes. A spectrum of possibilities is available to the firm (as discussed in chapter 4), from a wholly owned subsidiary built as a greenfield operation at one end, to rapid entry via acquisition or partnership at the other end. A second aspect involves the firm's integration within the target market, such as its attraction of local customers, or if a production operation, its ability to build a local supply network. This aspect appears to be neglected in the internationalization literature, and yet in practice it is one of the most important strategic dimensions of the firm's international involvement. For many fledgling MNEs building a worldwide production network, the issue as to whether to use local suppliers or not is one of the most critical. From the perspective of the host country, the use of local supplier networks is one of the most visible indexes of commitment to that market. A third aspect would involve consideration of the firm's engagement in various kinds of international alliances.[20] The firm that is engaged in one international alliance is, at first sight, less internationalized than one that is engaged in ten such alliances.

In each case, the condition that sustains the ability of the firm to expand and enrich its linkages is its organizational capacities and organizational resources devoted to internationalization. The firm that simply clones its domestic products and operations abroad, without regard to local linkages or market adaptations, may well become very profitable—take the case of Dell Computer. Yet its degree of internationalization, and its organizational commitment to the international sphere, is surely inferior to that of a firm which expands its linkages to local suppliers, which enters into partnerships with local distributors, which adapts products to the tastes of local customers, and which engages in many forms of international collaborative exercises. The organizational commitment of resources to internationalization in the latter case surely exceeds that involved in the former.

Organizational resources, like resources in general, cannot easily be measured. But that is not to say that they are unimportant. Indeed, we are clearly of the view that the most important dimension to the process of internationalization is the organizational. And it is our view that it is on this dimension that latecomers score extremely well, in terms of successfully accelerating their degree of internationalization, precisely through the attention that they pay to the organizational dimension and the strategic resources which it opens up.

To be concrete, one can view Acer's global cellular organizational model as a commitment of organizational resources which underpins the corporation's global expansion and rapid market entry. It makes Acer a more truly "global" firm than an incumbent that has simply replicated its existing products and operations abroad. In this sense, our third dimension of organizational commitment echoes Perlmutter's earlier concerns in capturing management attitudes in terms of their ethnocentric, polycentric, or, eventually, geocentric character.

Dynamics of Internationalization

The firm can expand its resources by internationalizing through the mechanisms that we have called linkage and leverage. In complementary fashion, these represent ways in which the established firm can expand the scope of its exploitation of strategic assets—which is the situation almost always discussed in the literature. In either case, whether internationalization involves gaining access to new resources, or exploiting existing resources on a wider international scale, it is a case of internationalization broadening the firm's strategic resources and hence its options.

To illustrate, take the case of global integration and the sourcing of components from the most cost-effective suppliers. As the firm internationalizes, so the option of global sourcing of supplies, to obtain the best prices and best delivery terms, becomes a source of strategic advantage—an option, in other words—that is not available to the domestic competitor. In this sense we conceive strategic resources as expanding as the firm internationalizes.

Acer has been able to utilize each of these aspects—linkage, and leverage—in its internationalization experiences. It has utilized *linkage* in its accelerated market entry strategy, linking up with local distributors so as not to have to create its own distribution channels *ab initio*, country by country. It has utilized *leverage* in its manner of entering new fields, like semiconductor manufacturing or CD-ROM production or LCD flat panels production. In each case, Acer has skillfully acquired the requisite technology from an established company through strategic partnership, such as offering advanced OEM contracting services, in a manner which provides advantages to the technology donor and enables Acer to leverage the required technological capabilities.

Strategic Choices in Internationalization

The point of the three-dimensional depiction of the firm's internationalization developed here, with time as the fourth dimension, is that it allows us to identify and demonstrate different strategic choices involving varying emphasis along the different dimensions. Strategic choices thus mark out different trajectories through the three-dimensional "internationalization" space.

Consider the different internationalization trajectories marked out in I-space as depicted in Fig. 8.1. This illustration shows a slightly internationalized firm at point A (a1 in terms of coverage, e.g., five countries; a2 in terms of commitment, e.g., three subsidiaries and two export markets; and a3 in terms of strategic resources, e.g., membership in two international

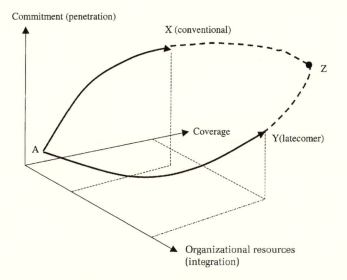

Figure 8.1 Internationalization trajectories: strategic choices. In I-space (internationalization), the conventional MNE follows a trajectory from A to X, while the latecomer emphasizes rapid coverage and integration and moves from A to Y. Both could eventually end up at Z, where they have substantial degrees of commitment, coverage, and integration.

collaborative alliances). What are this firm's strategic options for moving to a "more internationalized" point in the space? One strategy, depicted as curve X, moves out along the commitment (penetration) dimension and the coverage dimension, for example, through the building of a series of national subsidiaries, but not very much along the organizational resources (integration) dimension. This reflects the experience of the typical or conventional MNE, where its international activities might be bundled together in an "international division" rather than integrated with its product strategies. A quite different set of strategic choices is depicted in trajectory Y, where the firm moves out rapidly along the coverage dimension and organizational resources dimension (e.g., through linkage), but only a short way along the commitment (penetration) dimension. This shows a typical latecomer MNE strategic trajectory, achieving accelerated international coverage, but leaving the deepening or penetration for later. Both firms can be expected to end up eventually at point Z in I-space, where they have reached substantial degrees of commitment, coverage, and integration—but their ways of reaching this point involve very different strategic choices.

A Resource-Based, Process-Oriented Account of Accelerated Internationalization

We are now in a position to discuss a process-oriented approach to internationalization that is able to make sense of the processes being pursued by newcomers and latecomers in the global economy. Our approach will demonstrate what is common to all the cases of international expansion, in terms of the decisions to be made, the options available, and the factors which impinge on those decisions. Four fundamental features may be identified, namely:

1. The decision to expand internationally (i.e., why the firm expands abroad; the factors that prompt it)
2. The strategic options available for the process (i.e., how international expansion can enhance the competitive position of the firm)
3. The sequence of strategic choices to be made and the options that present themselves (i.e., the institutional embodiment of the process)
4. The factors involved in why some options are chosen over others

This account has to be able to demonstrate plausibility not only in terms of its coverage of known and future cases, but also in terms of such processes as organizational learning (or accumulation of organizational knowledge) involved, that is, as a synthesis of the firm's previous internationalization experiences as preparation for the next phase of expansion.

These features *exclude* consideration of certain matters, such as how the firm reorganizes itself as its international coverage grows. We see this as belonging to the sphere of international organization, particularly global organization, and wish to treat it separately from the process of international expansion itself.

The Decision to Expand Internationally: Pull Rather than Push

Recall that the process of internationalization was defined in chapter 2 as one that draws the firm into closer integration within the worldwide economy. This definition was provided as an alternative to previous definitions offered in the literature, where the emphasis has been on firms' needing to overcome barriers, of being "pushed" rather than "pulled."[21] It accommodates international expansion as an autonomous activity, as well as expansion through strategic linkage. All these kinds of activity, in which connections are being established between firms across national borders, fall within the purview of our concept of "internationalization."

Strategic Options Available

The conventional literature makes assumptions about the "modes" of market entry which then shape subsequent theoretical discussion. The "internalization" approach has recognized three such market entry options, namely (1) export from home base; (2) development of local subsidiary (i.e., foreign direct investment); and (3) licensing of a product to a local firm which then develops the market itself, paying a royalty to the firm which seeks a wider market for its product. Rugman later broadened the range to include a fourth option: international joint ventures.[22] Likewise, the "internationalization" approach, even broadened as discussed above to encompass new variants, still seeks to impose some deterministic sequence on the establishment chain.[23] Even allowing for the fact that these models were formulated more than 20 years ago and would encompass more options if formulated today, nevertheless, the choice of options continues to be considered within a remarkably narrow theoretical framework.[24]

A theoretical framework for internationalization needs to accommodate a wider range of options and possibilities, consistent with those observed in reality by newly internationalizing firms. Thus, it is convenient to present the options in terms of a spectrum, ranging from one extreme, where there is no partnership at all and the firm relies entirely on its own resources for market entry, to permanent partnership, where the firm seeks to build its presence in the market through building and enhancing its partner. In between these extremes are a range of agency and partnership agreements which evolve in different ways toward either full self-sufficiency or permanent partnership. The key to making the differentiation between options within this spectrum is to view them as offering increasing levels of resources from international players. The options, with their varying levels of commitment to a foreign market and resource deployment (or leverage) by the expanding firm, are shown in Table 8.3.

Decision Points and Options Chosen

The process of international expansion can be viewed not only as a search and learning process—learning about the needs of foreign markets—but also about how the firm may deploy and build its competencies (resources) as it grows and expands abroad, applying the lessons of its experiences in one market as it seeks to enter the next.[25] Such a framework needs to be concerned with laying out the strategic options available to the firm and the critical decision points through which it must pass—rather than with dictating a deterministic sequence of steps or stages or insisting on one modal form over another.

Actual choices made by a firm accumulate to map out a pathway of international expansion (dubbed the "establishment chain" by Nordic researchers), which in turn will shape future choices available to the firm. We seek to capture this sequence in the following four decision points, each of which requires choices to be made by the firm as it expands its international links: (1) Search; (2) Experiment and validate; (3) Select; and (4) Build and enhance. The process of international expansion is shown in Fig. 8.2, where it is depicted as one that unfolds across two dimensions, namely, time and resource commitment.

Search   The process of entering a new market is a process of making new linkages—with potential agents (for sales and promotion), with potential

Table 8.3   International Expansion: Strategic Options Available

Options	Commitment of Firm to Market	Resource-Based View
Export/licensing through agent	Very low	Resources deployed abroad
Merger/acquisition	Low	Resource deployment
Subsidiary formation	Medium	Resource deployment
Partnership	Medium-high	Resource sharing; leverage
Joint venture	High	Resource sharing
Full subsidiary (sales, production, customer service)	High	Resource sharing (e.g., with suppliers)
Independent operation grown from partnership (e.g., as part of world-wide group)	Highest	Resource sharing (cellular; "client-server")

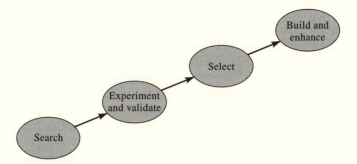

Figure 8.2 Sequence of decision points for the firm's international expansion. *Note:* This figure was developed jointly with C. Snow.

partners (for market development or joint production), with potential suppliers (for a manufacturing operation), or with targets (for merger or acquisition). The search for potential partners is something that has to be done by every firm, whether it be a start-up in its first overseas market or the most experienced multinational looking to bid for a contract in an emerging market.

If the firm wishes to expand abroad exclusively through "internalizing" its own resources, then that may well be strategically optimal for the firm—but it is as well to consider the range of alternatives available, and whether some might work better than others. From this perspective, it makes little sense for the firm to expand through the creation of its own subsidiaries, except in very special cases. It makes much more sense to draw on the local knowledge of firms in the target market and work through them to acquire and internalize this knowledge. A partnership arrangement allows such partner firms to grow, while expanding the business of the initiating firm; they enrich each other.

Experiment and Validate   Initially, the firm cannot tell who will be the most reliable partners, agents, suppliers, or merger targets, and so any attempt to enter a new market will probably proceed through a trial stage where multiple links are entertained. If it is a case of building a sales operation, then dealerships (or agency agreements) will be entered into with many firms, each of which has nonexclusive rights to the expanding firm's products. If it is a case of building a production network, then multiple suppliers will be tested to see which ones can offer the most reliable service and the highest quality and commitment.

Select   A process of selection can then take place, based on observing which of the agents or suppliers or partners devotes more energy to the task and has greater success in the business of promoting the firm's products and expanding its market share or expanding its supply base. The most successful can then be approached to discuss a full-scale partnership based on mutual exclusivity. In the case of marketing, this means that the expanding firm distributes only through the partner firm, and the partner firm distributes only the products of the firm. In the case of supplying to a production operation, it means that the expanding firm builds a partnership with the supplier, and the supplier works only for its new partner (or at least limits its customers to two or three). Such an arrangement can last for many years, like any other strategic alliance or joint venture.

Build and Enhance   Partnerships and cooperative arrangements for market entry can evolve in many directions. In the case of marketing arrangements, it might evolve toward greater independence on the part of the partner (which might want to develop its own products) or toward greater integration, with the partner firm being absorbed as part of the firm's growing worldwide network. It may take its place in this network as an autonomous entity that agrees to obey the network rules or as a wholly owned subsidiary (in effect, through the principals of the partner firm selling out their equity to the expanding firm). It might evolve toward full merger or outright acquisition. On the other hand, a partnership arrangement may last for several years, with each party profiting from the arrangement.

In the case of production systems, various "vendor partnership" arrangements in emerging markets tie suppliers closer and closer to their multinational customers, in long-term arrangements which are based on building and enhancing the capabilities (core resources) of the partner firm.[26]

In either case, then, the process of expanding linkages in a new market culminates in a process of enhancing some of the linkages and cutting others off. This is a dynamic process that keeps pace with the fortunes of the firm in this new market. As its presence in the market expands, so its network of linkages can be expected to grow—contrary to the predictions of the dominant theoretical accounts which see the long-term result of entry into a new market as being the stand-alone success of the expanding firm. In our framework (as in the real global economy), this case can be considered an exception.

Factors Involved in the Choice of Options at Each Stage

The context within which choices will be made between the different options available is that of strategy. The usual framework within which strategic choices are made is that of an established firm considering its market entry options.[27] But such an approach tends to exclude the case of firms which are expanding precisely in search of such advantages or which may be opting to scale back their international exposure for tactical reasons.[28] How do latecomer firms like Acer from Taiwan or Ispat from India acquire global reach—become Top 10 players in their industries—all within the space of a decade? Certainly not by following conventional strategies.

Ispat, for example, reached the Top 10 within the world steel industry not by pursuing strategies based on huge steel complexes competing through the achievement of economies of scale. Instead, it globalized rapidly, creating a worldwide network of ministeel mills which specialize in steel market segments. It located plants close to customers rather than engaging in long-distance trade.[29] Likewise, Acer reached the Top 10 in the PC industry within a decade of going international from its base in Taiwan, not through establishing large, centralized production plants but through a clever "fast food" business model of supplying "fresh" PC components close to points of final assembly. Acer was able to enter a huge range of new markets in accelerated fashion through partnering with local distributors, some of which became permanent members of Acer's worldwide group.

Thus, it is strategy that determines the particular resource configuration of an internationally expanding firm. In some cases, it will expand rapidly in its quest for the resources needed to underpin new capabilities in new technologies, for example, or the partners and distributors needed to accelerate global coverage.[30] The latecomer MNEs offer a dazzling display of such innovative strategies combined with resource leverage across the globe in order to accelerate their internationalization.

Ultimately, it is the global economy itself with its richness of interconnections that provides the opportunity and the impetus for the internationalization of so many firms which would have been confined in earlier times, because of their resource poverty, to a domestic competitive environment. This is why we describe the process of internationalization as one of "integration" within this wider global economic sphere.[31].

Validation of the Process-Account The framework offered is sufficiently general to accommodate the experiences of earlier MNE incumbents and also those of the more recent newcomers and latecomers. Moreover, it allows the different strategic options chosen to be highlighted. The framework is consistent with empirical studies of international expansion by firms from emergent markets.[32] It is also consistent with recent longitudinal studies of MNEs' trajectories, such as Matsushita, Eli Lilly, and, as noted earlier, Upjohn.[33] It is ultimately empirical studies that will determine the utility of the model developed.[34]

Moreover, the framework offered is consistent with recent accounts of internationalization that view it as a process of organizational learning, or organizational knowledge management, or as an evolutionary process.

Organizational Learning in Internationalization

Existing models of the internationalization process are couched in terms of sequential market entry and thereby fail to capture the organizational learning that may enable an experienced MNE to enter its 101st market somewhat more rapidly and efficiently than its 51st or its 21st. The Nordic "process" model certainly captures the experiential learning of a firm within a given market, but in its classic formulation neglects the overall learning involved as internationalization experience accumulates.[35] The process model as presented is driven by such considerations through allowing for an evolutionary process of market entry and for iteration of the "search, experiment and validate, select, build and enhance" sequence. Thus, the *process* of internationalization can be speeded up as internationalization accumulates—in line with the near universal experience of internationalizing firms.

Such acceleration of internationalization calls for the accumulation of resources and organizational capabilities; these remain the principal barriers to successful achievement of internationalization when viewed as a process. Incremental expansion can be equated with gradual resource commitment to foreign markets, and the accelerated internationalization of newcomers and latecomers is thus seen as a case of fast resource commitment.[36] In this case, we are concerned with capabilities of international partner identification, testing, choice, and further development.[37] Whereas scholars like Madhok are concerned to elaborate a theorization of foreign market entry mode in terms of the contrast between the development of organizational capabilities on the one hand, and the choice of strategy dictated by the minimization of a priori transaction costs on the other, our concern is with the elaboration of the decision sequence involved. But in each case, there is an emphasis on the process of internationalization (or foreign market entry) as a process of organizational learning that involves the development and improvement of certain organizational routines (such as a routine for identifying and selecting potential marketing partners or agents in a new foreign market). In many cases, the decision to enter a foreign market will be made with explicit reliance on a particular partner, formalized as an international joint venture. This arrangement represents an explicit form of internationalization that is not contemplated by either of the existing theoretical elaborations of the process—but is, of course, contemplated as a likely eventuality in actual business decisions.

An Evolutionary View

Evolutionary economic theorizing (Nelson & Winter 1982) has emerged as a powerful antidote to the static and a priori frameworks of neoclassical economics—which provide the context for the internalization approach to the firm's international expansion. In its most general formulation, the proposed schema for the process of internationalization mimics an evolutionary sequence, through spurts of variation, followed by competitive selection, and then operation until a new shift in environment provokes a new spurt of variation. The shift in environment corresponds to the shift into a new market or series of markets by the firm or the firm's attachment to a global player such as a global customer or global contractor. This provokes a burst of "variation" in the sense of a series of opportunities for outward expansion being presented to the firm—a variety of partners for JVs, say, or a variety of marketing agents, or a variety of potential OEM contracting partners, or a variety of global customers. The point is, that once the firm is attuned to these possibilities, then the potential for international expansion appears to be unlimited. But some choice has to be made, and some choices make more strategic sense than others, given the firm's existing endowments, its past experiences, and its strategic objectives.

Choices are made, but not necessarily definitive choices. A global start-up (GSU) might have several industrial customers for its new software system, but only two or three turn out to be collaborators in its further development; thus, the firm grows closer to these customers and more distant from others, which eventually cut themselves off or are cut off. A firm expanding its product range into a new market might utilize three distribution agents at first, all with strong local knowledge, but find that only one of these gives the product real attention and promotion and generates real market success; this is the firm to which the expanding firm grows closer, eventually to the point of contemplating a JV, while its ties to the others diminish (and they perhaps grow closer to the firm's competitors). If this JV proves to be successful, then some even stronger tie, such as incorporation within the expanding firm, may be contemplated. Such was the Acer approach to international expansion in Asia.

Thus, the choices are made from the initial set of "variations," and eventually through a process of competitive "selection" a certain configuration for the international expansion is established, which works for this firm. This configuration then dictates the course of further expansion experiences, as the firm repeats its success in one set of markets with further searching, testing, and choosing in subsequent markets. This process can continue indefinitely, through one set of markets after another, until learning enables the firm to eliminate some of the steps involved, or a further environmental shift (such as the arrival of a new competitor with a quite different form of market expansion or new set of products) provokes a new round of evolutionary variation, selection, and playing out of a new configuration.

International Interfirm Networks

Our account of the internationalization process is thus both dynamic and evolutionary. It is incremental, like the Scandinavian school's approach, without prespecifying a set number of stages. It allows for a number of end-points, including the formation of a wholly owned subsidiary, but also encompassing other end-points widely observed in practice, such as strategic alliances and various licensing arrangements, as well as contracted manufacturing arrangements which can expand to cover logistics and customer service as well, or even R&D. It is an account that is biased toward learning, both in terms of the sequence passed through in any one country, and as the process of expansion proceeds from one market to another.

The account offered is also oriented toward the possibilities of internationalization being achieved through connection or integration in international interfirm networks.[38] The process of international expansion can be viewed as being guided and stimulated by a series of connections with a preexisting network of firms constituting the international economy. Thus, there is a strong overlap between a process theory of international network formation and operation (Johanson & Mattsson 1988) and the process of internationalization itself. In certain instances, they represent two ways of seeing the same thing. In each case, connections are established (e.g., as industrial supplier, or industrial customer, or partner, or agent) that take a firm into a new set of relationships (and thus a role in a new and expanded network) that at the same time cross borders (and thus carry the firm into engagement with the international economy).

Concluding Remarks

The conceptual model presented in this chapter remains to be validated further in empirical studies. It is presented in order to stimulate such studies, where the processes investigated and the options examined may be somewhat more broadly based than those envisaged in the theoretical frameworks that still prevail in the field of international business.

The process-oriented account of internationalization then is a second fruit of our examination of the novel practices and experiences of the latecomer MNEs from the Periphery. It provides us with a fresh perspective that would otherwise not have been forthcoming. But once it is made explicit, then it becomes clear that many cases of internationalization can indeed be accommodated within this framework. It can thus be used not only as a tool of analysis and description but also as a framework for framing internationalization strategy, which will increasingly be an issue for firms as the international economy globalizes. How then do the experiences of the latecomer MNEs mesh with the current debates over globalization? This is a final set of ideas where we can find some useful and telling engagement with the novel experiences of the latecomer MNEs from the Periphery.

Notes

   1. See Caves (1982/1996) for an authoritative exploration of the economics of the MNE, and Caves (1998) for a retrospective on the issue.
   2. Buckley and Casson (1976) was a pioneering study of this kind.
   3. For further engagement with the Stopford and Wells model, see Egelhoff (1988).

4. See for example, Kojima (1978); Ozawa (1979); Tsurumi (1983); and Yoshino (1974; 1976).

5. See the discussion on this topic in chapter 7.

6. See Bilkey (1978) and Bilkey and Tesar (1977) or Cavusgil (1980) as early examples; Leonidou and Katsikeas (1996) provide a comprehensive review of such studies.

7. The major contributors are discussed in the text following. For reviews of the Scandinavian approach and of the status of the claims of the "Uppsala" school, see for example Andersen (1993; 1997) as well as Petersen and Pedersen (1997).

8. This account appeared first in Swedish accounts by scholars such as Hornell, Johanson, and Wiedersheim-Paul; it was given its authoritative English expression in Johanson and Vahlne (1977).

9. Attempts to validate the internalization account, by demonstrating a causal relationship, in terms of the accumulation of assets preceding the internationalization of the firm, have been rare—Berry and Sakakibara (1999) being a recent exception. These two scholars took a sample of 141 Japanese manufacturing firms expanding abroad over a twenty-four year period (1974–1997) and claimed to demonstrate that asset accumulation preceded and "caused" the firms' entry into foreign markets. But it should be noted that "assets" were in fact measured by proxies, in this case advertising expenditure (as proxy for marketing assets such as brands) and R&D expenditure (as proxy for firm-specific technological or product assets). So what the study actually revealed was that increases in R&D expenditure and advertising expenditure preceded these Japanese firms' foreign expansion rather than coming after their foreign expansion. Granted all the difficulties involved in demonstrating social scientific hypotheses in actual settings, one must concede that to take this to be confirmation of the "internalization" argument is tenuous at best. Other case studies directed toward confirmation of the internalization arguments have given again mixed results. The study by Fina and Rugman (1996) claims to "test" the theory against the experience of the U.S. MNE, Upjohn, and finds that it matches the predictions of both the internalization as well as the internationalization accounts. But the striking conclusion from our perspective is that they find that Upjohn's expansion abroad was principally through "strategic alliances"—a partnership form of accelerated expansion that does not figure in either of the conventional accounts.

10. See for example Petersen and Pedersen (1997); Sullivan and Bauerschmidt (1990).

11. On the empirical shortcomings of the "stages" theories of internationalization, see for example Bell (1995); Andersen (1993) provides a comprehensive review.

12. These comments, which are more or less completely accurate, were made in the context of developing a third "process account" of internationalization, namely, through network formation (Johanson and Mattsson 1988). We elaborate on this alternative viewpoint below.

13. This is my own interpretation, not the stated view of the Uppsala scholars.

14. There is a substantial technical literature on this topic of "establishment mode" in foreign markets. As representative studies, see Andersen and Gatignon

(1986) for an analysis using static Transaction Cost Economics reasoning; Agarwal and Ramaswami (1992) for an analysis linked to OLI factors; Chang (1997) for links with foreign direct investment; Cho and Padmanabhan (1995) for analysis of Japanese experience; Erramilli and Rao (1990) for the case of service firms; Hennart and Reddy (1997) for the choice between JVs and mergers, using the experience of Japanese investment in the U.S.; and Kim and Hwang (1992) for the link between entry mode and global strategy. For a plea to go beyond narrow static comparisons of various "modes," see Benito and Welch (1994).

15. In line with contributions like that of Chi & McGuire (1996) and, although Buckley and Casson do not mention them, those of Kogut & Zander (1993) and Madhok (1997).

16. On international joint ventures (IJVs), see for example Kogut (1988; 1991); Beamish and Banks (1987); Geringer (1991); Geringer and Hebert (1989); and Blomstrom and Zejan (1991). On partnership arrangements in general, see Contractor (1990); Hamel (1991); and Cavusgil (1998) for recent reviews.

17. In the model presented by Kutschker and Baurle (1997), there were again three dimensions along which the firm internationalizes, this time with the dynamic dimension (time) being made explicit as a "fourth" dimension. The three dimensions were

- number of countries and their geographic-cultural distance from the home base—the degree of internationalization increasing with the number of countries covered;
- value-added across different national boundaries—as a measure of degree of involvement in cross-border activities, from mere export to completely self-sustaining subsidiaries; and
- integration across borders—as a measure of the firm's commitment to sustaining its international presence through organizational coordination of its disparate activities.

In this case, some in-principle remarks are offered regarding actual measurement of the firm's degree of internationalization. The point of the exercise is to discuss the dynamics of the process of internationalization, and the impact of strategic calculations by the firm (and its rivals) on this process.

The model developed by Jarillo and Martinez (1991) is also couched in three dimensions, where this time the firm's "externalization" is considered, by which is meant the ". . . extent of external resources used by the firm in a systematic way" (1991: 283). Such external resources can be tapped (we would say leveraged) from other firms in the international economy via such arrangements as licensing, joint ventures, and franchises. This has clear significance for our own framework and the patterns of international expansion pursued by latecomer MNEs.

18. The term used by Johanson and Mattsson (1988) is "international extension" which they define in network terms as the firm establishing positions in relation to counterparts in national nets that are new to the firm, i.e., making links with new firms across borders.

19. Note the various indices of internationalization discussed so far in the literature, such as in Sullivan (1994a;-b) and their critique by Ramaswamy, Galen, and Renforth (1996). The ratio of international sales as a proportion of total

sales is used as a measure of "international intensity" of early-stage technology-based firms by Preece et al. (1999).

20. See for example Doz and Hamel (1998) for a discussion of the dynamics of international strategic alliances.

21. Such a definition encompasses the experience of a firm becoming attached to a global customer (Millman 1997); a firm expanding its operations as a "global start-up" (Oviatt & McDougall 1995) or "born global" (Knight & Cavusgil 1996; Madsen & Servais 1997); a firm entering into an international joint venture (Kogut 1988); a firm locating a supplier in a foreign market (Korhonen, Luostarinen, & Welch 1996); or a firm entering into a subcontracting relationship with a foreign contractee (Andersen, Blenker, and Christensen 1997).

22. See Rugman (1986) and Rugman, D'Cruz, and Verbeke (1995).

23. The choice of entering a new market via a full-blown joint venture partnership agreement is not even considered, at least in the theoretical accounts. It is of course considered in papers specifically addressed to this option, such as in Coviello and Munro (1997), Smith and Reney (1997) or Inkpen and Beamish (1997).

24. Barkema and Vermeulen (1998), for example, examined the foreign market entry strategies of 25 Dutch multinationals over a period spanning nearly three decades (1966 to 1994) and involving 829 separate incidents of foreign market entry in 72 countries. But inexplicably they explore foreign entry only in terms of acquisition or (greenfield) start-up, including agency and partnership agreements in the "start-up" classification. Thus their data are able to shed little light on the actual range of alternatives these Dutch firms faced—and correspondingly, their conclusions regarding the effects of multinationality and multiproduct influences are rendered weaker as a result.

25. Luostarinen (1980; 1994) has emphasized such a process approach in the analysis of the internationalization behavior of Finnish firms. For a discussion, and more recent empirical results based on a sample of 196 small high-technology firms internationalizing from the UK, see Jones (1999), or Berra, Piatti, and Vitali (1995) in the case of small firms internationalizing from Italy.

26. See Martin, Mitchell, and Swaminathan (1994) and Martin, Swaminathan, and Mitchell (1998) for discussion of the internationalization of buyer-supplier production links.

27. See for example the approach of Hill, Hwang, and Kim (1990).

28. This latter case is explicitly dealt with by Benito and Welch (1997), while it is the source of the "oscillation" in the internationalization of the Swedish firm Alfa Laval (Zander and Zander 1997). Tactical retreat, often for very sound reasons, is far more common than the literature would indicate.

29. See the discussion on this point in Stopford (1998).

30. This point is reinforced by the study of a sample of 246 technology-based start-up firms internationalizing from the UK (Burgel and Murray 2000), where it is found that firms may choose "entry modes" in the form of partnerships and distributors in foreign countries as a means of accessing a marketing resource that would otherwise lie beyond them. Similar results were reported by Bell (1995) and by Lindqvist (1991) in her study of "infant MNEs" expanding from Sweden.

31. Such an approach is consistent with a view of the international economy as a network of networks, and international expansion as a process of "strategic

linkage" (Nohria & Garcia-Pont 1991; Chen and Chen 1998a) or "network expansion" (Johanson & Mattsson 1988).

32. See for example studies of expansion strategies by firms from Taiwan (Chen & Chen 1998a;-b), and by small- and medium-sized MNEs (Fujita 1995).

33. See Craig (1997); Malnight (1995); and Fina and Rugman (1996) for these studies.

34. See, for example, the studies undertaken by Hitt, Hoskisson, & Kim (1997).

35. This is the feature explicitly discussed by more recent scholars such as Madhok (1997) and Kogut & Zander (1993).

36. See studies such as that by Petersen and Pedersen (1999), which is based on the experiences of Danish companies operating foreign subsidiaries.

37. See Madhok (1997) for a general account.

38. See for example Coviello and Munro (1997), who blend the internationalization process (in the case of small high-technology firms) with a network perspective.

9

GLOBALIZATION AND THE DRAGON MULTINATIONAL

Modern industry has established the world
market. . . . All old established national
industries have been destroyed or are daily
being destroyed. They are dislodged by new
industries, whose introduction becomes a life
and death question for all civilized nations, by
industries that no longer work up indigenous
raw material, but raw material drawn from the
remotest zones; industries whose products are
consumed, not only at home, but in every
quarter of the globe. . . . In place of the old local
and national seclusion and self-sufficiency, we
have intercourse in every direction, universal
interdependence of nations.
> Karl Marx and Friedrich Engels,
> *The Communist Manifesto*

At a very basic level, and however lustily they
sing from the same hymnbook when they gather
together in Davos or Aspen, the leaders of the
world's great business enterprises continue to
differ in their most fundamental strategic
behavior and objectives.
> Paul N. Doremus, William W. Keller,
> Louis W. Pauly, and Simon Reich,
> *The Myth of the Global Corporation*

The issue of what will be the outcome of the processes of world integration
of economic, industrial, and financial systems—the processes summarized
as globalization—continues to be the central issue of our time. Indeed, as
the words of Marx and Engels reveal, written on the eve of the 1848 revo-
lutions in Europe, it has been the central issue for a century and a half, at
least. The world has seen many upheavals since then—the rise of Germany
as a world industrial power in the nineteenth century and then of Japan in
the twentieth century; the continuing efforts to isolate countries from the
effects of globalization, through social democracy on the one hand, and

various kinds of communist, fascist, and nazi regimes on the other; the reestablishment of a world trading system in the postwar period, and the rise of East Asian industrial powers as principal beneficiaries of the system. But with the fall of the Berlin Wall in 1989, the long-delayed impetus toward the creation of world markets and a world economy was resumed. Geoeconomics reemerged as the global framework within which nations continue to assert their national interests; globalization reasserted its primacy as the central economic, financial, political, and industrial issue of our time.

The trend toward a "global system," spanning technological, economic, financial, political, and cultural tendencies, has been widely discussed in the 1990s.[1] There are two kinds of debates going on in the general cacophony surrounding the term "globalization." There is a debate (of sorts) being conducted between the evangelists of a single world system, led by Wall Street and the U.S. Treasury and propagated worldwide by the IMF, and opponents of such a system, led by labor movements, consumers' rights movements, and other citizen groups around the world, who see social dislocation and fragmentation as the price being paid for global convergence. One-sided as it is, this debate occupies most of the globalization airtime.[2]

The problem with much of the debate as it is conducted is that both sides share a fundamental belief in the uniformity and the convergence of the global system that is being generated. On the one side, the proponents of a global future as a desirable and inevitable outcome tend to see it as being shaped by unstoppable global forces such as the large, dominant multinational corporations that are shaping the world in their own image. Their opponents, vehemently protesting against such a future, seem equally convinced of the powers of the forces and instruments at work, namely, the global corporation, as a force of such dominance that it needs to be constrained by social checks and regulatory balances. There is little room in this debate for an intermediary range of views that query the actual power and dominance of the supposedly global corporations involved or the prospects for the supposedly borderless world that is emerging.

But such views are indeed expressed, and perhaps they are receiving more attention as the shrillness of the debates over globalization is becoming tedious. There is another approach to an analysis of emerging global futures and that is one that accepts the premises of globalization—namely, the destruction of trade barriers and financial barriers and the accelerated integration of world economic and financial systems—but does not accept that this process is necessarily creating a single, uniform, convergent world system nor that it spells the end of nation-state influence on economic dynamics.[3] In the field of international political economy and comparative politics, for example, there are voices raised against the supposed collapse of the salience of the nation-state.[4] Indeed, many of what appear to be "strong" claims for globalization, namely, the emergence of a single world economy and the disappearance of borders as meaningful economic barriers, turn out to be claiming only that a global economy based on uniform rules and transparency, for example, for investment purposes, is emerging. Such claims do not necessarily translate into an argument for strong convergence—although this is frequently the subtext of the debate or the popular interpretation.

Indeed, there is a strong point of view, encapsulated in the quotation from Doremus et al., that the concept of a "global corporation" is a figment created by the imagination of the apologists of globalization. From this perspective, it is salient to point to the continuing—and undeniable—differences that are sustained between the leading firms from the United States, Europe, and Japan. It is also salient to point to the manifest shortcomings of many of the firms dubbed "global" in remaining tied to a home base, if not explicitly in terms of production and trade operations, then certainly in terms of patterns of corporate governance. So there is indeed something of a myth concerning the "globality" of many if not most of the MNEs emanating from the Triad countries.

The starting point for this book, and the appropriate point on which to bring the discussion to a close, is that such views fail to capture the reality of what firms from the Periphery have accomplished—indeed, what they have had to accomplish in order to become players in the globalizing international economy. So while the existence of global corporations might have a mythical side to it when considering MNEs from the Triad, my point is that MNEs from the Periphery *have to be global* in their outlook, in their corporate governance, and in their operations, if they are to flourish in the new kind of international economy being created. Their globality is no myth, but indeed their passport to success.

The Global Corporation

The global corporation was first seen in the 1960s as a threat to both national governments and aspiring domestic companies. But this perspective could not last. Singapore and then other developing countries showed that MNEs could be harnessed very effectively for their own development. Then in the 1970s and 1980s, it was seen as a promise, and the global corporation emerged as a vehicle for countries' advancement and as an efficient form through which to conduct business. In the 1990s, the elusive goal of globality has been revealed as achieved actually by very few players. The supremacy of the traditional MNE has been challenged, as its vulnerabilities and lumbering slowness have become all too apparent. Even more significant, its truly "global" status has been challenged, as study after study has revealed the continuing attachment of even the most apparently global corporations to their U.S., European, or Japanese home bases. It turns out that truly global status is a rare attainment.[5]

The debate has now shifted so that from the perspective of the Periphery the global corporation is not seen as a threat but as a highly desirable attainment. It is the argument of this book that it is the latecomer firms from the Periphery that reveal the outlines of what it means to be truly global. The largest multinationals in the world today have little institutional memory of how they acquired and how they sustain their international scale. But this is the most pressing issue for the latecomers. Issues which appear as management problems for existing global corporations—such as the reconciliation of the dilemma of maintaining global integration alongside local responsiveness—become the means for latecomers to define their internationalization strategy. The concept of "global" in all its complexity is laid bare through the analysis of their experiences.

The Global Network Economy and Latecomer Strategies

Our argument now comes full circle. The network features of the emergent global economy support and underpin the strategic and organizational innovations of newcomers and latecomers. Four aspects of this complementarity may be identified. There is first the emergence of new forms of MNEs (TNEs) that have been able to take advantage of new opportunities. Second, they have been able to successfully "colonize" and insert themselves within the worldwide web of the international economy through their accelerated internationalization. Third, they have utilized organizational innovations and strategic innovations such as linkage and leverage which mesh with the interlinked character of the global economy. Finally their ability to sustain their advantages is translated from initial peripheral advantages into the advantages that stem from global coverage, global organization, and global strategy.

The Networked Global Economy and Emergence of New MNE Forms

The conventional literature on the global economy (such as is found in texts on international business and political economy) depicts the growth of MNEs as driven by their strategic goal of exploiting their assets and advantages internationally. The view of MNEs as behemoths trampling over domestic competitors is one that is now deeply rooted—and yet it is quite at odds with the reality (which is that most MNEs are quite small) and with the dynamics of the global economic system (which sees global firms sprouting up everywhere in response to wholly new opportunities and challenges to which behemoths are far too slow to respond). Thus, we depict the arrival of so many new forms of MNEs, of which latecomers from East Asia like Acer are prominent examples, as linked to the emergence of new dynamics in the global economy that presents new opportunities for firms.

There are opportunities connected with cross-border industrial contracting; with the globalization of functions such as production, R&D, logistics, and customer service; and there are the new opportunities generated by the demands of global firms themselves. Our argument is that the emergence of new forms of MNEs is simply the obverse face of these changes in the dynamics of the global economy.

The Networked Global Economy and Accelerated Internationalization

Seeing the emerging global economy as networks of multiply interlinked firms provides a fresh perspective on the process of internationalization. The key characteristic of the newcomers and latecomers is that they do not build solid international structures piece by piece, but rather they engage in "lattice" construction, with accelerated expansion as the key goal. They build their global operations extremely quickly through linking up with existing players rather than creating everything over again, through partnership or acquisition, and with an organizational capability that rapidly assimilates such acquisitions or partners to their global processes. It is as if there is an existing network template in the global economy with linkages waiting to be created and which are created by the rapidly expanding newcomers and latecomers.

The Networked Global Economy and Global Clusters— the Cellular Form

The counterpart to rapid expansion by the MNE through the creation or addition of new external linkages is a pattern of organizational growth based on internal networks as well. This is what I am calling the "cellular model." It is a network form of organizational architecture in which the parts of the corporation grow independently, adapting autonomously to new situations and taking advantage of new opportunities. It is as natural for the business units (BUs) within such a network or cellular structure to construct links with each other, as it is with firms outside the corporation. The network or cellular form of the corporation on a global scale solves the problem that is much discussed in the MNE literature, namely, the problem of (lack of) subsidiary initiative and the converse problem of maneuvering between corporate HQ and disgruntled subsidiaries looking to evade headquarters control. It solves it by treating the subsidiary as an autonomous entity, subject to the discipline that is imposed on the entire corporation. This in turn is based on the capacity of the business units, or cells, to take strategic initiatives of their own consistent with the overall strategy of the global corporation.

The Networked Global Economy and Strategic Innovation

The global economy seen as networks of interlinked firms provides the setting in which newcomer and latecomer MNEs can rapidly establish themselves through taking strategic advantage of these novel structures and network processes. A firm like Acer expands internationally with an eye on the possibilities of creating points of concentration around which it builds strength. Acer, as we have seen, developed partner firms in Central America and Southeast Asia and then used these partnerships, which flourished, to expand the corporation's reach into neighboring countries. This pattern of building strength around points of concentration, and linking one part of the network with another, is highly reminiscent of stratagems used in the Eastern game of GO—a game with which Acer founder Stan Shih is most familiar. It is through strategic innovations that the latecomer MNE acquires a stake and a presence in the global economy. As a global cluster its success is dependent on the ability of its parts (cells) to take strategic initiatives for themselves, consistent with the overall strategy of the global corporation.

The Networked Global Economy and Resolution of the
Organizational Problems of Global Scale

Conventional solidly built MNEs with strong hierarchical and centralized organizational processes have found it extremely difficult to solve the organizational problems that come with global scale, and in particular what Bartlett and Ghoshal call the global integration–local responsiveness dilemma. While this is an issue that must be addressed by all MNEs, whether latecomers, or early comers, the latecomer, with a loose, network structure and an accelerated expansion strategy of creating linkages, can resolve the GI-LR dilemma as it expands and use its resolution precisely as a means of accelerating its expansion. The nodes within the global economy to which the latecomers and newcomers connect are precisely the source of local responsiveness (e.g., local distributors in new markets), while the corporation can concentrate on building coordination capabilities that can hold such a loose structure together.

Strategic and Organizational Innovations as Adaptations to the Global Network Economy

The strategic and organizational innovations that we have been describing as emanating from the newcomers and latecomers in the global economy now have greater plausibility. They are not one-off innovations with transient or ephemeral appeal. They are in fact deeply rooted in the tendencies within the global economy itself. The newcomers and latecomers that we have identified, and whose strategies and organizational architectures appear to be so innovative, are in fact the *early adapters to the new conditions of the global networked economy.* They are the firms that have taken advantage of the new opportunities for linkage and leverage, as the worldwide web of the global economy has emerged.

The conclusion then is that these latecomers (and newcomers) are the first truly global firms. They are equipped not just with a geocentric attitude and a global reach embodying global economies and synergies, but they have strategies and organizational architectures that draw their strength and efficacy from their complementarity with the weblike character of the global economy. They have been able to take maximum advantage of the new opportunities presented by the interlinkages of the global economy.[6]

So my concluding thesis or proposition is that it is the changing global environment which has hastened the appearance of newcomers and latecomers and which has provided opportunities for expansion and penetration for firms that can take advantage of, and complement, the weblike character of the multiple networks of the global economy. The globally interlinked character of the latecomer MNE is the outcome of its accelerated internationalization through linkage and leverage, and both strategy and structure complement perfectly the globally interlinked character of the global economy.

This is actually a *stunning* conclusion. It goes completely against the grain of conventional wisdom that sees globalization as a dominant tendency, driven by a handful of huge global firms creating a uniform world in their own image. On the contrary, the picture developed is of the global incumbents struggling to keep up with a fast-changing world economy, where they are being outwitted by the more nimble newcomers and latecomers. If this is the case, then the forces shaping the global economy in the twenty-first century are very different from those that were generally recognized as having been the dominant influences in the past.

The Argument Summarized

We are now in a position to summarize the main findings of this study. The work began with the realization that the global economy is being transformed through the sudden arrival of many new and relatively unknown firms. Case studies revealed that these new arrivals do not fit the pattern of conventional MNEs, in that they have become global very fast; they are not huge (and sometimes are very small); and they do not follow the same kinds of organizational and strategic logic as the large, established incumbents. Moreover, many of them originate from peripheral parts of the world economy, rather than—as expected—from the Triad countries. Acer, in particular, provided unprecedented access to managers at all levels to generate a picture of how a firm originating from the Periphery views the world.

For the purposes of this study, these "new MNEs" have been assembled into a small representative group which includes Acer, as well as other latecomers like Ispat, Cemex, Li and Fung, or Hong Leong (as examples from various NICs). These examples are buttressed by the cases of newcomers like Gemplus, Fresenius, Nutreco, or CMS Energy, and of niche players like Barth & Sohn, or Krones, or Hauni. These firms may be taken as representative of a "new zoology" of the global economy, which is populated not only by global incumbents but also by various new "species" such as born globals, niche players, global contractors, latecomers, and newcomers of various kinds.

The sudden appearance of these firms, and their capacity to create a competitive position in the teeth of opposition from giant incumbents, is the phenomenon that provided the central puzzle and starting point for this study. Why, at a time of unparalleled interest in giant firms and globalization, should these latecomers and newcomers make their sudden and dramatic entry? On reflection, many of the obvious kinds of explanations do not seem able to resolve this puzzle. Issues like low costs, or the harnessing of internal resources, or simply "luck" did not seem to provide satisfactory explanations.

This study has therefore concerned itself with strategic and organizational innovations that have been developed by the newcomers and latecomers. These successfully globalizing firms share some important and distinctive characteristics. First, they all internationalized very rapidly. It was as if they had executed a "gestalt switch" from domestic to global player—even if their actual pattern of internationalization was incremental. Thus, they benefited from surprise in creating their global presence. Second, they adopted a variety of global organizational forms, from highly unconventional global cellular clusters (Acer, Li and Fung) to weblike integrated global operations like Ispat. In all cases, they dispensed with conventional "international division"–style organization, which demonstrates that they began their internationalization already equipped with a global outlook. Third, they adopted a variety of innovative strategies for achieving global reach, from piggybacking on incumbent global firms as customers, through subcontracting arrangements, and various other linkage and leverage devices.

These characteristics provided the starting point for an analysis of what could account for their success, in the face of such overwhelming opposition from very competitive incumbents. The newcomers and latecomers have had to find innovative ways to make space for themselves in markets that were already crowded with very capable firms. Viewed in their own terms, the firms found new ways to "complement" the strategies of the incumbents, such as through offering contract services, through licensing new technologies to forming joint ventures and strategic alliances. It is plausible that it was through the implementation of these "complementary" strategies that newcomers and latecomers were able to win a place in the emergent global economy, not on the basis of their existing strengths, but on the basis of their capacity to leverage resources from the strengths of others, through making international connections. These internationalization strategies, designed to enhance firms' resource bases rather than to exploit existing assets, represent a fundamental departure in thinking by firms about what "globalizing" means and how it can be accomplished.

This study appeals to the recent "resource-based view" of firms' competitive positions to provide a more general account of the successes of the newcomers and latecomers in their quest for international reach. From a resource perspective, what these firms have in common is that their internationalization is not based on the possession of overwhelming domestic assets which can be exploited abroad—as has been common with conventional MNEs. Rather, their international expansion has been undertaken as much for the search for new resources to underpin new strategic options, as it has been to exploit existing resources. And this is why they have to expand quickly to consolidate gains that are fleetingly won. And this is why they tend to rely on partnerships and joint ventures to reduce the high level of risk involved in their leveraged strategies.

It is worth underlining that the differences between these two approaches are profound. On the one hand, incumbent giants exploit their domestic resources in order to move abroad, while on the other hand, nimble newcomers and latecomers venture abroad to access resources that would otherwise be unavailable—particularly marketing resources but also access to R&D facilities, production facilities, and partner firms—and thereby create a global position for themselves. Global giants see themselves as having much to lose, and little to gain, by sharing their resources in partnerships and other contractual alliances. The newcomers and latecomers, by contrast, have everything to gain by tapping the resources of others and can be seen to internationalize explicitly with this goal. The incumbents see the world as full of competitors who are trying to imitate their success. The newcomers and latecomers see the world as full of resources to be tapped, provided the appropriate complementary strategies and organizational forms can be devised. This thinking is quite different from earlier "resource access" strategies (where the resources involved were raw materials, often in former colonial possessions). It is also quite different from earlier internationalization strategies of "Third World Multinationals" that relied heavily on exploitation of their cost advantages rather than on accessing overseas resources. It is, quite simply, a new model for global growth.

Such innovative patterns of outward expansion in search of new resources can be captured in a set of principles that mirror the OLI framework as developed by Dunning et al. for conventional MNEs. In terms of resource leverage, the newcomers and latecomers have been Outward-oriented—searching for new sources of resources in the wider global economy (rather than exploiting their existing internal resources through purely internalized processes). They have sought to access new resources through patterns of Linkage and Leverage, that is, through establishing innovative links such as subcontracting or licensing arrangements that have the effect of complementing the strategies of incumbents. And as they have expanded, they have found ways to tightly Integrate their operations with a consistent global perspective and strategy. This alternative OLI* framework as developed in this study for latecomer and newcomer MNEs thus differs significantly from the framework developed by Dunning et al. to account for the expansion of incumbent MNEs from the Triad. It captures the novelty and distinctiveness of the rationale for international expansion undertaken by newcomers and latecomers and their organizational and strategic approach to operating internationally. More to the point, the alternative framework invites the appropriate questions in seeking answers to the puzzle as to how these newcomers and latecomers managed their rapid internationalization in the face of such resistance.

The demonstration of characteristic patterns of expansion and international reach would not, on its own, be sufficient to account for the success of the latecomers and newcomers. The critical issue is that their OLI* characteristics are very well adapted to the character of the emergent global economy, with its multiple linkages and weblike interfirm connections. Their outward orientation and their propensity to form linkages and to leverage resources through these linkages are ideally suited to a world economy of multiple connections. Firms form cross-boundary linkages through connections with suppliers, customers, and each other, forming complex and multipronged value chains that span national boundaries. The critical organizational capacities involved in this global networking are those to do with managing the accelerated process of making connections (e.g., through management of partnerships) and integrating the light, latticelike dispersed organizational structures that result. The newcomers and latecomers all exhibit a capacity to resolve in novel ways the major organizational obstacle that has held back incumbents, namely, the simultaneous resolution of the global integration–local responsiveness dilemma. It is a striking fact that firms from the Periphery have been so prominent in finding ways to resolve this dilemma, while incumbent giants have found it so difficult.

This book therefore provides suggestive evidence that firms are internationalizing in ways that generate novel dynamics and opportunities in the emergent global economy. It thus generates fresh insights into the multiple processes that are labeled "globalization." There is a widespread view that globalization—insofar as it is driven by MNEs creating cross-border production, trade, and knowledge flow networks—is being driven by giant firms and by relentless convergence pressures, creating uniform global markets inhabited by oligopolies of giants which have no "home base." It is difficult to sustain such a picture in the face of the evidence established by the newcomers and latecomers investigated.

While this study is based on a very small sample of firms and therefore cannot be regarded in any way as definitive, nevertheless, it is reasonable to claim that the firms chosen are representative of many more global players to come, whose patterns of expansion and mode of drawing advantages from their international involvement are and will be very different from those ascribed to conventional, incumbent MNEs. The insights generated are suggestive of trends that make it more plausible to argue that globalization is being driven as much by firms from the Periphery as by giants from the Triad economies. The giants are still very much tied to a "home base" and to date have demonstrated little appetite for engaging in truly "global" competition. By contrast, newcomers and latecomers—like the firms in our sample—are definitely global in their outlook and their strategy and organization. This is giving them rapidly acquired advantages over slower-moving and less-focused incumbents—even in markets that have traditionally been viewed as "global." In markets that have traditionally been domestic-oriented, like steel and cement, the Peripheral firms are demonstrating how significant advantages can be secured through globalized operations and service.

If they can be corroborated, these insights have striking implications. If indeed globalizing processes are being driven by Peripheral as much as by Triad firms, then rather than resulting in uniformity, globalization processes are more likely to result in a vast array of different outcomes, offering unprecedented opportunities for small- and medium-sized latecomers and newcomers. The world economy at the beginning of the twenty-first century has never been more open and richer in productive resources that can be tapped by clever and nimble small players. This is very different from an outcome where there is economic dominance by a few. The same reasoning holds that many of the fears associated with political, industrial, and cultural dominance, discussed under the broad rubric of "globalization," may be equally wide of the mark.

Globalization in the twenty-first century is thus likely to be characterized by the increasing integration of a variety of small- and medium-sized players in international networks of production, movement of goods, and flows of information and knowledge. These in themselves will continue to throw up new opportunities for involvement on the part of innovative small- and medium-sized players, who will create constant pressure on incumbents. The international economy is likely to become the source of endless novelty and innovation, creating ever new opportunities but also pressures on incumbents to adapt or disappear. The fear that MNEs would become bloated giants beyond control, shaping the world in their own image, may thus be viewed as a response to a very brief period of dominance by a handful of giant U.S. firms going abroad. More important, they helped to create the global economic trends that have created opportunities for the newcomers and latecomers, and these players in turn are now helping to shape the global trends that will create yet more opportunities in the future. This is a prospect to be welcomed, not feared.

Notes

1. For general treatments of globalization and of the emergent global system (economic, political, cultural), see for example Axford (1995); Dicken (1992/98); Ruigrok and Van Tulder (1995); and Boyd and Dunning (eds) (1999). Hirst and Thompson (1996) provide a critical overview of the notion of globalization, while Veseth (1998) gives a healthy dose of skepticism. Gold and Islam (1995) provide an overview of TNC evolution as both cause and effect of globalization, while Kozul-Wright and Rowthorn (1998) offer a range of essays on the inter-action between the globalizing economy and MNEs. Accounts which emphasize the conflicts (real and potential) between globalizing tendencies and national governance systems include Friedman (1999); Luttwak (1999); Yergin and Stan-islaw (1999) and Mickelthwait and Woodridge (2000). Zysman (1996) queries the salience of a "global economy" at a time of enduring national and regional economic realities.

2. For representative works that emphasize the social costs of globalization processes (intended or unintended), see Greider (1997), Martin and Schumann (1997), Gray (1998), and from a sociological perspective, Sassen (1998).

3. Reich (1992) and Ohmae (1989; 1990/99; 1995a;-b) are frequently cited as two such "strong globalization" authors. While they certainly spend a lot of time and energy denying the future relevance of borders, or that there is any distinc-tion between "them" and "us" in a global economy, they do not actually go so far as to say that what is emerging is a completely uniform, convergent global economy peopled by uniform, convergent MNEs. Hyperglobalization enthusiasts do say such a thing, however; see for example Bryan and Farrell (1996): "We are moving toward a world where the capital markets constrain what govern-ment can do—not the other way around. . . . The engine behind this change is the growing power of the global capital market. . . . Individual national financial markets are losing their separate identities as they merge into a single, over-powering marketplace" (1996: 1–8).

4. See Weiss (1998; 1999a;-b; 2001) for a strong defense of the continuing role for state economic policies, e.g., for industrial upgrading, in adaptation to and in complementary fashion to emerging global tendencies. This is consistent with the view that national interests continue to be promoted by states in an era of "geoeconomics" (Luttwak 1999).

5. Such a view is supported by the evidence as presented by UNCTAD in the *World Investment Report*. Year after year, this report reveals that the most globalized firms, as measured by the Transnationality Index (TNI), come from smaller countries such as Switzerland or Sweden or The Netherlands, or from noncore countries such as Canada. Significantly, in *WIR99*, none of the Top 10 globalized TNCs came from the U.S., UK, or Japan (Table 3.6, p. 83, UNCTAD 1999).

6. This pattern of world industrial development, couched in terms of linkage, leverage, and learning by internationalizing firms from the Periphery, is dis-cussed in the forthcoming UNIDO *World Industrial Development Report* (2002).

BIBLIOGRAPHY

Acs, Z. and Preston, L. 1997. Small and medium-sized enterprises, technology and globalization: Introduction. *Small Business Economics (*Special Issue: Small and Medium-sized Enterprises in the Global Economy), 9 (1): 1–6.

Acs, Z., Morck, R., Shaver, J. M., and Yeung, B. 1997. The internationalization of small and medium-sized enterprises: A policy perspective. *Small Business Economics*, 9: 7–20.

Agarwal, J. P. 1985. Intra-LDCs foreign direct investment: A comparative analysis of Third World multinationals. *The Developing Economies*, 23 (3).

Agarwal, S. and Ramaswami, S. N. 1992. Choice of foreign market entry mode: Impact of ownership, location and internalization factors. *Journal of International Business Studies*, 23: 1–27.

Aggarwal, R. and Agmon, T. 1990. The international success of developing country firms: Role of government-directed comparative advantage. *Management International Review*, 30 (2): 163–180.

Agmon, T. and Kindleberger, C. P. (eds) 1977. *Multinationals from Small Countries*. Cambridge, MA: The MIT Press.

Agren, L. 1990. Swedish direct investment in the U. S. Ph.D. diss., Institute of International Business, Stockholm School of Economics.

Aharoni, Y. 1966. *The Foreign Investment Decision Process*. Boston: Harvard Graduate School of Business Administration.

Andersen, O. 1993. On the internationalization process of firms: A critical analysis. *Journal of International Business Studies*, 24(2): 209–231.

Andersen, O. 1997. Internationalization and market entry mode: A review of theories and conceptual frameworks. *Management International Review*, 37 (Special issue on Internationalization processes): 27–42.

Andersen, O. and Kheam, L. S. 1998. Resource-based theory and international growth strategies: An exploratory study. *International Business Review*, 7: 163–184.

225

Andersen, P. H., Blenker, P., and Christensen, P. R. 1997. Generic routes to sub-contractors' internationalisation. In I. Bjorkman and M. Forsgren (eds), *The Nature of the International Firm*. Copenhagen: Copenhagen Business School Press.

Anderson, E. and Gatignon, H. 1986. Modes of entry: A transactions cost analysis and propositions. *Journal of International Business Studies*, 17 (3): 1–26.

Anderson, P. and Tushman, M. L. 1990. Technological discontinuities and dominant designs: A cyclical model of technological change. *Administrative Science Quarterly*, 35: 604–633.

Andersson, A. 2000. The internationalization of the firm from an entrepreneurial perspective. *International Studies of Management & Organization*, 30 (1): 63–92.

Andersson, U., Johanson, J., and Vahlne, J.-E. 1997. Organic acquisitions in the internationalization process of the business firm. *Management International Review*, 37 (Special issue on Internationalization processes): 67–84.

Aron, D. J. 1991. Using the capital market as a monitor: Corporate spinoffs in an agency framework. *The RAND Journal of Economics*, 22 (4): 505–519.

Attman, A., Kuuse, J., and Olsson, U. 1976. *L.M. Ericsson 100 Years*. (Volume 1: The Pioneering Years, Struggle for Concessions, Crisis 1876–1932). Stockholm: L.M. Ericsson.

Attman, A. and Olsson, U. 1976. *L.M. Ericsson 100 Years*. (Volume 2: Rescue, Reconstruction, Worldwide Enterprise 1932–1976). Stockholm: L.M. Ericsson.

Axelsson, B. and Johanson, J. 1992. Foreign market entry: The textbook vs. the network view. In B. Axelsson, and G. Easton (eds), *Industrial Networks: A New View of Reality*. London and New York: Routledge.

Axford, B. 1995. *The Global System: Economics, Politics and Culture*. New York: St. Martin's Press.

Bain, J. S. 1956. *Barriers to New Competition*. Cambridge, MA: Harvard University Press.

Baird, I. S., Lyles, M. A., and Orris, J. B. 1994. The choice of international strategies by small business. *Journal of Small Business Management*, 32 (1): 48–59.

Barham, K. and Heimer, C. 1998. *ABB The Dancing Giant: Creating the Globally Connected Corporation*. London: Financial Times Management.

Barkema, H. G. and Vermeulen, F. 1998. International expansion through start-up or acquisition: A learning perspective. *Academy of Management Journal*, 41 (1): 7–26.

Barnet, R. J. and Mueller, R. E. 1974. *Global Reach: The Power of the Multinational Corporations*. New York: Simon & Schuster.

Barnet, R. J. and Cavanagh, J. 1994. *Global Dreams: Imperial Corporations and the New World Order*. New York: Simon & Schuster.

Barney, J. B. 1986. Strategic factor markets: Expectations, luck, and business strategy. *Management Science*, 32 (10): 1231–1241.

Barney, J. B. 1991. Firm resources and sustained competitive advantage. *Journal of Management*, 17 (1): 99–120.

Barney, J. B. 1995. Looking inside for competitive advantage. *Academy of Management Executive*, 9 (4): 49–61.

Barney, J. B. 1997. *Gaining and Sustaining Competitive Advantage*. Reading, MA: Addison-Wesley.

Bartlett, C. A. 1979. Multinational structural evolution: The changing decision environment in international divisions. Ph.D. diss., Graduate School of Business Administration, Harvard University.

Bartlett, C. A. 1986. Building and managing the transnational: The new organizational challenge. In M. Porter (ed), *Competition in Global Industries*. Boston: Harvard Business School Press.

Bartlett, C. A., Doz, Y. L., and Hedlund, G. (eds). 1990. *Managing the Global Firm*. London and New York: Routledge.

Bartlett, C. A. and Ghoshal, S. 1987. Managing across borders: New organizational responses. *Sloan Management Review*, (Fall): 43–53.

Bartlett, C. A. and Ghoshal, S. 1989. *Managing Across Borders: The Transnational Solution*. Boston: Harvard Business School Press.

Bartlett, C. A. and Ghoshal, S. 2000a. *Transnational Management: Text, Cases, and Readings in Cross-Border Management*. (Third edition). New York: McGraw-Hill.

Bartlett, C. A. and Ghoshal, S. 2000b. Going global: Lessons from late movers. *Harvard Business Review*, (Mar-Apr): 132–142.

Beamish, P. W. and Banks, J. C. 1987. Equity joint ventures and the theory of the multinational enterprise. *Journal of International Business Studies*, 19 (2): 1–16.

Beamish, P. W., Delios, A., and Lecraw, D. J. 1997. *Japanese Multinationals in the Global Economy*. Cheltenham, UK: Edward Elgar.

Belanger, J., Berggren, C., Bjorkman, T., and Kohler, C. (eds). 1999. *Being Local Worldwide: ABB and the Challenge of Global Management*. Ithaca, NY: Cornell University Press.

Bell, J. 1995. The internationalisation of small computer software firms: A further challenge to "stage" theories. *European Journal of Marketing*, 29 (8): 60–75.

Benito, G. R. G. and Welch, L. S. 1994. Foreign market servicing: Beyond choice of entry mode. *Journal of International Marketing*, 2 (2): 7–27.

Benito, G. R. G. and Welch, L. S. 1997. De-internationalization. *Management International Review*, 37 (Special issue on Internationalization processes): 7–25.

Berra, L., Piatti, L., and Vitali, G. 1995. The internationalization process in the small and medium-sized firm: A case study of the Italian clothing industry. *Small Business Economics*, 7 (1): 67–75.

Berry, H. and Sakakibara, M. 1999. Resource accumulation and overseas expansion by Japanese multinationals: An empirical analysis of the internalization theory. Working paper S&O 99–26, Anderson Graduate School of Management, UCLA.

Bilkey, W. J. 1978. An attempted integration of the literature on the export behavior of firms. *Journal of International Business Studies*, 9 (1): 33–46.

Bilkey, W. J. and Tesar, G. 1977. The export behavior of smaller-sized Wisconsin firms. *Journal of International Business Studies*, 8 (1): 93–98.

Birkinshaw, J. 1997. Entrepreneurship in multinational corporations: The characteristics of subsidiary initiatives. *Strategic Management Journal*, 18 (3): 207–229.

Birkinshaw, J. and Hood, N. (eds). 1998a. *Multinational Corporate Evolution and Subsidiary Development*. London: Macmillan; and New York: St. Martin's Press.

Birkinshaw, J. and Hood, N. 1998b. Multinational subsidiary evolution: Capability and charter change in foreign-owned subsidiary companies. *Academy of Management Review*, 23 (4): 773–795.

Birkinshaw, J. and Ridderstråle, J. 1999. Fighting the corporate immune system: A process study of subsidiary initiatives in multinational corporations. *International Business Review*, 8: 149–180.

Birkinshaw, J., Hood, N., and Jonsson, S. 1998. Building firm-specific advantages in multinational corporations: The role of subsidiary initiative. *Strategic Management Journal*, 19: 221–241.

Björkman, I. and Forsgren, M. (eds). 1997. *The Nature of the International Firm: Nordic Contributions to International Business Research*. Copenhagen Studies in Economics and Management, No. 11. Copenhagen: Handelshøjskolens Forlag.

Blomström, Magnus, 2000. Internationalization and growth: Evidence from Sweden. Working paper #90, European Institute of Japanese Studies, Stockholm School of Economics.

Blomström, M. and Zejan, M. 1991. Why do multinational firms seek out joint ventures? *Journal of International Development*, 3: 53–63.

Bloodgood, J. M., Sapienza, H. J. and Almeida, J. G. 1996. The internationalization of new high-potential U.S. ventures: Antecedents and outcomes. *Entrepreneurship Theory and Practice*, 20 (4): 61–76.

Boyd, G. and Dunning, J. H. (eds). 1999. *Structural Change and Cooperation in the Global Economy*. Aldershot, UK: Edward Elgar.

Bryan, L. and Farrell, D. 1996. *Market Unbound: Unleashing Global Capitalism*. New York: John Wiley.

Buckley, P. J. 1988. The limits of explanation: Testing the internalization theory of the multinational enterprise. *Journal of International Business Studies*, 19 (2): 181–193.

Buckley, P. J. 1991. The frontiers of international business research. *Management International Review*, 31 (Special Issue): 7–22.

Buckley, P. J. and Casson, M. C. 1976. *The Future of the Multinational Enterprise*. London: Holmes & Meier.

Buckley, P. J. and Casson, M. C. 1985. *The Economic Theory of the Multinational Enterprise*. London: Macmillan.

Buckley, P. J. and Casson, M. C. 1998. Analyzing foreign market entry strategies: Extending the internalization approach. *Journal of International Business Studies*, 29 (3): 539–562.

Buckley, P. J. and Mirza, H. 1988. The strategy of Pacific Asian Multinationals. *The Pacific Review*, 1 (1): 50–62.

Burgel, O. and Murray, G. C. 2000. The international market entry choices of start-up companies in high-technology industries. *Journal of International Marketing*, 8 (2): 33–62.

Burgelman, R. 1994. Fading memories: A process theory of strategic business exit in dynamic environments. *Administrative Science Quarterly*, 39 (1): 24–56.

Calof, J. L. 1993. The impact of size on internationalization. *Journal of Small Business Management*, 31 (4): 60–69.

Calof, J. L. and Beamish, P. W. 1995. Adapting to foreign markets: Explaining internationalization. *International Business Review*, 4 (2): 115–131.

Cantwell, J. A. 1989. The changing form of multinational enterprise expansion in the twentieth century. In A. Teichova et al. (eds), *Historical Studies in International Corporate Business*. Cambridge: Cambridge University Press.

Cantwell, J. A. 1991. A survey of theories of international production. In C. N. Pitelis and R. Sugden (eds), *The Nature of the Transnational Firm*. London: Routledge.

Cantwell, J. and Iammarino, S. 1998. MNCs, technological innovation and regional systems in the EU: Some evidence in the Italian case. *International Journal of the Economics of Business*, 5 (3): 383–408.

Cantwell, J. and Santangelo, G. D. 1999. The frontier of international technology networks: Sourcing abroad the most highly tacit capabilities. *Information Economics and Policy*, 11 (1): 101–123.

Carlson, S. 1977. Company policies for international expansion: The Swedish experience. In T. Agmon and C. P. Kindleberger (eds), *Multinationals from Small Countries*. Cambridge, MA: The MIT Press.

Carlson, C. 1979. *Swedish industry goes abroad: An essay on industrialization and internationalization*. Lund: Studentlitteratur.

Casson, M. 1982. Transaction costs and the theory of MNEs. In A. Rugman (ed), *New Theories of the Multinational Enterprise*. New York: St. Martins Press.

Casson, M. 1986. General theories of the MNE: Their relevance to business history. In P. Hertner and G. Jones (eds), *Multinationals: Theory and History*. Aldershot: Gower.

Casson, M. 1987. *The Firm and the Market: Studies on Multinational Enterprise and the Scope of the Firm*. Oxford: Basil Blackwell.

Caves, R. E. 1982. *Multinational Enterprise and Economic Analysis*. (First/Second edition). Cambridge: Cambridge University Press.

Caves, R. E. 1998. Research on international business: Problems and prospects. *Journal of International Business Studies*, 29 (1): 5–20.

Cavusgil, S. T. 1980. On the internationalisation process of firms. *European Research*, 8(6): 273–281.

Cavusgil, S. T. 1998. International partnering: A systematic framework for collaborating with foreign business partners. *Journal of International Marketing*, 6 (1): 91–107.

Chandler, A. D. 1986. Technological and organizational underpinnings of modern industrial multinational enterprise: The dynamics of competitive advantage. In A. Teichova et al. (eds), *Multinational Enterprise in Historical Perspective*. Cambridge: Cambridge University Press.

Chandler, A. D., Hagström, P., and Sölvell, O. (eds). 1998. *The Dynamic Firm: The Role of Technology, Strategy, Organization, and Regions*. Oxford: Oxford University Press.

Chang, M. H. 1997. The choice of entry modes and theories of foreign direct investment. *Journal of Global Marketing*, 11 (2): 43–64.

Chang, S. J. 1995. International expansion strategy of Japanese firms: Capability building through sequential entry. *Academy of Management Journal*, 38 (2): 383–407.

Chang, S. J. and Rosenzweig, P. M. 1998. Functional and line of business evolution processes in MNC subsidiaries: Sony in the USA, 1972–95. In J. Birkinshaw and N. Hood (eds), *Multinational Corporate Evolution and Subsidiary Development.* London: Macmillan; and New York: St. Martin's Press.

Chen, E. K. Y. 1981. Hong Kong multinationals in Asia: Characteristics and objectives. In K. Kumar and M. G. McLeod (eds), *Multinationals from Developing Countries.* Lexington, MA: Lexington Books.

Chen H. M. and Chen, T. J. 1998a. Foreign direct investment as a strategic linkage. *Thunderbird International Business Review*, 40 (1): 13–30.

Chen H. M. and Chen, T. J. 1998b. Network linkages and location choice in foreign direct investment. *Journal of International Business Studies*, 29 (3): 445–468.

Chen, R. H. 1998. *Made in Taiwan: The Story of Acer Computers.* Taipei: McGraw-Hill.

Chen, T. J. 1992. Determinants of Taiwan's direct foreign investment: The case of a newly industrialized country. *Journal of Economic Development*, 39 (2): 397–408.

Chi, T. L. and McGuire, D. J. 1996. Collaborative ventures and value of learning: Integrating the transaction cost and strategic option perspectives on the choice of market entry modes. *Journal of International Business Studies*, 27 (2): 285–307.

Cho, D. S. 1987. *The General Trading Company: Concept and Strategy.* Lexington, MA: Lexington Books.

Cho, K. R. and Padmanabhan, P. 1995. Acquisition versus new venture: The choice of foreign establishment mode by Japanese firms. *Journal of International Management*, 1: 255–285.

Clark, T., Pugh, D. S., and Mallory, G. 1997. The process of internationalization in the operating firm. *International Business Review*, 6 (6): 605–623.

Collis, D. J. 1991. A resource-based analysis of global competition: The case of the bearings industry. *Strategic Management Journal*, 12: 49–68.

Collis, D. J. and Montgomery, C. 1998. Creating corporate advantage. *Harvard Business Review*, 76 (3): 70–83.

Contractor, F. J. 1990. Contractual and cooperative forms of international business: Towards a unified theory of modal choice. *Management International Review*, 30 (1): 31–54.

Coviello, N. and McAuley, A. 1999. Internationalisation and the smaller firm: A review of contemporary empirical research. *Management International Review*, 39 (3): 223–256.

Coviello, N. and Munro, H. 1997. Network relationships and the internationalisation process of small software firms. *International Business Review*, 6 (4): 361–386.

Craig, C. S. and Douglas, S. P. 1996a. Developing strategies for global markets: An evolutionary perspective. *Columbia Journal of World Business*, 31 (1): 70–81.

Craig, C. S. and Douglas, S. P. 1996b. Responding to the challenges of global markets: Change, complexity, competition and conscience. *Columbia Journal of World Business*, 31 (4): 6–18.

Craig, C. S. and Douglas, S. P. 1997. Executive insights: Managing the transnational value chain—strategies for firms from emerging markets. *Journal of International Marketing*, 5(3): 71–84.

Craig, T. 1997. Location and implementation issues in support function FDI: The globalisation of Matsushita Electric Industrial Co., Ltd. *Asia Pacific Journal of Management*, 14: 143–164.

Cyert, R. M. and March, J. G. 1963. *A Behavioral Theory of the Firm*. New York: Prentice-Hall.

D'Aveni, R. 1994. *Hypercompetition: Managing the Dynamics of Strategic Maneuvering*. New York: The Free Press.

De Geus, A. 1997. *The Living Company*. London: Nicholas Brealey Publishing.

De La Torre, J., Doz, Y., and Devinney, T. 2000. *Managing the Global Corporation: Case Studies in Strategy and Management*. (Second edition). New York: McGraw-Hill.

Dell, M. (with C. Fredman). 1999. *Direct from Dell: Strategies that Revolutionized an Industry*. New York: HarperCollins.

Dicken, P. 1992. *Global Shift: Transforming the World Economy*. (Second/Third edition). London: Paul Chapman/SAGE.

Dierickx, I. and Cool, K. 1989. Asset stock accumulation and the sustainability of competitive advantage. *Management Science*, 35: 1504–1511.

Doremus, P. N., Keller, W. W., Pauly, L. W., and Reich, S. 1998. *The Myth of the Global Corporation*. Princeton, NJ: Princeton University Press.

Doz, Y. L. 1986. *Strategic Management in Multinational Companies*. Oxford: Pergamon.

Doz, Y. L. and Hamel, G. 1998. *Alliance Advantage*. Boston: HBS Press.

Doz, Y. L. and Prahalad, C. K. 1991. Managing DMNCs: A search for a new paradigm. *Strategic Management Journal*, 12: 145–164.

Doz, Y. L., Bartlett, C. A., and Prahalad, C. K. 1981. Global competitive pressures and host country demands: Managing tensions in MNCs. *California Management Review*, 24 (3): 63–74.

Drucker, P. F. 1997. The global economy and the nation state. *Foreign Affairs*, 76 (5): 159–171.

Dunning, J. H. 1980. Toward an eclectic theory of international production: Some empirical tests. *Journal of International Business Studies*, 11(1): 9–31.

Dunning, J. H. 1981. *The Eclectic Theory of the MNC*. London: Allen & Unwin.

Dunning, J. H. 1988. The eclectic paradigm of international production: A restatement and some possible extensions. *Journal of International Business Studies*, 19 (1): 1–31.

Dunning, J. H. 1993a. *Multinational Enterprises and the Global Economy*. Wokingham, UK and Reading, MA: Addison-Wesley.

Dunning, J. H. (ed). 1993b. *The Globalization of Business: The Challenge of the 1990s*. London: Routledge.

Dunning, J. H. 1995. Reappraising the eclectic paradigm in an age of alliance capitalism. *Journal of International Business Studies*, 26 (3): 461–492.

Dunning, J. H. (ed). 1997. *Governments, Globalization, and International Business*. Oxford: Oxford University Press.

Dunning, J. H. and Narula, R. 1996. The investment development path revisited: Some emerging issues. In J. Dunning and R. Narula (eds), *Foreign Direct Investment and Governments: Catalysts for Economic Restructuring*. London: Routledge.

Dunning, J. H. and Narula, R. 1997. Developing countries versus multinationals in a globalizing world: The dangers of falling behind. In P. Buckley and P.

Ghauri (eds), *Multinational Enterprises and Emerging Markets*. London: Dryden Press.

Dunning, J. H., van Hoesel, R., and Narula, R. 1997. Third World multinationals revisited: New developments and theoretical implications. Discussion papers in International Investment and Management #227. University of Reading, Department of Economics.

Egelhoff, W. G. 1988. Strategy and structure in multinational corporations: A revision of the Stopford and Wells model. *Strategic Management Journal*, 8 (1): 1–14.

Egelhoff, W. G. 1993. Great strategy or great strategy implementation—two ways of competing in global markets. *Sloan Management Review*, 34 (2): 37–50.

Encarnation, D. J. 1982. The political economy of Indian joint industrial ventures abroad. *International Organization*, 36 (1): 31–59.

Encarnation, D. J. 1989. *Dislodging Multinationals: India's Strategy in Comparative Perspective*. (Cornell Studies in Political Economy). Ithaca, NY: Cornell University Press.

Eriksson, K., Johanson, J., Majkgard, A., and Sharma, D. D. 1997. Experiential knowledge and cost in the internationalization process. *Journal of International Business Studies*, 28 (2): 337–360.

Eriksson, K., Johanson, J., Majkgard, A., and Sharma, D. D. 2000. Effect of variation on knowledge accumulation in the internationalisation process. *International Studies of Management & Organization*, 30 (1): 26–44.

Erramilli, M. K. and Rao, C. P. 1990. Choice of foreign market entry modes by service firms: Role of market knowledge. *Management International Review*, 30 (2): 135–150.

Fahy, J. 1996. Competitive advantage in international services: A resource-based view. *International Studies of Management & Organization*, 26 (2): 24–37.

Fairtlough, G. 1995. *Creative Compartments: A Design for Future Organisation*. London: Adamantine Press.

Fieldhouse, D. K. 1986. The multinational: A critique of a concept. In A. Teichova et al. (eds), *Multinational Enterprise in Historical Perspective*. Cambridge: Cambridge University Press.

Fina, E. and Rugman, A. M. 1996. A test of internalization theory and internationalization theory: The Upjohn company. *Management International Review*, 36 (3): 199–213.

Fleenor, D. 1993. The coming *and going* of the global corporation. *Columbia Journal of World Business*, 28 (4): 6–16.

Forsgren, M. 1989. *Managing the Internationalisation Process: The Swedish Case*. London: Routledge.

Forsgren, M. 1990. Managing the international multi-centre firm: Case studies from Sweden. *European Management Journal*, 8 (2): 261–267.

Forsgren, M. 1999. Some critical notes on learning in the Uppsala internationalization process model. Working paper #99/23, Institute of International Business, Stockholm School of Economics.

Forsgren, M. and Johanson, J. 1992. Managing internationalization in business networks. In M. Forsgren and J. Johanson (eds), *Managing Networks in International Business*. Philadelphia: Gordon and Breach.

Forsgren, M., Holm, U., and Johanson, J. 1995. Division headquarters go abroad—A step in the internationalization of the multinational corporation. *Journal of Management Studies*, 32 (4): 475–491.

Forsgren, M., Pedersen, T., and Foss, N. J. 1999. Accounting for the strengths of MNC subsidiaries: The case of foreign-owned firms in Denmark. *International Business Review*, 8: 181–196.

Foss, N. J. (ed). 1997. *Resources, Firms and Strategies*. New York: Oxford University Press.

Franko, L. G. 1974a. The move toward a multinational structure in European organizations. *Administrative Science Quarterly*, 19: 493–506.

Franko, L. G. 1974b. The origins of multinational manufacturing by continental European firms. *Business History Review*, 48 (Autumn): 277–302.

Franko, L. G. 1976. *The European Multinational: A Renewed Challenge to American and British Big Business*. London: Harper & Row; Stamford, CT: Greylock.

Friedman, T. L. 1999. *The Lexus and the Olive Tree*. New York: Farrar, Straus & Giroux.

Fujita, M. 1995a. Small and medium-sized transnational corporations: Trends and patterns of foreign direct investment. *Small Business Economics*, 7 (3): 183–204.

Fujita, M. 1995b. Small and medium-sized transnational corporations: Salient features. *Small Business Economics*, 7 (3): 251–271.

Fujita, M. 1998. *The Transnational Activities of Small and Medium-Sized Enterprises*. Dordrecht: Kluwer Academic.

Geringer, J. M. 1991. Strategic determinants of partner selection criteria in international joint ventures. *Journal of International Business Studies*, 22 (1): 41–62.

Geringer, J. M. and Hebert, L. 1989. Control and performance of international joint ventures. *Journal of International Business Studies*, 20 (2): 235–254.

Geringer, J. M., Beamish, P. W., and daCosta, R. C. 1989. Diversification strategy and internationalization: Implications for MNE performance. *Strategic Management Journal*, 10: 109–119.

Geringer, J. M, Tallman, S., and Olsen, D. M. 2000. Product and international diversification among Japanese multinational firms. *Strategic Management Journal*, 21: 51–80.

Gerschenkron, A. 1962. *Economic Backwardness in Historical Perspective*. Cambridge: The Belknap Press of Harvard University Press.

Ghoshal, S. 1986. The innovative multinational: A differentiated network of organizational roles and management processes. Ph.D. diss., Graduate School of Business Administration, Harvard University.

Ghoshal, S. 1987. Global strategy: An organizing framework. *Strategic Management Journal*, 8: 425–440.

Ghoshal, S. and Bartlett, C. A. 1988. Creation, adoption, and diffusion of innovations by subsidiaries of multinational corporations. *Journal of International Business Studies,* 19 (3): 365–388.

Ghoshal, S. and Bartlett, C. A. 1990. The multinational corporation as a differentiated inter-organizational network. *Academy of Management Review*, 15 (4): 603–625.

Ghoshal, S. and Bartlett, C. A. 1997. *The Individualized Corporation: A Fundamentally New Approach to Management.* New York: Harper Business.

Ghoshal, S. and Nohria, N. 1993. "Horses for courses: Organizational forms for multinational corporations." *Sloan Management Review*, 34 (2): 23–36.

Ghymn, K. I. 1980. Multinational enterprises from the Third World. *Journal of International Business Studies*, 11 (2): 118–122.

Gold, D. and Islam, A. 1995. The evolving nature of the transnational corporation: Cause and effect of globalization. In D. F. Simon (ed), *Corporate Strategies in the Pacific Rim: Global versus Regional Trends.* London and New York: Routledge.

Gomes-Casseres, B. 1997. Alliance strategies of small firms. *Small Business Economics*, 9: 33–44.

Gomes-Casseres, B. and Kohn, T. 1998. Small firms in international competition: A challenge to traditional theory. In P. J. Buckley et al. (eds), *International Technology Transfer by Small and Medium Sized Enterprises: Country Studies.* London: Macmillan.

Gomez, P. Y. and Korine, H. 1999. The leap to globalization: An economic explanation and a management framework. Paper presented at Academy of Management Annual Meeting, Chicago (August).

Grant, R. M. 1996. Toward a knowledge-based theory of the firm. *Strategic Management Journal*, 17 (Special Issue, Winter): 109–122.

Gray, J. 1998/99. *False Dawn: The Delusions of Global Capitalism.* London: Granta Books.

Greider, W. 1997. *One World, Ready or Not: The Manic Logic of Global Capitalism.* New York: Simon & Schuster.

Håkanson, L. 1995. Learning through acquisitions: Management and integration of foreign R&D laboratories. *International Studies of Management & Organization*, 25 (1–2): 121–157.

Håkansson, H. 1982. *International Marketing and Purchasing of Industrial Goods: An Interaction Approach.* New York: Wiley.

Håkansson, H. 1989. *Corporate Technological Behaviour: Cooperation and Networks.* London: Routledge.

Halal, W. 1994. From hierarchy to enterprise: Internal markets are the new foundation of management. *Academy of Management Executive*, 8 (4): 69–83.

Hamel, G. 1991. Competition for competence and inter-partner learning within international strategic alliances. *Strategic Management Journal*, 12: 83–103.

Hamel, G. and Prahalad, C. K. 1985. Do you really have a global strategy? *Harvard Business Review*, 63 (4): 139–148.

Hamel, G. and Prahalad, C. K. 1994. *Competing for the Future.* Boston: Harvard Business School Press.

Hamid, E. and Wright, R. W. 1999. Internationalization of SMEs: Management responses to a changing environment. *Journal of International Marketing*, 7 (4): 4–10.

Harzing, A.-W. 2000. An empirical analysis and extension of the Bartlett and Ghoshal typology of multinational companies. *Journal of International Business Studies*, 31 (1): 101–120.

Hedlund, G. 1986. The hypermodern MNC: A heterarchy? *Human Resource Management*, 25 (1): 9–25.

Hedlund, G. 1993a. Assumptions of hierarchy and heterarchy—with applications to the management of the multinational corporation. In S. Ghoshal and D. E. Westney (eds), *Organization Theory and the Multinational Corporation*. London: Macmillan.

Hedlund, G. 1993b. Introduction. In G. Hedlund (ed), *Organization of Transnational Corporations*. United Nations Library on Transnational Corporations, Volume 6. London: Routledge.

Hedlund, G. and Kogut, B. 1993. Managing the MNC: The end of the missionary era. In G. Hedlund (ed), *Organization of Transnational Corporations*. London: Routledge.

Hedlund, G. and Rolander, D. 1990. Actions in heterarchies: New approaches to managing the MNC. In C. A. Bartlett, Y. Doz, and G. Hedlund (eds), *Managing the Global Firm*. London and New York: Routledge.

Hennart, J. F. and Reddy, S. 1997. The choice between mergers /acquisitions and joint ventures: The case of Japanese investors in the United States. *Strategic Management Journal*, 18: 1–12.

Hertner, P. 1986. German multinational enterprise before 1914: Some case studies. In P. Hertner and G. Jones (eds), *Multinationals: Theory and History*. Aldershot: Gower.

Hertner, P. and Jones, G. (eds). 1986. *Multinationals: Theory and History*. Aldershot: Gower.

Hill, C. W., Hwang, P. and Kim, W. C. 1990. An eclectic theory of the choice of international entry mode. *Strategic Management Journal*, 11: 117–128.

Hirst, P. and Thompson, G. 1996/99. *Globalisation in Question* (First/second edition). Cambridge, UK: Polity Press.

Hitt, M. A., Hoskisson, R. E., and Kim, H. 1997. International diversification: Effects on innovation and firm performance in product-diversified firms. *Academy of Management Journal*, 40 (4): 767–798.

Hobday, M. 1995. *Innovation in East Asia: The Challenge to Japan*. Aldershot, UK: Edward Elgar.

Holm, U., Johanson, J., and Thilenius, P. 1995. Headquarters' knowledge of subsidiary network contexts in the multinational corporation. *International Studies of Management & Organization*, 25 (1–2): 97–119.

Holm, U. and Pedersen, T. (eds). 2000. *The Emergence and Impact of MNC Centres of Excellence: A Subsidiary Perspective*. New York: St. Martins Press.

Holmlund, M. and Kock, S. 1998. Relationships and the internationalisation of Finnish small and medium-sized companies. *International Small Business Journal*, 16 (4): 46–63.

Hörnell, E. and Vahlne, J.-E. 1986. *Multinationals: The Swedish Case*. London: Croom Helm.

Hout, T., Porter, M. E., and Rudden, E. 1982. How global companies win out. *Harvard Business Review*, 60 (5) (Sep-Oct): 98–108.

Hu, Y.-S. 1992. Global or stateless corporations are national firms with international operations. *California Management Review*, 34: 107–26.

Hymer, S. 1976. *The International Operations of National Firms: A Study of Direct Foreign Investment*. Cambridge, MA: MIT Press. [Originally presented as Ph.D. thesis, MIT, 1960.]

Hymer, S. 1979. *The Multinational Corporation: A Radical Approach*. Papers. Cambridge: Cambridge University Press.

Inkpen, A. C. and Beamish, P. W. 1997. Knowledge, bargaining power, and the instability of international joint ventures. *Academy of Management Review,* 22 (1): 177–202.

Itaki, M. 1991. A critical assessment of the eclectic theory of the MNE. *Journal of International Business Studies,* 22: 445–460.

Itami, H. 1994. The globalization of Japanese firms. In N. Campbell and F. Burton (eds), *Japanese Multinationals: Strategies and Management in the Global Kaisha.* London and New York: Routledge.

Jarillo, J. C. and Martinez, J. I. 1991. The international expansion of Spanish firms: Towards an integrative framework for international strategy. In L.-G. Mattsson and B. Stymne (eds), *Corporate and Industry Strategies for Europe.* Amsterdam: North-Holland.

Johanson, J. and Mattsson, L.-G. 1988. Internationalisation in industrial systems—a network approach. In N. Hood and J.-E. Vahlne (eds), *Strategies in Global Competition.* London: Croom Helm.

Johanson, J. and Mattsson, L.-G. 1991. Strategic adaptation of firms to the European single market: A network approach. In L.-G. Mattsson and B. Stymne (eds), *Corporate and Industry Strategies for Europe.* Amsterdam: North-Holland.

Johanson, J. and Mattsson, L.-G. 1992. Network positions and strategic action: An analytical framework. In B. Axelsson and G. Easton (eds), *Industrial Networks: A New View of Reality.* London and New York: Routledge.

Johanson, J. and Mattsson, L.-G. 1994. The markets-as-networks research tradition in Sweden. In G. Laurent, G. Lilien, and B. Pras (eds), *Research Traditions in Marketing.* Boston: Kluwer Press.

Johanson, J. and Vahlne, J. E. 1977. The internationalisation process of the firm: A model of knowledge development and increasing foreign market commitments. *Journal of International Business Studies,* 8(1): 23–32.

Johanson, J. and Vahlne, J. E. 1990. The mechanism of internationalisation. *International Marketing Review,* 7(4): 11–24.

Johanson, J. and Wiedersheim-Paul, F. 1975. The internationalization of the firm: Four Swedish case studies. *The Journal of Management Studies,* 12(3): 305–322.

Johnson, G. A., Brown, R. M., and Johnson, D. J. 1994. The market reaction to voluntary corporate spinoffs—revisited. *Quarterly Journal of Business and Economics,* 33 (4): 44–60.

Johnston, R. and Lawrence, P. R. 1990. Beyond vertical integration—The rise of the value-adding partnership. *Harvard Business Review,* 66 (4): 94–101.

Jones, G. (ed). 1993. *Transnational Corporations: A Historical Perspective.* United Nations Library on Transnational Corporations, Volume 2. London and New York: Routledge.

Jones, G. 1996. *The Evolution of International Business: An Introduction.* London and New York: Routledge.

Jones, G. and Schroeter, H. G. (eds). 1993. *The Rise of Multinationals in Continental Europe.* Aldershot, UK: Edward Elgar.

Jones, M. V. 1999. The internationalization of small high-technology firms. *Journal of International Marketing,* 7 (4): 15–41.

Juul, M. and Walters, P. 1987. The internationalization of Norwegian firms: A study of the UK experience. *Management International Review,* 27 (1): 58–66.

Kahn, K. M. (ed). 1987. *Multinationals of the South: New Actors in the International Economy*. London: Francis Pinter.

Kanter, R. M. 1985. *The Change Masters*. New York: Simon & Schuster.

Kaplinsky, R. 1997. India's industrial development: An interpretative survey. *World Development*, 25 (5): 681–694.

Keeble, D., Lawson, C., Lawton-Smith, H., Moore, B., and Wilkinson, F. 1998. Internationalisation processes, networking and local embeddedness in technology-intensive small firms. *Small Business Economics*, 11 (4): 327–342.

Kim, W. C. and Hwang, P. 1992. Global strategy and multinationals' entry mode choice. *Journal of International Business Studies*, 23 (1): 29–53.

Kinch, N. 1992. Entering a tightly structured network: Strategic visions or network realities. In M. Forsgren and J. Johanson (eds), *Managing Networks in International Business*. Philadelphia: Gordon & Breach.

Kindleberger, C. P. 1969. *American Business Abroad: Six Lectures on Direct Investment*. New Haven: Yale University Press.

Kindleberger, C. P. 1970. *The International Corporation*. Cambridge: MIT Press.

Kindleberger, C. P. and Audretsch, D. B. (eds). 1983. *The Multinational Corporation in the 1980s*. Cambridge: MIT Press.

Kinugasa, Y. 1984. Japanese firms' foreign direct investment in the U.S.—The case of Matsushita and others. In A. Okuchi and T. Inoue (eds), *Overseas Business Activities: Proceedings of the Fuji Conference*. Tokyo: University of Tokyo Press.

Knight, G. A. and Cavusgil, S. T. 1996. The born global firm: A challenge to traditional internationalization theory. *Advances in International Marketing*, 8: 11–26.

Kobayashi, N. 1980. *Japanese Multinational Enterprises*. Tokyo: Chuo-Keizaisha.

Kobrin, S. J. 1991. An empirical analysis of the determinants of global integration. *Strategic Management Journal*, 12 (Summer special issue): 17–31.

Kobrin, S. J. 1997. The architecture of globalization: State sovereignty in a networked global economy. In J. H. Dunning (ed), *Governments, Globalization, and International Business*. Oxford: Oxford University Press.

Kogut, B. 1985a. Designing global strategies: Comparative and competitive value-added chains. *Sloan Management Review*, 26 (4): 15–28.

Kogut, B. 1985b. Designing global strategies: Profiting from operating flexibility. *Sloan Management Review*, 27 (1): 27–38.

Kogut, B. 1988. Joint ventures: Theoretical and empirical perspectives. *Strategic Management Journal*, 9(4): 319–332.

Kogut, B. 1999. What makes a company global? *Harvard Business Review*, 77 (1) (Jan-Feb): 165–170.

Kogut, B. and Chang, S. 1991. Technological capabilities and Japanese foreign direct investment in the United States. *The Review of Economics and Statistics*, 73 (Aug): 401–413.

Kogut, B. and Singh, H. 1988. The effect of national culture on the choice of entry mode. *Journal of International Business Studies*, 19: 411–432.

Kogut, B. and Zander, U. 1992. Knowledge of the firm, combinative capabilities and the reproduction of technology. *Organization Science*, 3: 383–97.

Kogut, B. and Zander, U. 1993. Knowledge of the firm and the evolutionary theory of the multinational corporation. *Journal of International Business Studies*, 24 (4): 625–645.

Kohn, T. O. 1997. Small firms as international players. *Small Business Economics*, 9: 45–51.

Kojima, K. 1978. *Direct Foreign Investment: A Japanese Model of Multinational Business Operations*. London: Croom Helm.

Kojima, K. and Ozawa, T. 1984. *Japan's General Trading Companies: Merchants of Economic Development*. Paris: Organisation for Economic Co-operation and Development.

Korhonen, H., Luostarinen, R., and Welch, L. 1996. Internationalization of SMEs: Inward-outward patterns and government policy. *Management International Review*, 36(4): 315–329.

Korine, H. 1999a. *Fresenius A.G.: Globalization*. Case 99-000-13, London Business School.

Korine, H. 1999b. *CMS Energy*. Case 99-000-17, London Business School.

Kozul-Wright, R. and Rowthorn, R. (eds). 1998. *Transnational Corporations and the Global Economy*. Basingstoke: Macmillan.

Kristensen, P. H. and Zeitlin, J. 2001. The making of a global firm: Local pathways to multinational enterprise. In G. Morgan, P. H. Kristensen, and R. Whitley (eds), *The Multinational Firm: Organizing across Institutional and National Divides*. Oxford: Oxford University Press.

Kumar, K. 1982. Third World multinationals: A growing force in international relations, *International Studies Quarterly*, 26 (3): 397–424.

Kumar, K. and McLeod, M. G. (eds). 1981. *Multinationals from Developing Countries*. Lexington, MA: Lexington Books.

Kutschker, M. and Baurle, I. 1997. Three plus one: Multidimensional strategy of internationalization. *Management International Review*, 37 (2): 103–125.

Lall, R. B. 1986. *Multinationals from the Third World*. Delhi: Oxford University Press.

Lall, S. 1982. The emergence of Third World Multinationals: Indian/Joint Ventures Overseas. *World Development*, 10 (2): 127–146.

Lall, S. in collaboration with E. Chen, J. Katz, B. Kosacoff, and A. Villela. 1983. *The New Multinationals: The Spread of Third World Enterprises*. New York: John Wiley.

Lall, S. (ed). 1993. *Transnational Corporations and Economic Development*. United Nations Library on Transnational Corporations, Volume 3. London: Routledge.

Lecraw, D. 1977. Direct investment by firms from less developed countries. *Oxford Economic Papers*, 29 (3): 442–457.

Lecraw, D. 1981. Internationalization of firms from LDCs: Evidence from the ASEAN region. In K. Kumar and M. G. McLeod (eds), *Multinationals from Developing Countries*. Lexington, MA: Lexington Books.

Leonard-Barton, D. 1995. *Wellsprings of Knowledge: Building and Sustaining the Sources of Innovation*. Boston: Harvard Business School Press.

Leonidou, L. C. and Katsikeas, C. S. 1996. The export development process: An integrative review of empirical models. *Journal of International Business Studies*, 27 (3): 517–551.

Levitt, T. 1983. The globalization of markets. *Harvard Business Review*, 61 (3): 92–102.

Liesch, P. W. and Knight, G. A. 1999. Information internalization and hurdle rates in small and medium enterprise internationalization, *Journal of International Business Studies*, 30 (2): 383–394.

Lindqvist, M. 1991. *Infant Multinationals: The Internationalization of Young, Technology-Based Swedish Firms.* Stockholm: Institute of International Business, Stockholm School of Economics.

Lundström, R. 1986. Swedish multinational growth before 1930. In P. Hertner and G. Jones (eds), *Multinationals: Theory and History.* Aldershot: Gower.

Luostarinen, R. 1980. *Internationalization of the Firm.* Helsinki: Helsinki School of Economics.

Luostarinen, R. 1994. *Foreign Operations of Finnish Industrial Firms.* Helsinki: Helsinki School of Economics.

Luostarinen, R. and Welch, L. S. 1990. *International Business Operations.* Helsinki: Helsinki School of Economics.

Luttwak, E. N. 1999. *Turbo-Capitalism: Winners & Losers in the Global Economy.* New York: HarperCollins.

Madhok, A. 1997. Cost, value and foreign market entry mode: The transaction and the firm. *Strategic Management Journal*, 18: 39–61.

Madsen, T. K. and Servais, P. 1997. The internationalization of born globals: An evolutionary process? *International Business Review*, 6 (6): 561–583.

Magretta, J. 1998. Fast, global, and entrepreneurial: Supply chain management, Hong Kong style: An interview with Victor Fung. *Harvard Business Review*, 76 (5) (Sep-Oct) 102–114.

Mair, A. 1994. *Honda's Global Local Corporation.* New York: St. Martin's Press.

Makadok, R. 1998. Can first-mover and early-mover advantages be sustained in an industry with low barriers to entry/imitation? *Strategic Management Journal*, 19 (7): 683–696.

Malnight, T. W. 1995. Globalization of an ethnocentric firm: An evolutionary perspective. *Strategic Management Journal*, 16 (2): 119–141.

Markides, C. 1997. Strategic innovation. *Sloan Management Review*, 38 (3): 9–24.

Martin, H.-P. and Schumann, H. 1997. *The Global Trap: Globalization and the Assault on Prosperity and Democracy.* London: Zed Books.

Martin, X., Mitchell, W., and Swaminathan, A. 1994. Recreating and extending buyer-supplier links following international expansion. *Advances in Strategic Management*, 10B: 47–72.

Martin, X., Swaminathan, A., and Mitchell, W. 1998. Organizational evolution in the inter-organizational environment: Incentives and constraints on international expansion strategy. *Administrative Science Quarterly*, 43 (3): 566–601.

Martinez, J. I. and Jarillo, J. C. 1991. Coordination demands of international strategies. *Journal of International Business Studies*, 22 (3): 429–444.

Mathews, J. A. 1996a. Holonic organisational architectures. *Human Systems Management*, 15 (1): 27–54.

Mathews, J. A. 1996b. The organizational foundations of economic learning. *Human Systems Management*, 15 (2): 113–124.

Mathews, J. A. 1998. Jack and the beanstalk: The creation of dynamic capabilities through knowledge leverage by latecomer firms. Paper presented at Academy of Management Annual Meeting, Business Policy and Strategy stream, San Diego. (Aug.).

Mathews, J. A. 1999. Silicon island of the East: Creating a semiconductor industry in Singapore. *California Management Review*, 41 (2): 55–74.

Mathews, J. A. 2000. Competitive dynamics and economic learning: An extended resource-based view. Paper presented at summer conference of Danish Research Unit for Industrial Dynamics (DRUID), Rebild, Denmark, (June).

Mathews, J. A. 2001a. From national innovations systems to national systems of economic learning: The case of technology diffusion management in East Asia, *International Journal of Technology Management*. Forthcoming.

Mathews, J. A. 2001b. Competitive interfirm dynamics within an industrial market system. *Industry and Innovation*, (1): 79–107.

Mathews, J. A. and Cho, D. S. 1999. Combinative capabilities and organizational learning in latecomer firms: The case of the Korean semiconductor industry. *Journal of World Business*, 34 (2): 139–156.

Mathews, J. A. and Cho, D. S. 2000. *Tiger Technology: The Creation of a Semiconductor Industry in East Asia*. Cambridge: Cambridge University Press.

Mathews, J. A. and Snow, C. C. 1998. A conversation with The Acer Group's Stan Shih on global strategy and management. *Organizational Dynamics*, (Summer): 65–74.

Mattsson, L.-G. 1995. Firms, "megaorganizations" and markets-as-networks view. *Journal of Institutional and Theoretical Economics*, 151 (4): 760–766.

Mattsson, L.-G. 1998. Dynamics of overlapping networks and strategic actions by the international firm. In A. C. Chandler, P. Hagström, and O. Sölvell (eds), *The Dynamic Firm*. Oxford: Oxford University Press.

McDougall, P. P. and Oviatt, B. M. 1991. Global start-ups: New ventures without geographic limits. *The Entrepreneurship Forum*, (Winter): 1–5.

McDougall, P. P. and Oviatt, B. M. 1997. International entrepreneurship literature in the 1990s and directions for future research. In D. L. Sexton and R. W. Smilor (eds), *Entrepreneurship 2000*. Chicago: Upstart Publishing.

McDougall, P. P. and Oviatt, B. M. 2000.International entrepreneurship: The intersection of two research paths. *Academy of Management Journal* 43(5) (Special Research Forum on International Entrepreneurship): 902–908.

McDougall, P. P., Shane, S., and Oviatt, B. M. 1994. Explaining the formation of international new ventures: The limits of theories from international business research. *Journal of Business Venturing*, 9: 469–487.

Melin, L. 1992. Internationalization as a strategy process. *Strategic Management Journal*, 13(2): 99–118.

Mickelthwait, J. and Woolridge, A. 2000. *A Future Perfect: The Challenge and Hidden Promise of Globalization*. New York: Crown Business.

Miles, J. A. and Woolridge, J. R. 1999. *Spin-Offs and Equity Carve-Outs: Achieving Faster Growth and Better Performance*. Morristown, NJ: Financial Executives Research Foundation.

Miles, R. E. and Snow, C. C. 1995. The new network firm: A spherical structure built on a human investment philosophy. *Organizational Dynamics*, 23: 5–18.

Miles, R. E. Snow, C. C., Mathews, J. A., Miles, G., and Coleman, H. J. 1997. Organizing in the knowledge age: Anticipating the cellular form. *Academy of Management Executive*, 11 (4): 7–20.

Millman, T. F. 1997. Global key account management and systems selling. *International Business Review*, 6: 631–645.

Monkiewicz, J. 1986. Multinational enterprises of developing countries: Some emerging characteristics. *Management International Review*, 26 (3): 67–80.

Montgomery, C. (ed). 1995. *Resource-based and Evolutionary Theories of the Firm: Towards a Synthesis*. Boston/Dordrecht/London: Kluwer Academic Publishers.

Mutinelli, M. and Piscitello, L. 1998. The entry mode choice of MNEs: An evolutionary approach, *Research Policy*, 27 (5): 491–506.

Mytelka, L. K. 2000. Local systems of innovation in a globalized world economy. *Industry and Innovation*, 7 (1): 15–32.

Narula, R. 1996. *Multinational Investment and Economic Structure*. London: Routledge.

Nelson, R. R. and Winter, S. G. 1982. *An Evolutionary Theory of Economic Change*. Cambridge, MA: The Belknap Press.

Nohria, N. and Garcia-Pont, C. 1991. Global strategic linkages and industry structure. *Strategic Management Journal*, 12 (Special Issue): 105–124.

Nohria, N. and Ghoshal, S. 1997. *The Differentiated Network: Organizing Multinational Corporations for Value Creation*. San Francisco, CA: Jossey-Bass.

Nonaka, I. 1990. Managing globalization as a self-renewing process: Experiences of Japanese MNCs. In C. Bartlett, Y. Doz, and G. Hedlund (eds), *Managing the Global Firm*. New York and London: Routledge.

Nordström, K. A. 1991. *The Internationalization Process of the Firm: Searching for New Patterns and Explanations*. Stockholm: Institute of International Business, Stockholm School of Economics.

O'Brien, P. 1980. The new multinationals: Developing country firms in international markets. *Futures*, 12 (4): 303–316.

OECD 1997. *Globalisation and Small and Medium-sized Enterprises (Vol. 1: Synthesis Report; Vol. 2; Country Studies)*. Paris: Organisation for Economic Co-operation and Development.

Ohishi, T. 1994. The internationalization of Japanese firms. *Management Japan*, 26 (2): 3–6.

Ohmae, K. I. 1990/99. *The Borderless World: Power and Strategy in the Interlinked Economy*. (First/revised edition). New York: Harper Business.

Ohmae, K. I. 1995a. Putting global logic first. *Harvard Business Review*, (Jan/Feb): 119–125.

Ohmae, K. I. (ed). 1995b. *The Evolving Global Economy: Making Sense of the New World Order*. Boston: Harvard Business School Press.

Okuchi, A. and Inoue, T. (eds). 1984. *Overseas Business Activities: Proceedings of the Fuji Conference*. Tokyo: University of Tokyo Press.

Oliver, C. 1997. Sustainable competitive advantage: Combining institutional and resource-based views. *Strategic Management Journal*, 18: 697–713.

Olsson, U. 1976. L. M. Ericsson as international concern. In A. Attman and U. Olsson (eds), *L.M. Ericsson 100 Years*. (Volume 2: Rescue, Reconstruction, Worldwide Enterprise 1932–1976). Stockholm: L.M. Ericsson.

Olsson, U. 1993. Securing the markets: Swedish multinationals in a historical context. In G. Jones and H. G. Schroeter (eds), *The Rise of Multinationals in Continental Europe*. Aldershot, UK: Edward Elgar.

Onida, F. and Viesti, G. (eds). 1988. *The Italian Multinationals*. London: Croom Helm.

Ostroff, Frank 1999. *The Horizontal Organization: What the Organization of the Future Actually Looks Like and How It Delivers Value to Customers*. New York: Oxford University Press.

Oviatt, B. and McDougall, P. P. 1994. Toward a theory of international new ventures. *Journal of International Business Studies*, 25(1): 45–64.

Oviatt, B. M. and McDougall, P. P. 1995. Global start-ups: Entrepreneurs on a worldwide stage. *Academy of Management Executive*, 9 (2): 30–44.

Oviatt, B. M. and McDougall, P. P. 1997. Challenges for internationalization process theory: The case of international new ventures. *Management International Review*, 37 (Special issue on Internationalization processes): 85–99.

Oviatt, B. M. and McDougall, P. P. 1999. A framework for understanding accelerated international entrepreneurship. In A. M. Rugman (Series editor) and R. W. Wright (Volume editor), *Research in Global Strategic Management, Volume 7. International Entrepreneurship: Globalization of Emerging Businesses*. Stamford, CT: JAI Press.

Ozawa, T. 1979. *Multinationalism: Japanese Style: The Political Economy of Outward Dependency*. Princeton, NJ: Princeton University Press.

Padmanabhan, P. and Cho, K. R. 1996. Ownership strategy for a foreign affiliate: An empirical investigation of Japanese firms. *Management International Review*, 36: 45–65.

Pananond, P. and Zeithaml, C. P. 1998. The international expansion process of MNEs from developing countries: A case study of Thailand's CP Group. *Asia Pacific Journal of Management*, 15 (2): 163–184.

Pearce, R. 1999. The evolution of technology in multinational enterprises: The role of creative subsidiaries. *International Business Review*, 8: 125–148.

Pedersen, T. and Petersen, B. 1998. Explaining gradually increasing resource commitment to a foreign market. *International Business Review*, 7: 483–501.

Penrose, E. 1959. *The Theory of the Growth of the Firm*. Oxford: Blackwell.

Penrose, E. 1968. *The Large International Firm in Developing Countries: The International Petroleum Industry*. Cambridge, MA: MIT Press.

Penrose, E. 1971. The state and the multinational enterprise in less-developed countries. In J. Dunning (ed), *The Multinational Enterprise*. London: Allen & Unwin.

Perlmutter, H. 1969. The tortuous evolution of the multinational corporation. *Columbia Journal of World Business*, 4 (Jan-Feb): 8–18.

Peteraf, M. 1993. The cornerstones of competitive advantage: A resource-based view. *Strategic Management Journal*, 14: 179–88.

Petersen, B. and Pedersen, T. 1997. Twenty years after—Support and critique of the Uppsala internationalisation model. In I. Björkman and M. Forsgren (eds), *The Nature of the International Firm*. Copenhagen: Handelshøjskolens Forlag.

Petersen, B. and Pedersen, T. 1999. Fast and slow resource commitment to foreign markets: What causes the difference? *Journal of International Management*, 5: 73–91.

Porter, M. E. 1985. *Competitive Advantage: Creating and Sustaining Superior Performance*. New York: The Free Press.

Porter, M. E. 1986a. Changing patterns of international competition. *California Management Review*, 28 (2): 9–40.

Porter, M. E. 1986b. Competition in global industries: A conceptual framework. In M.E. Porter (ed), *Competition in Global Industries*. Boston: Harvard Business School Press.

Porter, M. E. 1990. *The Competitive Advantages of Nations*. New York: The Free Press.

Powell, W. 1990. Neither market nor hierarchy: Network forms of organization. *Research in Organization Behavior*, 12: 295–316.

Prahalad, C. K. 1976. The strategic process in a multinational corporation. Ph.D. diss., Graduate School of Business Administration, Harvard University.

Prahalad, C. K. and Doz, Y. L. 1981. An approach to strategic control in MNCs. *Sloan Management Review*, 22 (4): 5–13.

Prahalad, C. K. and Doz, Y. L. 1987. *The Multinational Mission: Balancing Local Demands and Global Vision*. New York: The Free Press.

Prahalad, C. K. and Hamel, G. 1990. "The core competence of the corporation". *Harvard Business Review*, 68 (3): 79–91.

Prasad, S. B. 1999. Globalization of smaller firms: Field notes on processes. *Small Business Economics*, 13: 1–7.

Preece, S. B., Miles, G., and Baetz, M. C. 1999. Explaining the international intensity and global diversity of early-stage technology-based firms. *Journal of Business Venturing*, 14 (3): 259–281.

Pugel, T. A., Kragas, E. S., and Kimura, Y. 1996. Further evidence on Japanese direct investment in U.S. manufacturing. *The Review of Economics and Statistics*, 78 (2): 208–213.

Ramaswamy, K., Galen, K. K., and Renforth, W. 1996. Measuring the degree of internationalization of a firm: A comment. *Journal of International Business Studies*, 27 (1): 167–178.

Randøy, T. 1997. Towards a firm-based model of foreign direct investment. In I. Björkman and M. Forsgren (eds), *The Nature of the International Firm: Nordic Contributions to International Business Research*. Copenhagen: Handelshøjskolens Forlag.

Reed, R. and De Fillippi, R. J. 1990. Causal ambiguity, barriers to imitation, and sustainable competitive advantage. *Academy of Management Review*, 15 (1): 88–102.

Reich, R. 1992. *The Work of Nations*. New York: Vintage Books.

Ridderstråle, J. 1996. *Global Innovation: Managing International Innovation Projects at ABB and Electrolux*. Stockholm: Institute of International Business, Stockholm School of Economics.

Rodrik, D. 1999. *The New Global Economy and Developing Countries: Making Openness Work*. Policy Essay #24. Washington, DC: Overseas Development Council.

Roos, J., von Krogh, G., and Yip. G. 1994. An epistemology of globalizing firms. *International Business Review*, 3 (4): 395–409.

Rugman, A. M. 1980. A new theory of the multinational enterprise: Internationalization versus internationalization. *Columbia Journal of World Business*, 15(1): 23–29.

Rugman, A. M. 1986. New theories of the multinational enterprise: An assessment of internalization theory. *Bulletin of Economic Research*, (May): 101–118.

Rugman, A. M. 1999. Multinational enterprises and the end of global strategy. Keynote address, ANZ International Business Academy, *Proceedings of the Second Annual Conference*. Australian Centre for International Business, University of New South Wales.

Rugman, A. M. 2000. *The End of Globalization*. New York: Random House Business Books.

Rugman, A. M., D'Cruz, J. R., and Verbeke, A. 1995. Internalisation and de-internalisation: Will business networks replace multinationals? In G. Boyd (ed), *Competitive and Cooperative Macromanagement: The Challenge of Structural Interdependence*. Aldershot: Edward Elgar.

Ruigrok, W. and Van Tulder, R. 1995. *The Logic of International Restructuring*. London and New York: Routledge.

Sachs, J. and Warner, A. 1995. Economic reform and the process of global integration. *Brookings Papers on Economic Activity*, 1: 1–118.

Sadtler, D., Campbell, A., and Koch, R. 1997. *Breakup! How Companies Use Spinoffs to Gain Focus and Grow Strong*. New York: The Free Press.

Sakai, K. and Sekiyama, H. 1985. *Bunsha—Company Division: What Good is a Stuffed Tiger?* Tokyo: Taiyo.

Sakai, K. and Russell, D. 1993. *To Expand, We Divide: The Practice and Principles of Bunsha Management*. Tokyo: Intercultural Group.

Sassen, S. 1998. *Globalization and its Discontents: Essays on the New Mobility of People and Money*. New York: The New Press.

Schmitz, H. and Cassiolato, J. (eds). 1992. *Hi-Tech for Industrial Development: Lessons from the Brazilian Experience in Electronics and Automation*. London: Routledge.

Schumpeter, J. 1934. *The Theory of Economic Development*. Cambridge: Harvard University Press.

Shih, Stan 1996. *Me-Too Is Not My Style: Challenge Difficulties, Break Through Bottlenecks, Create Values*. Taipei: The Acer Foundation.

Simon, H. 1996. *Hidden Champions: Lessons from 500 of the World's Best Unknown Companies*. Boston: Harvard Business School Press.

Slywotzky, A. J. and Morrison, D. J. 1997. *The Profit Zone: How Strategic Business Design Will Lead You to Tomorrow's Profits*. New York: Times Books.

Smith, A. and Reney, M. C. 1997. The mating dance: A case study of local partnering processes in developing countries. *European Management Journal*, 15 (2): 174–182.

Smith, A. and Zeithaml, C. 1999. The intervening hand: Contemporary international expansion processes of the regional Bell operating companies. *Journal of Management Inquiry*, 8 (1): 34–64.

Snow, C. C., Mathews, J. A., and Miles, R. E. 1999. The concept of the corporation in the twenty-first century. Working paper 99–01, Carnegie-Bosch Institute, Carnegie-Mellon University.

Sölvell, O. and Zander, I. 1995. Organization of the dynamic multinational enterprise: The home-based and the heterarchical MNE. *International Studies of Management & Organization*, 25 (1–2): 17–38.

Spruyt, H. 1994. *The Sovereign State and its Competitors: An Analysis of Systems Change*. Princeton, NJ: Princeton University Press.

Stopford, J. M. 1998. Think again: Multinational corporations. *Foreign Policy*, (Winter 1998/99): 12–24.

Stopford, J. M. and Wells, L. T. 1972. *Managing the Multinational Enterprise: Organization of the Firm and Ownership of the Subsidiaries*. New York: Basic Books.

Sugiura, H. 1990. How Honda localizes its global strategy. *Sloan Management Review*, 32 (1): 77–82.

Sull, D. 1999. Spinning steel into gold: The case of Ispat International N.V. *European Management Journal*, 17 (4) (Aug): 368–382.

Sullivan, D. 1994a. The "threshold of internationalization": Replication, extension and reinterpretation. *Management International Review*, 34: 165–186.

Sullivan, D. 1994b. Measuring the degree of internationalization of a firm. *Journal of International Business Studies*, 25 (2): 325–342.

Sullivan, D. and Bauerschmidt, A. 1990. Incremental internationalization: A test of Johanson and Vahlne's thesis. *Management International Review*, 30 (1): 19–30.

Tallman, S. B. and Shenkar, O. 1990. International cooperative venture strategies: Outward investment and small firms from NICs. *Management International Review*, 30 (4): 299–316.

Teece, D. J. 1998. Design issues for innovative firms. In A. C. Chandler, P. Hagström, and O. Sölvell (eds), *The Dynamic Firm*. Oxford: Oxford University Press.

Teece, D. J., Pisano, G., and Shuen, A. 1997. Dynamic capabilities and strategic management. *Strategic Management Journal*, 18: 509–534.

Teichova, A., Levy-Leboyer, M., and Nussbaum, H. (eds). 1986. *Multinational Enterprise in Historical Perspective*. Cambridge: Cambridge University Press.

Teichova, A., Levy-Leboyer, M., and Nussbaum, H. (eds). 1989. *Historical Studies in International Corporate Business*. Cambridge: Cambridge University Press.

Tolentino, P. E. E. 1993. *Technological Innovation and Third World Multinationals*. London and New York: Routledge.

Tsang, E. 1999. Internationalization as a learning process: Singapore MNCs in China. *Academy of Management Executive*, 13 (1): 91–101.

Tsurumi, Y. 1976. *The Japanese Are Coming: A Multinational Interaction of Firms and Policies*. Cambridge, MA: Ballinger.

Tsurumi, Y. 1983. *Multinational Management: Business Strategy and Government Policy*. Cambridge, MA: Ballinger.

Turnbull, P. W. 1987. A challenge to the stages theory of the internationalization process. In P. J. Rosson and S. D. Reed (eds), *Managing Export Entry and Expansion*. Westport, CT: Greenwood.

Ulgado, F. M., Yu, C. M. J., and Negandhi, A. R. 1994. Multinational enterprises from Asian developing countries: Management and organizational characteristics. *International Business Review*, 3 (2): 123–133.

UNCTAD. 1998. *World Investment Report 1998: Trends and Determinants*. New York and Geneva: United Nations Conference on Trade and Development.

UNCTAD. 1999. *World Investment Report 1999: Foreign Direct Investment and the Challenge of Development.* New York and Geneva: United Nations Conference on Trade and Development.

Ungson, G. R., Steers, R. M., and Park, S. H. 1997. *Korean Enterprise: The Quest for Globalization.* Boston: Harvard Business School Press.

UNIDO 2002. *World Industrial Development Report.* New York and Vienna: United Nations Industrial Development Organization (forthcoming).

Vernon, R. 1966. International investment and international trade in the product life cycle. *Quarterly Journal of Economics,* 80: 190–207.

Vernon, R. 1971. *Sovereignty at Bay: The Multinational Spread of U.S. Enterprises.* New York: Basic Books.

Vernon, R. 1977. *Storm Over the Multinationals: The Real Issues.* Cambridge: Harvard University Press.

Vernon, R. 1992. Transnational corporations: Where are they coming from, where are they headed? *Transnational Corporations,* 1 (2): 7–35.

Vernon, R. 1998. *In the Hurricane's Eye: The Troubled Prospects of Multinational Enterprises.* Cambridge: Harvard University Press.

Vernon-Wortzel, H. and Wortzel, L.H. 1988. Globalizing strategies for multinationals from developing countries. *Columbia Journal of World Business,* 23 (1): 27–36.

Veseth, M. 1998. *Selling Globalization: The Myth of the Global Economy.* Boulder, CO: Lynne Rienner.

Viesti, G. 1988. International strategies of Italian multinationals. In F. Onida and G. Viesti (eds), *The Italian Multinationals.* London: Croom Helm.

Warwick, M. 1998. AT&T—Unisource: The local company everywhere. *Communications International,* 25 (2): 15–22.

Weiss, L. 1998. *The Myth of the Powerless State: Governing the Economy in a Global Era.* Ithaca, NY: Cornell University Press; and Cambridge, UK: Polity Press.

Weiss, L. 1999a. State power and the Asian crisis. *New Political Economy,* 4 (3): 317–343.

Weiss, L. 1999b. Globalization and national governance: Antinomy or interdependence? *Review of International Studies,* 25 (5): 59–88.

Weiss, L. (ed). 2001. *States in the Global Economy: Bringing Domestic Institutions Back In.* Cambridge: Cambridge University Press.

Welch, D. E. and Welch, L. S. 1996. The internationalization process and networks: A strategic management perspective. *Journal of International Marketing,* 4 (3): 11–28.

Welch, L. S. and Luostarinen, R. K. 1988. Internationalization: Evolution of a concept. *Journal of General Management,* 14 (2): 34–55.

Wells, L. T. 1977. The internationalization of firms from developing countries. In T. Agmon and C. P. Kindleberger (eds), *Multinationals from Small Countries.* Cambridge, MA: The MIT Press.

Wells, L. T. 1981. Foreign investors from the Third World. In K. Kumar and M. G. McLeod (eds), *Multinationals from Developing Countries.* Lexington, MA: Lexington Books.

Wells, L. T. 1983. *Third World Multinationals: The Rise of Foreign Investment from Developing Countries.* Cambridge, MA: The MIT Press.

Wells, L. T. 1998. Multinationals and the developing countries. *Journal of International Business Studies*, 29 (1):101–114.

Wernerfelt, B. 1984. A resource-based view of the firm. *Strategic Management Journal*, 5: 171–180.

Wilkins, M. 1970. *The Emergence of Multinational Enterprise: American Business Abroad from the Colonial Era to 1914*. Cambridge: Harvard University Press.

Wilkins, M. 1974. *The Maturing of Multinational Enterprise: American Business Abroad from 1914 to 1970*. Cambridge: Harvard University Press.

Wilkins, M. 1986a. European multinationals in the United States: 1875–1914. In A. Teichova et al. (eds), *Multinational Enterprise in Historical Perspective*. Cambridge: Cambridge University Press.

Wilkins, M. 1986b. Japanese multinational enterprise before 1914. *Business History Review*, 60: 199–231.

Wilkins, M. 1988. European and North American multinationals, 1870–1914: Comparisons and contrasts. *Business History Review*, 30: 8–45.

Wilkins, M. (ed). 1991. *The Growth of Multinational Enterprise*. Aldershot, UK: Edward Elgar.

Williamson, P. J. 1997. Asia's new competitive game. *Harvard Business Review*, (Sep–Oct): 55–67,

Yamawaki, H. 1994. Japanese multinationals in U.S. and European manufacturing. In M. Mason and D. Encarnation (eds), *Does Ownership Matter? Japanese Multinationals in Europe*. New York: Oxford University Press.

Yates, R. E. 1998. *The Kikkoman Chronicles: A Global Company with a Japanese Soul*. New York: McGraw-Hill.

Yergin, D. and Stanislaw, J. 1999. *The Commanding Heights: The Battle between Government and the Marketplace that is Remaking the Modern World*. New York: Simon & Schuster.

Yeung, A. K., Ulrich, D. O., Nason, S. W., and Von Glinow, M. A. 1999. *Organizational Learning Capability*. New York/Oxford: Oxford University Press.

Yeung, H. W. C. 1994a. Third World multinationals revisited: A research critique and future agenda. *Third World Quarterly*, 15: 297–317.

Yeung, H. W. C. 1994b. Transnational corporations from Asian developing countries: Their characteristics and competitive edge. *Journal of Asian Business*, 10 (4): 17–58.

Yeung, H. W. C. 1997. Business networks and transnational corporations: A study of Hong Kong firms in the ASEAN region. *Economic Geography*, 73: 1–25.

Yeung, H. W. C. 1998. The political economy of transnational corporations: A study of the regionalization of Singaporean firms. *Political Geography*, 17 (4): 389–416.

Yeung, H. W. C. 1999a. The internationalization of ethnic Chinese business firms from Southeast Asia: Strategies, processes and competitive advantage. *International Journal of Urban and Regional Research*, 23 (1): 88–102.

Yeung, H. W. C. 1999b. Singapore's global reach. Working paper, Department of Geography, National University of Singapore.

Yeung, H. W. C. (ed). 1999c. *The Globalization of Business Firms from Emerging Economies*. Cheltenham, UK: Edward Elgar.

Yoshida, M. 1987. *Japanese Direct Manufacturing Investment in the United States*. New York: Praeger.

Yoshino, M. Y. 1974. The multinational spread of Japanese manufacturing investment since World War II. *Business History Review*, 48: 357–381.

Yoshino, M. Y. 1976. *Japan's Multinational Enterprises*. Cambridge: Harvard University Press.

Yoshino, M. Y. 1984. The evolution of United States multinational enterprises. In A. Okuchi and T. Inoue (eds), *Overseas Business Activities: Proceedings of the Fuji Conference*. Tokyo: University of Tokyo Press.

Young, S., Huang, C. H., and McDermott, M. 1996. Internationalization and competitive catch-up processes: Case study evidence on Chinese multinational enterprises. *Management International Review*, 36(4): 295–314.

Yu, C.-M. J. 1990. The experience effect and foreign direct investment. *Weltwirtschaftliches Archiv*, 126 (3): 561–579.

Zacharakis, A. L. 1997. Entrepreneurial entry into foreign markets: A transaction cost perspective. *Entrepreneurship Theory & Practice*, 21 (3): 23–39.

Zahra, S. A., Ireland, R. D., and Hitt, M. A. 2000. International expansion by new venture firms: International diversity, mode of market entry, technological learning and performance. *Academy of Management Journal* 43 (5): 925–950. (Special Research Forum: International Entrepreneurship).

Zander, I. 1994. *The Tortoise Evolution of the Multinational Corporation: Foreign Technological Activity in Swedish Multinational Firms 1890–1990*. Stockholm: Institute of International Business, Stockholm School of Economics.

Zander, I. 1999a. Whereto the multinational? The evolution of technological capabilities in the multinational network. *International Business Review*, 8: 261–291.

Zander, I. 1999b. How do you mean "global"? An empirical investigation of innovation networks in the multinational corporation. *Research Policy*, 28: 195–213.

Zander, I. and Zander, U. 1997. "The oscillating multinational firm: Alfa Laval in the period 1890–1990". In I. Bjorkman and M. Forsgren (eds), *The Nature of the International Firm: Nordic Contributions to International Business Research*. Copenhagen: Copenhagen Business School Press.

Zander, U. and Kogut, B. 1995. Knowledge and the speed of transfer and imitation of organizational capabilities: An empirical test. *Organization Science*, 6 (1): 76–92.

Zysman, J.1996. The myth of a "global economy": Enduring national foundations and emerging regional realities. *New Political Economy*, 1 (2): 157–184.

INDEX